Cross-Cultural Technology Design

Oxford Series in Human-Technology Interaction

Series Editor
Alex Kirlik, University of Illinois at Urbana–Champaign and the
Beckman Institute

*Adaptive Perspectives on Human-Technology Interaction: Methods and
Models for Cognitive Engineering and Human-Computer Interaction*
Edited by Alex Kirlik

Computers, Phones, and the Internet: Domesticating Information Technology
Edited by Robert Kraut, Malcolm Brynin, and Sara Kiesler

Attention: From Theory to Practice
Edited by Arthur F. Kramer, Douglas Wiegmann, and Alex Kirlik

Neuroergonomics: The Brain at Work
Edited by Raja Parasuraman and Matthew Rizzo

Information Foraging Theory: Adaptive Interaction with Information
Peter Pirolli

Human-tech: Ethical and Scientific Foundations
Kim Vicente
Edited by Alex Kirlik

Being There Together: Social Interaction in Virtual Environments
Ralph Schroeder

*Exposing the Magic of Design: A Practitioner's Guide to the Methods and
Theory of Synthesis*
Jon Kolko

*Cross-Cultural Technology Design: Creating Culture-Sensitive Technology
for Local Users*
Huatong Sun

Cross-Cultural Technology Design

Creating Culture-Sensitive Technology for Local Users

HUATONG SUN

OXFORD
UNIVERSITY PRESS

OXFORD
UNIVERSITY PRESS

Oxford University Press, Inc., publishes works that further
Oxford University's objective of excellence
in research, scholarship, and education.

Oxford New York
Auckland Cape Town Dar es Salaam Hong Kong Karachi
Kuala Lumpur Madrid Melbourne Mexico City Nairobi
New Delhi Shanghai Taipei Toronto

With offices in
Argentina Austria Brazil Chile Czech Republic France Greece
Guatemala Hungary Italy Japan Poland Portugal Singapore
South Korea Switzerland Thailand Turkey Ukraine Vietnam

Published by Oxford University Press, Inc.
198 Madison Avenue, New York, New York 10016
www.oup.com

Oxford is a registered trademark of Oxford University Press

Library of Congress Cataloging-in-Publication Data
Sun, Huatong.
  Cross-cultural technology design : creating culture-sensitive technology for local users / Huatong Sun.
    p. cm. — (Oxford series in human-technology interaction)
  Includes bibliographical references and index.
  ISBN 978–0–19–974476–3 (hbk. : alk. paper)
    1. Technology—Sociological aspects. 2. User-centered system design—Cross-cultural studies.
  3. Human-computer interaction—Cross-cultural studies. 4. Information technology—Cross-cultural
studies. I. Title.
  HM846.S85 2012
  303.48'3—dc23   2011036791

9 8 7 6 5 4 3 2 1
Printed in USA
on acid-free paper

To my mother Huirui and father Peiran

Contents

Part III   Implications

List of Figures

List of Tables

Preface

It is striking for American adults to realize that the same mobile text messaging technology used in the States primarily by teenagers for social grooming and fun chat is also used by a Chinese bride-to-be to send wedding invitations to friends of her age, by a migrant Filipino nanny to "mother" her children half a world away with dozens of daily text messages, by an amateur Japanese writer to compose and publish *keitai* (cell phone) novels followed by thousands of readers online, by a Malaysian Islamic court as a legitimate announcement of divorce, and by doctors in South Africa to monitor and prescribe medications to HIV/AIDS patients.

It is also hard to find another technology like mobile text messaging that has engendered such diverse uses across the globe, been portrayed by so many faces in different locales, and formed such myriad articulations and identities. Unlike email, pagers, instant messaging, and blogging, which seem to have similar uses across cultures, mobile text messaging technology can be defined dramatically differently in diverse cultural contexts in terms of public vs. private, formal vs. casual, orality vs. literacy, and social vs. technical.

The phenomenon of mobile text messaging use represents one of many demanding challenges that cross-cultural technology design has faced in this increasingly globalized world with a rising participatory culture. Nowadays, cross-cultural design has become a standard practice and a daily test in many Information Technology (IT) companies as follows.

First, a large number of today's IT products are consumer-oriented. Compared to the applications and technologies used to manage computing tasks and coordinate business processes for large organizations (e.g., enterprise information systems), these products are expected to fit into the fabric of an individual user's everyday life. While the local uses of IT enterprise products might share similarities in work flows and organizational structures across cultures, the local uses of IT consumer products take on numerous cultural and social meanings in different cultural contexts.

Second, individual users are the heroes of this era of participatory culture, as profiled as "the person of the year" by *Time* magazine in 2006. They are not passive users but active designers who shape, redesign, and localize an available technology to fit into their local contexts. The dynamic user efforts of incorporating a technology into one's life are called *user localization* in this book, which differs from *developer localization*—the localization work that occurs at the developer's site to which we commonly refer. These endeavors of *user localization* continue from *developer localization* and often determine the market success or failure of an IT product. The practice of ending the development and production cycle at the moment of shipping is forever gone.

Third, while localizing an IT product to different local cultures is already difficult, the fact that a user would use a technology according to his or her lifestyle raises intriguing questions for cross-cultural design: How can a technology be designed as both usable and meaningful to culturally diverse users? How can a technology both reach diverse cultural groups and touch individual users? How can we strike a balance between local cultural ethos and individual subjectivity in a design? How could such a design appeal to a local context without stereotyping the local culture in an essentialist fashion?

All of these challenges urge researchers and practitioners to develop an effective approach to design appropriately localized products that meet the cultural expectations of local users, support their complex activities in concrete contexts, empower their agency, and mediate their identities. In this book, I present the design philosophy and model of Culturally Localized User Experience (CLUE), which integrates action and meaning through the cyclical design process in order to make a technology both usable and meaningful to local users, as an attempt to address the challenges and answer the questions above. Regarding local culture as the dynamic nexus of contextual interactions, the CLUE approach incorporates key concepts and methods from activity theory, British cultural studies, and genre theory, and argues that a technology created for a Culturally Localized User Experience mediates not only instrumental practices but social meanings as well. This approach places concrete use activities on center stage, which is often missing in current cross-cultural design literature and practice.

To illustrate, enrich, and fully develop the CLUE approach, I present a comparative study of mobile text messaging use in American and Chinese contexts, which investigates a technology that is poorly localized at the developer's site but is then rescued by users' localization efforts. The study was conducted at an interesting moment, when text messaging reached a point of being widely adopted by a larger population of users in many places of the world, and when the technology became a seamless part of the lives of many users, who used it in different ways according to their lifestyles. Forty-one frequent users from the U.S. and China participated in the study, five of whom are profiled as individual cases of user localization in this book.

The global traffic of mobile messaging is expected to reach 8.7 trillion messages in 2015, rising from 5 trillion in 2010 (Informa Telecoms & Media, 2011). After text messaging has been part of many people's lives, it is illuminating to study concrete use activities at sites of technology-in-use and listen to individual voices of local users behind the numbers and patterns, trend charts, and interview quotes that are commonly found in mobile messaging research, not to mention the similarities in modes of use between then and now (see Chapter 4). This book is an effort to fill that gap, offering ways for researchers and practitioners to think about how to reach culturally diverse users in this *glocalization* age and help local users to consummate Culturally Localized User Experiences of an emerging technology like mobile messaging. At the same time, these vivid user stories demonstrate how an emerging technology was adopted, used, consumed, and localized in a global context; how an object of instrumentality traversed through social circulation, obtaining and altering meanings, sustaining and eradicating practices, and constituting and destabilizing the structure; and how user needs arose, were cultivated, evolved, and/or disappeared.

By examining and comparing the *user localization* of mobile text messaging in two distinctly different cultural contexts, I search for ways to improve the *developer localization* and advocate a cyclical, open-ended design process that connects design and use, starting the dialogue between designers and users and helping the cross-cultural design community to better meet the demanding challenges of satisfying local cultural expectations in this participatory culture.

Cultural diversity in this book refers to the fact that we live in a multicultural global society; a variety of local users for a global technology form *culturally diverse* users. This applies to design situations of localizing a technology for assorted local cultures and those of designing a technology for collaborative use between users from different cultures at the same time.

Intended Audience

I am writing this scholarly book for people who work in the fields of human–computer interaction (HCI), technical and professional communication, user experience design, translation and localization, cross-cultural communication, information design, information studies, information systems, social computing, computer supported collaborative work (CSCW), writing and literacy studies, industrial design, science and technology studies, mobile communication, and Internet studies, to name a few; for people who share a passion for and an interest in making technologies that serve the needs of and give meaning to the lives of culturally diverse users; and for people who believe that designing a more culturally sensitive technology creates a better future for this global village. In the book I generally refer to this cohort of people as the cross-cultural design community.

For readers with a primary interest in cross-cultural issues, I would like to highlight the pervasive technological impact and illustrate the dynamic articulations of technology and culture in our contemporary situation. For readers with a background in technology design, I would like to emphasize technology design as a cultural practice rooted in the local and show its complicacy. For critical communication scholars and technologists, I would like to stress the emancipating power of design as the primary activity of human beings, which, deeply interwoven with the technology use decisions we make daily, will help us build a better technological order and design a better life and future in this technological culture.

While the book is mainly targeted at an academic audience, I hope thoughtful practitioners who are interested in the challenges caused by multicultural or cultural issues will also find the discussion useful.

The Structure of the Book

The book is divided into three parts: theoretical grounding, case histories, and scholarly implications. The first four chapters develop conceptual foundations for the framework of Culturally Localized User Experience. Chapter 1 looks at the subject of local culture, and Chapters 2 and 3 study the subject of user experience. For both subjects, I survey the current status of the studied topic, trace the conceptual movement for a broader vision of the notion, and develop and advance my view in the end. In Chapter 1 I establish a dialogic view of culture that connects action and meaning and describes local culture as the dynamic nexus of contextual interactions for requirements gathering in cross-cultural design practices. Chapters 2 and 3 develop a holistic vision of user experience that integrates action and meaning in cross-cultural design: Chapter 2 particularly looks at *why* to have a holistic vision, and Chapter 3 investigates the *how* and *what* in constructing this holistic vision by weaving intellectual traditions of activity theory, British cultural studies, and genre theory. The seven defining features of CLUE are outlined at the end of Chapter 3. Chapter 4 introduces the case of the book, the cross-cultural study of mobile messaging use, and discusses how CLUE worked as a framework for cross-cultural user experience research in this case study.

Individual case studies are brought forth to contextualize theoretical development. While reading all five cases as a whole provides a more complete vision of Culturally Localized User Experience, readers could pick up any of them and group them as they like to complement the reading of the theories and implications.

I begin with two cases that elucidate how action and meaning are interwoven in local uses, with a focus on the dialogic interactions of technology affordances. Chapter 5 looks at how American business professional Sophie used mobile text messaging for emotional support in various work settings in order to juggle work, family life, and friendship. The "artful integration" process was accomplished through her successful negotiation between instrumental and social affordances. Chapter 6 examines Chinese teacher Lili's messaging use in her daily social network. The meaning of the technology conveyed from its social affordance was so important to her that she would ignore the poor usability of the technology. This chapter also introduces a complex picture of various cultural influences during technology use.

Chapters 7 and 8 continue exploring the complexities of local culture beyond the models of cultural dimensions. Chapter 7 studies American graduate student Brian's texting use for coordinating with friends and examines how a precedent genre (instant messaging) shaped the local use of a new technology (text messaging) and the perception of the writing practices engendered (i.e., text messages as conversations) in the American context. Chapter 8 regards Chinese graduate student Mei's late-night message exchanges as a new form of fan innovation and a literacy practice. In comparison to Brian's orality practice, this chapter discusses how different cultural preferences lead to different use and genre patterns of text messaging and contribute to different meanings. Therefore, these two chapters illuminate the complicacy of a dual mediation process influenced by complex local cultural factors.

Chapter 9 traces the messaging use of American college student Emma for three years. It looks at meaning construction and identity work in cross-cultural design in a postmodern era and discusses how multiple identities were constructed in numerous layers of cultural contexts through a process of becoming, where the user was constantly looking for a technology to fit her lifestyle.

Broader implications of the empirical study are explored in the last two chapters. Chapter 10 further develops the framework of CLUE with a consolidated discussion of use cases and investigates how Culturally Localized User Experience is accomplished through user localization at the users' sites. Chapter 11 suggests future directions for the research and practice of cross-cultural technology design in a glocalization age. Centering on a dialogical approach, it analyzes what the cross-cultural design community could learn from the user localization efforts to design for, invoke, nurture, encourage, support, and sustain Culturally Localized User Experience for emerging technologies.

One of my goals in writing this book is to advocate an activity approach that places concrete user activities on the center stage of design in order to enrich the cultural dimensions approach that has dominated cross-cultural technology design research and practices. A taxonomic view of culture has its own value, but I do not agree on the simplistic tabulation of complex cultural situations in terms of cultural variables or the narrow and literal translation of cultural dimensions into interface features. For me, the cultural dimensions approach is a useful method, but we need a more rigorous design methodology to apply this tool effectively and avoid stereotyping local culture, which is what I have attempted to do in this book.

I remember taking an international business communication course shortly after I arrived in the U.S. In one class we "role-played" a business meeting where I was asked to play "myself," a Confucian Asian woman who would keep silent and only nod at meetings. While I do not speak a lot at meetings, I immediately saw how invalid that widely accepted image and cultural stereotype was: I had an urge to speak during the role-played "meeting," and I still vividly remember that strong urge. That realization has pushed me to voice my opinions about popular cross-cultural design myths over the years, and what follows is one of the utterances. . . .

Acknowledgments

Writing and publishing one's first scholarly book from a dissertation project could be a daunting process. I owe my genuine thanks to many people who helped me, advised me, believed in me, and pulled me through the puddles for the past few years.

I especially thank the following people who gave me sage advice and smart directions at the various key stages of book-making. I have benefited greatly from many enlightening discussions with my dissertation advisor Bill Hart-Davidson. This book and the empirical study from which the book is based would not have happened without his guidance. I have learned a lot from my committee Cheryl Geisler, Bob Krull, and Linnda Caporael, whose insights are reflected here. I am grateful to Clay Spinuzzi who believed this work would turn into an interesting book and encouraged me to think further and beyond borders. He helped me develop and define an interdisciplinary book project targeted to multiple fields. My former colleagues at Miami University Michele Simmons, LuMing Mao, and Jim Porter walked me through the writing and revision process: Simmons was a great sounding board as I worked from the early stage of the book proposal to the final manuscript review; Mao guided me to navigate between and connect the Eastern Asian and Western intellectual traditions; and Porter, as my "book advisor," read the earlier drafts and offered concrete writing suggestions that spruced up the book. It was my fortune as a first-time author to work with the Series Editor Alex Kirlik, who strongly supports my idea and tremendously helped steer the book project through the whole process with his sharp vision and wise directions.

I am grateful for the help and feedback from many people to this piece of work. I am indebted to the anonymous prospectus reviewers and manuscript reviewers from multiple fields who helped me remedy my disciplinary myopia. I am thankful for Rebecca Rickly from Texas Tech and her graduate students in Spring 2007 Field Methods course for the feedback on my dissertation and their particular suggestion for the name of the CLUE. The graduate students in my Information Design course in Spring 2010 gave me useful feedback for an earlier draft of the first chapter.

I have been very fortunate to work with many wonderful people along the way. I feel grateful to all participants in this study. Without them, this empirical study would not be as interesting as it is. I am thankful for the nurturing community of the writing program and beyond at Miami University including Jean Lutz, Heidi McKee, Katherine Durack, Paul Anderson, Jason Palmeri, Cindy Lewiecki-Wilson, Kate Ronald, Keith Tuma, and Kerry Powell. I appreciate the warm support and encouragement from my former Writing colleagues at Grand Valley State University Dan Royer, Kay Losey, Carol Kountz, and Ellen Schendel, and that from my colleagues in the Interdisciplinary Arts and Sciences program at the University of Washington Tacoma such as Bill Kunz and Divya McMillin. I want to thank James Zappen, Jason Swarts, and Mark Zachry for their help and advice. I am grateful to the editors and their proficient staff of the Oxford University Press for good support.

The fieldwork of this project was partially funded by the Joanne Wagner Memorial Dissertation Fellowship of Rensselaer Polytechnic Institute and the Research Grant-in-Aid of Grand Valley State University. The Assigned Research Appointment from Miami University allowed me to work on manuscript revision intensively.

Most of all, I am deeply indebted to my family. I thank my parents and my brother for their unflagging support and belief in me in many ways. I thank Irisa for realizing the importance of mommy's work as a little girl. And to Zhouxuan, who texted me a photo of a beautiful rainbow he took on the road trip to attend my dissertation defense, I would like to say, "yes, I can see it!"

PART I

GROUNDING

I

Approaching Culture in Cross-Cultural Technology Design

A Chinese college student was learning to use the Chinese version of Windows 3.2—the first graphical user interface (GUI) she had ever encountered—on her new computer. With the help of the translated *The Complete Idiot's Guide to Windows,* she made fast progress. However, every time she opened and moved a file, she was a bit puzzled as to why she needed to click a small yellow rectangular icon on the desktop. She was told that the yellow rectangle was *wen jian jia* (a Chinese translation of file folder), and its function was to organize files. But what is a file folder? Why did she need to organize her files? She had no idea. As someone who was unfamiliar with American office culture, she had never used a file folder before nor had any experience with filing documents—Chinese culture was not as obsessed with paper trails as American culture, at least not at this time in the 1990s. In rare situations, she used a Chinese file pocket, which looked like an American heavy-duty manila mailing envelope, to store her writing papers. Of course, she did not know that the yellow rectangle represented a horizontal tabbed manila folder, a mundane artifact in the American office environment, until she came to the United States for graduate study a few years later. She experienced that "Wow!" moment when she matched the yellow rectangle on her desktop interface with a real manila folder. But for a long time after her arrival, she still put all her computer files under one large folder with a one-level flat structure, just as she had in China—technically a same-sized Chinese file pocket cannot be placed inside another one, whereas a same-sized manila folder can be. It was after she became more familiar with the filing activity of American office culture that she learned to create various folders and subfolders to get her files organized hierarchically.

That student was me. And I was not alone as a confused local user for that file folder icon. I found later that users from some European countries experienced similar confusion (A. Marcus, 1996). In those countries, documents were stored vertically in a cardboard box-like container with a small finger hole located on the side panel of the box. Those users would prefer to see the vertical container's face with the finger hole as the icon for file collection.

The example above is one of many that show how complex and challenging it can be to design for users from another culture. Cross-cultural technology design is not just about translating a dialogue box or localizing an icon—a process of transferring meaning. A visual inter-face is built on the discursive practices and cultural values it represents (see Selfe & Selfe, 1994). For some local users who are unfamiliar with an activity embodied in design, such as organizing documents in this case, how could they understand what an icon represents? How could they enjoy the functionality of a program and appreciate the affordance of a technology? Therefore, how could the designed technology meet the cultural expectations of local users, support their complex activi-ties in concrete contexts, and empower their agency and mediate their identities in a contemporary situation?

In this book I will investigate the interactions and relationships between action and meaning in cross-cultural technology design. I argue that a design philosophy and model that attends to both action and meaning through the cyclical design process will help the cross-cultural design community to create a technology both usable and meaningful to local users, and I call this integrated approach Culturally Localized User Experience (CLUE). I hope it will bring timely clues and inspira-tions to this rapidly developing community and serve as a conceptual foundation and resource at a time when so many challenges await.

The central argument of this book is that we need to integrate action and meaning in cross-cultural technology design to augment the everyday lives of local users. This opening chapter explores the unin-tegrated situation of cross-cultural technology design from the angle of culture, the core of cross-cultural design. My goal is to establish a dialogic view of culture that connects action and meaning in cross-cultural design practices. I first assess the status of culture in cross-cultural design practices, discuss how narrow representations of local culture result in poor user experience of localized technologies, and review the movement of capturing local culture from the surface to its core with case studies of three approaches commonly adopted in cross-cultural design. This discussion is further contextualized in a contemporary situation, where I examine the complex interactions between culture, technology, and design and develop a position for technology design that attends to both instrumentality and social circulation. Building on that, I outline a dialogic vision of culture as a semantic space that bridges implementation and interpretation in the end.

The Problem of Culture in Cross-Cultural Design Practices

Culture is a heavily contested term with myriad connotations from different fields such as communication, psychology, sociology, anthropology, science and technology studies, and information systems. It can be used either in a singular form, when we want to regard culture as one constituting entity and highlight its characteristics as a whole; or in a plural form, when we want to emphasize different varieties of culture. Before further developing a dialogic view of culture later in this chapter, I briefly preview my take on culture here. Informed by research in anthropology and ethnomethodology, I regard culture as the meanings, behaviors, and practices that groups of people develop and share over time as well as the tangible manifestations of a way of life, such as artifacts, values, and states of consciousness (Geertz, 1973). In this sense, local culture includes broad sociocultural factors from national/ethnic culture (e.g., collectivism vs. individualism, universalist vs. particularist orientations) and from subgroup culture (e.g., age group, gender, and organizational affiliation), individual factors (e.g., personal background, values, and interests), ways of life, daily activities, and interpretations of these.

Because of the complexities of the notion of culture itself and its multi-voiced connotations from different fields, accounting for local culture is not easy in cross-cultural design: Even though culture takes a central role in a cross-cultural design process, it remains one of the major problems constantly hurting design practices.

The good news is that the essential role of culture has been claimed, proven, and validated in an extensive amount of research literature and real-world cases of market failures where companies did not carefully consider local cultural issues (e.g., DeVoss, Jasken, & Hayden, 2002; Hofstede & Hofstede, 2005; Hoft, 1995; Taylor, 1992; Victor, 1992). As a matter of fact, we see the pervasive term "culture" frequently appearing in cross-cultural design literature. One could expect to encounter the word "culture" in almost every piece of literature, and usually more than once. For example, the importance of culture is well recognized in the set of three official definitions of cross-cultural design provided by the former Localization Industry Standards Association (LISA), an international nonprofit organization founded in 1990 to develop industry standards for IT localization:[1]

> Globalization... refers to all of the business decisions and activities required to make an organization truly international in scope and outlook. Globalization is the transformation of business and processes to support customers around the world, in whatever language, country, or culture they require. (LISA, 2007, p. 1)

> Internationalization is the process of enabling a product at a technical level for localization. (p. 17)

> Localization is the process of modifying products or services to account for differences in distinct markets. (p. 11)

For a product/service to go global, the process of globalization[2] usually consists of two parts, *internationalization* and *localization*. The first step is "isolating and extracting all cultural context from a product" (Taylor, 1992, p. 34); the second step is "infusing a specific cultural context into a previously internationalized product" (ibid). According to LISA, localization covers four main categories: linguistic issues (linguistic adaptation for genres such as user interface, online help, user documentation, and marketing and product collateral materials); physical issues (physical modification); business and cultural issues (the presentation of information, such as local currencies, formats of name, number, time, etc., icons, graphics, and colors); and technical issues (redesigning and re-engineering a technological product to accommodate issues such as double byte characters). Put simply, the localization industry believes cross-cultural design practice should either remove culture-related modules (e.g., in internationalization) or add them (e.g., in localization) at some point along the design cycle, and culture plays an important role in the processes of both reduction and addition.

In some ways, the concept of culture actually creates more opportunities for the field of IT localization. At an online conference on localization and translation training in 2003, researchers suggested that localization does not have to be limited to the adapting process when translation is involved. It can be "a process of adapting anything to a target locale" (Clark, Drugan, Hartley, & Wu, 2003) or "an interdisciplinary process of adapting an information technology (IT) product to the needs or expectations of a specific target audience" (Drouin, 2003) as long as there is a distinctive culture and locale there; for example, technology design for senior citizens or young children can be regarded as localization.

The bad news is that regardless of the consensus about the importance of culture in cross-cultural design, the application of culture work remains within a narrow scope and on a surface level (Sun, 2002b). Practitioners spend most of their energy on a technological product's form, such as what colors would not work for an audience in a specific country and what page layout would be preferred by some ethnic cultures. As I have argued elsewhere (Sun, 2006), professionals design for operational convenience, without careful consideration of how to support meaningful activity in a local context for social affordance.

To better explain this, let us turn to a popular analogy, the iceberg metaphor, which has been used widely in intercultural communication to describe the complexity of culture. Hoft (1995) proposes that issues of translation, punctuation, color, page layout, and aesthetic appeal are just the tip of the iceberg, and this visible section above the water is only 10 percent of the whole. In contrast, its huge submerged body, invisible to designers and manufacturers, accounts for the other 90 percent of the iceberg and consists of unspoken and unconscious rules (e.g., common knowledge and values shared within a culture). This huge underwater iceberg—the broader cultural context where technological products are situated, designed, produced, distributed, and consumed—needs to be well attended to by designers. The shortsightedness of looking at only the tip of the iceberg results in a product-oriented localization process that separates product design from product use, and the resultant technological products are detached from their contexts. Many manufacturers do not have an overall vision of localization strategies in product design: Their localization work occurs only at the developer's site, and it ends when the product ships. They are not aware of either the complex interactions between use and design or user localization.

Moving beyond Narrow Representations of Local Culture

Behind this shortsightedness and resultant decontextualization, there is a profound problem in technology design: a disconnect between action and meaning (see Bødker & Andersen, 2005; Svanæs, 2000). In this section, I probe one side of this unintegrated situation: the narrow representation of local culture. When local culture is approached in a confined way, the actual practices of social activities are missing in this understanding, and we see the narrow scope of localization work discussed above. Here I go over three common approaches for capturing local cultural contexts in cross-cultural design, represented by a case each, through which I show the focus of these three approaches move from the tip to the deeper level of the iceberg and explain why they still neglect to portray a more complete picture of local cultural contexts due to their methodological limitations.

DOs and DON'Ts, Anecdotes, and Business Cases

Much of the local cultural knowledge designers have developed over years resides in various forms of DOs and DON'Ts, anecdotes, and business cases.

To envision a local culture, we might want to think of walking into a friend's messy room: Initially the messiness strikes us as strange, yet it shows traces of familiarity, and after a while we might be able to discern the structure behind the apparent messiness. One approach is to see the messiness and then log, categorize, and organize it into ad-hoc cross-cultural communication guides. Lengthy lists of DOs and DON'Ts, oft-repeated warning boxes, and industry case studies make up the staple for topics on intercultural communication and international business in many textbooks. They come from personal experiences, informal observations, numerous encounters, and even friends' stories. A typical list of DOs and DON'Ts would include items such as do be punctual when meeting German businesspeople, but be prepared for the late arrival of a Mexican collaborator. And an industry case might look like this: "American toothpaste manufacturer Colgate introduced a product called 'Cue' in France, but it turned out to be the same name as a well-known adult magazine. Oops!" These intensive efforts on cultural details often lead to guidelines, rules, advice, warnings, standards, and handbooks of cross-cultural design in translation, coding conventions, layouts, fonts, graphics, and testing (e.g., Lingo Systems, 2000, 2009; MultiLingual, 2010; Schumacher, 2010).

Nobody can deny the value of this type of experiential knowledge; we all know that a deep understanding always begins from initial encounters and interactions. However, these manifestations of culture usually represent only the cultural conventions of a dominant culture in a country (the tip of the huge iceberg). One example is applying "cultural markers" to website localization (Barber & Badre, 1998; Sheppard & Scholtz, 1999). Barber and Badre define cultural markers as interface design elements that stand for local cultural conventions, including national symbols, colors, spatial organizations, etc. They recommend incorporating cultural markers in web design to increase web usability and acceptability. For example, an American bank website might want to use the color green to attract Egyptian customers because green is associated with fertility and growth in Egypt. Taking the conventions for granted, this approach tends to neglect the nuances and dynamics of an ever-changing culture. In some cases, people blindly follow the old rules without realizing that they are outdated. Barber and Badre cite a color-culture chart from previous research in which the color white is associated with death for Japanese culture; however, the connotation of white has expanded as more and more Japanese brides choose to wear white Western-styled gowns at their weddings.

Most of the time, cultural manifestations are presented as they are, without further justification about why we see them. It would be helpful to know that a Mexican would show up late to a business meeting because Mexican culture has a less formal perception of time than

German culture does. In a similar way, while designers appreciate DOs and DON'Ts about conducting user research in countries with which they are not familiar, such as not scheduling tests in a particular month, they would find a list of DOs and DON'Ts based on cognitive differences and cultural expectations more valuable than that of logistics information, like this example: A usability test moderator in India needs to dress differently to match the socioeconomic status of the test participants because Indian daily interactions function upon social status. Either a "dressed up" or "dressed down" situation could hinder data collection (Beaton & Kumar, 2010).

This view of local culture captures neither action nor dynamic meaning from the angle of technology design. The validity of the findings is also sometimes questionable, as there are no rigorous methods used to obtain this type of knowledge. Generally this approach is built on a technical/engineering frame of mind, which favors efficiency over culture sensitivity. For Barber and Badre, culture is "a means of distinguishing among the different countries and their respective web-sites" (1998). When the richness of culture is reduced to some means, the whole process of localization is simplified as part of the engineering cycle from the planning stage to the testing stage, detached from its use context. In the pursuit of engineering and automating this process, practitioners need only to attend to delivery and style, such as translating the user interface and resizing a dialogue box, as shown in many internationalization and localization manuals (e.g., Esselink, 2000; Kano, 1995; Lingo Systems, 2000; Musale, 2001). The resulting phenomenon is that localized products and services are usually not appropriate for use contexts.

Value-Oriented Cultural Dimensions

Unsatisfied with shallow manifestations of local culture, researchers seek to understand the structure behind the messiness to better capture local culture, and a series of models of cultural dimensions are thus developed (e.g., E. Hall, 1983; Hofstede, 2001; Trompernaars, 1993; Victor, 1992), among which is Hofstede's landmark study (Hofstede, 2001; Hofstede & Hofstede, 2005). Hofstede regards culture as "collective programming of the mind" (2001, p. 1) and associates culture with values, "a broader tendency to prefer certain states of affairs over others" (p. 3). Based on survey results collected from IBM in 72 countries in the 1970s, he developed the following five cultural dimensions to compare local culture:

- *Power distance* refers to the extent to which less powerful members of a culture expect and accept unequal power and authority distribution.
- *Uncertainty avoidance* measures the (in)tolerance level when the members of a culture face ambiguous and unknown situations.
- *Individualism and collectivism* describes the ties between an individual member and his or her various groups.
- *Masculinity and femininity* refers to traditional gender roles associated with work goals. For example, earnings and recognition are associated with a masculine type, and cooperation and employment security are associated with a feminine type.
- *Long- versus short-term orientation*[3] describes the tendency to foster virtues oriented toward future rewards versus toward more immediate results.

Applying a quantitative research methodology, Hofstede generated cultural indexes for the five dimensions and normalized them to values of 0 to above 100. For example, a high power distance index (PDI), like 104 for Malaysia, shows that the vertical structure of authority in this country is more rigid than other countries. Compared to anecdotal evidence of cultural knowledge, Hofstede's framework of cultural dimensions helps designers to focus on "the regularities between cultures" by reducing "cultural differences to a manageable number" (Gould, 2004, p. 67) and provides vocabularies and structured models to assess cultural patterns across nations. It is the most popular approach used in cross-cultural design among the three reviewed here (for example, Choi, Lee, Kim, & Jeon, 2005; Ess & Sudweeks, 2005; Faiola, 2002; A. Marcus & Gould, 2000; Singh & Pereira, 2005; Zahedi, Pelt, & Song, 2001).

A report of cross-cultural information systems research published in 2002 found that 24 of 36 pieces of literature reviewed used some or all of Hofstede's cultural dimensions (Myers & Tan, 2002). As revealed by Hofstede in the preface to his second edition of *Culture's Consequences* (2001), the first edition, published in 1980, is one of the most cited in the entire *Social Science Citation Index* since its publication. Indeed, Hofstede's work is so influential that at least two other larger projects of cross-cultural comparative surveys followed to study cultural values, testing and enriching Hofstede's findings in the 1990s—the Global Leadership and Organizational Behavior Effectiveness (GLOBE) research project, conducted among 62 societies with 150 researchers involved (House, Hanges, Javidan, Dorfman, & Gupta, 2004); and the World Values Survey (WVS), undertaken in 43 societies and with multiple researchers involved (Inglehart, 1997).

While these cultural models help designers see more of the submerged iceberg, they also introduce methodological inaccuracies to design practices: They promote a positivist view of culture,[4] which strips rich contextual data away during the formation of the formal structure. First, only the dominant cultural values in a national culture are represented in cultural models; other subcultural factors, such as the individual user's gender, age, organizational affiliation, or ethnic group, are ignored. It is an "overly simplistic" treatment of culture (Myers & Tan, 2002). For example, the nation–state is actually a relatively recent phenomenon, occurring in the later part of human history. In cross-cultural design practices, we often see local cultures that are related to a subculture in a country (e.g., text messaging is more popular among teenagers than other age groups in the Western world), but these cultural models cannot help design and localization processes if they are obscured by a set of national culture dimensions.

Second, these views of culture place concrete cultural realities into static dimensions, with an emphasis on cognitive schemas of ethnic groups. Some information systems researchers notice that those value-oriented variables could not fully explain the complex cultural phenomena found in the field when the messiness and complexities of the local contexts (e.g., immediate context) are often neglected and only general patterns originating from the broader social contexts are attended to. For example, Harvey (1997) concludes her research on a comparative study of geographic information systems between German and American users this way: "Hofstede's dimensions of national culture are a good basis for understanding the influence of national culture on organizations' self-representation, but miss the actual practice of social activities" (p. 145). Weisinger and Trauth (2002) agree that "such broad dimensions are perhaps useful only at a high level of analysis (i.e., at the country level) but not at the level of interaction where a variety of contextual factors can affect behavior" (p. 315). From an anthropological point, Batteau (2010) comments that culture is treated by Hofstede as "a storehouse filled with collective attitudes cut from similar parts templates," and thus "the dials and knobs of culture can be adjusted to meet the demands of modern industry" (p. 85).

In fact, missing the actual practice of social activities is a common problem in cross-cultural design literature, as we can see from the two representations reviewed so far. As an example, Hoft's book *International Technical Communication* (1995) covers many aspects of internationalization and localization with "international variables," but none of them comes from field studies of use activities in context. In her mapping of international variables (p. 114), all of the variables are static and abstract. When designers follow her suggestions of cultural editing (p. 123), they can only beautify buttons with local translations, though the real goal here is to support complex user activities in their local contexts. When culture is operationalized into abstract dimensions separated from concrete user activities in the localization process, culture is not situated in practices anymore. Moreover, this narrowness misses the use moment when certain kinds of local uses are engendered by particular sociocultural settings and when certain technologies are adopted in a locale to reinforce or transform the social-structural configurations. For example, some East Asian users think mobile text messaging is more suitable for Asian people to express implicit feelings and emotions.

While action is missing, the value-oriented meaning is not rich enough either. The survey Hofstede and his colleagues conducted explored employee attitudes in an organizational context (IBM), rather than in a broader sociocultural context. Survey participants, most of whom were middle class, shared many cultural values and interests concerning their careers and working contexts. Some of the cultural dimensions were developed based on the responses to a limited number of questions; for example, the power distance index was derived from the answers to only three questions. Trompernaars, Hofstede's student, collected his data in a similar way, developing his model based on a 16-question survey and participants made up of managers and administrative staff (Hoft, 1995). Furthermore, E. Hall's model came from personal observation, and Victor's model primarily came from secondary sources. The GLOBE project and the WVS project have similar limitations as Hofstede's. If we regard Hofstede's study as a form of usability research, then we would have to conclude that the test participants Hofstede chose for his "usability tests" might not match the profiles of our targeted users most of the time, and that the test objectives and focuses might not fit our design situations either.

Clearly, these models were advanced to study cross-cultural communication, usually in an international business context, rather than for cross-cultural design; therefore we need to be more careful when using them to inform design decisions. A literal translation of cultural dimensions into interface design patterns—for example, a website for a local culture with a high uncertainty avoidance index should have a simple and structured layout—might miss other design opportunities to address richer cultural issues and end up falling into the trap of the DOs and DON'Ts approach again. In the conceptual framework for cross-cultural web design that Zahedi and his colleagues proposed (2001), Hofstede's cultural dimensions are synthesized with social constructionist theory to study individual factors and address complex cultural interactions, which can be seen as a move toward the goal of depicting local culture more thoroughly.

Structured Fieldwork Methods

The method of fieldwork is an approach introduced to avoid a positivist view of culture and to capture rich activities at local sites. With a focus on the richness and texture of everyday life, this approach is concerned with the production and exchange of meanings between the members of a society or group in an ethnomethodological sense. Fieldworkers study how users use a product in their natural contexts, just as anthropologists observe aboriginal people, and thus provide thick descriptions of users using a technology in their surrounding culture. Of course this type of design ethnography (see Salvador, Bell, & Anderson, 1999) brings its own disciplinary baggage to HCI design. For example, it lacks formal models for data analysis and knowledge reuse related to IT product design. Dray and Siegel (2007) also note that it risks ambiguous fieldwork data and premature closure in data analysis. As Sullivan (1989) pointed out long before, successful adaptations are needed before the fieldwork method can really contribute to usability research.

Contextual design (Beyer & Holtzblatt, 1998; Holtzblatt, Wendell, & Wood, 2005) is a successful adaptation in many ways. The idea of contextual design is to enter the user's world as an "apprentice" in order to learn and to make observations and inquiries related to the selected focus areas of a client project. Through having a typical two- or three-hour contextual inquiry of each carefully selected individual user by various team members, the design team develops a collaborative understanding of a local context based on five work models: (1) the *flow model* surveying the communication and coordination in which people are engaged at work, (2) the *sequence model* studying the task sequence of work, (3) the *artifact model* investigating the assumptions and role of artifacts in the work, (4) the *cultural model* examining the issues of cultural context in a workplace, and (5) the *physical model* reviewing the physical environment of the workplace.

A contextual inquiry usually employs qualitative methods such as observation, walkthrough, and interview. Compared to ethnographic fieldwork, contextual design maintains a hermeneutic stance in seeking to understand in-situ user experience through empathetic interpretation of a local culture, as well as contextualizes the messiness and richness of a local culture via a set of structured methods. Thus it has been a very popular design approach adopted by big IT companies including Ericsson, Intel, Microsoft, Nokia, and SK Telecom as a participatory method to gather design requirements in general design and cross-cultural design (e.g., Blom, Chipchase, & Lehikoinen, 2005; Jokinen, Karimäki, & Kangas, 2003; Nieminen-Sundell & Vaananen-Vainio-Mattila, 2003; Page, 2005; Vaananen-Vainio-Mattila and Ruuska, 2000; Yi, 2010; Yu & Tng, 2003).

"Context" is a key principle that defines the approach of contextual design. According to Beyer and Holtzblatt (1998), this principle advocates immersing designers into the studied workplace and observing the unfolding work. It is a way of obtaining "ongoing experience" and "concrete data" (p. 47). While the central focus on context contributes to the popularity of contextual design in industry, the scope of the proposed context is limited in the following ways. First, this context refers only to the workplace. As originated to answer design calls for enterprise information systems, the work models of contextual design were developed to examine work practices in an organizational context, but not to understand social computing practices in an individual context like mobile phones and other information appliances.

Second, this context has "the problem of unintegrated scope," as Spinuzzi assesses (2002, p. 4). The "macroscopic" understanding of a local context, an understanding of the level of cultural–historical activity, is accomplished through data-collection methods (e.g., targeted observations, walkthroughs, and interviews) that function at the "mesoscopic" level—a level of situated, goal-directed action.[5] The mismatch between the project focus and the data-collection tools implies that there is an underlying work structure that has "a causal, foundational relationship with the other levels." This conflicts with sociocultural theories that support "co-constitutive" relationships between levels and thus causes "the problem of unintegrated scope." Furthermore, it misses "the reciprocal changes" across different levels (p. 13).

Third, as something significantly relevant to context, culture is unfortunately given insincere support in this design methodology. Guidelines about cultural issues are superficial and brief, and the cultural model primarily studies policy, power influence, and group frictions. It is doubtful how this cultural model can help to collect data hidden in the underwater iceberg without deep engagement (see Sullivan & Porter, 1997); Randall, Harper, and Rouncefield (2007) comment that this use of context lacks "a sociological sensibility" and claim that "[c]ulture is perhaps the most ambiguously articulated concept in Beyer and Holtzblatt's exposition" (p. 29). As a matter of fact, the cultural model is skipped in the process of rapid contextual design (Holtzblatt et al., 2005).

Therefore, a structured fieldwork method like contextual design is still narrow in its scope, as it contextualizes only half of the process. Its interpretation of the local culture tends to focus on the immediate context of where a user is situated, and it fails to connect the immediate context with the broader sociocultural context, which is important in localization practices. This is also a common limitation for current fieldwork methods, i.e., those methods that focus just on the aspect of tool-mediated production of an IT artifact in context, but rarely explore its sign-mediated communication, though they come from a hermeneutical stance that values meaning creation in cultural practices. Thus they are good for gathering design requirements for instrumental convenience but are poor at exploring design options for social affordances. Other limitations include studying product use either only at certain stages or for a short period. Long-term research with a focus on a developmental aspect is also very hard to find in this approach.

Compared to large-scale, cross-cultural studies on value-oriented cultural dimensions, most projects employing structured fieldwork methods remain as scattered case studies. While there emerges reports of cultural factors (e.g., Thomas, Haddon, Gilligan, Heiznmann, & de Gournay, 2005) assembling case studies to "make sense of national differences" (p. 13) with a sociological sensibility, it is still too early to expect coherent interpretations of the findings on the global level for two reasons. First, it is more difficult to conduct a large-scale, qualitative study across societies and cultures than to do a quantitative project like the GLOBE study methodologically. Second, there is an internal tension between "contextualized interpretations" brought by fieldwork methods and "standardized data collection" of multinational comparisons (Livingstone, 2003, p. 494).

In summary, the three ways of capturing local culture are presented in a chronological order; at the same time, they form a lucid trajectory directing design research from the surface to the deeper level of the underwater iceberg, and thus make a continuum of local cultural knowledge from limited to more complete. Applying Geertz's view of culture to assess the representations of local culture in terms of action and meaning, the approach of DOs and DON'Ts does not have a systematic way of sorting out action and meaning; the approach of value-oriented cultural dimensions looks only at a static view of meaning; and the approach of structured fieldwork methods intends for both action and meaning, but ends up depicting action with an unintegrated scope and meaning just coming out of an immediate context. Clearly a richer and more dynamic view of local culture is needed for the success of cross-cultural design.

Technology Design in a Technological Culture

To be more accurate, as the three approaches aim to better capture and present local cultural contexts for technology design in order to create products appealing to local users, what they investigate for culture is actually part of collecting requirements and determining needs of the design process. So the representation and manifestation of local culture should be fully examined in the nexus of technology, design, and culture. Questions thus arise: What is technology? What is technology design? And what does technology design mean to our contemporary situation?

Technology is a modern word; for example, Karl Marx never used this word in his work of the early 19th century (Murphie & Potts, 2003), but no philosopher and thinker of today could skip it. To the same extent, *technology* is as much a challenged notion as *culture*, which deserves a standalone book just for the review of its numerous connotations. Indeed, cultural studies scholars Slack and Wise (2005) claim that, since technology assumes a crucial role in our everyday life (culture is a whole way of life for the school of cultural studies), it is meaningless to treat culture and technology as "separate entities" when examining the complex relationship between technology and culture (p. 4). For them, technology should be defined "in terms of articulations[6] among the physical arrangements of matter, typically labeled technologies, and a range of contingently related practices, representations, experiences, and affects" (p. 128). Because "the particular articulations that constitute a technology *are* its context" (p. 128–129, emphasis as it is), *technological culture* depicts the reality of our contemporary situation better than culture and technology treated separately. To put it this way, the relationship of technology and culture forms "the central problem of technological culture" (p. 4).

From an anthropological standpoint, though the term "technology" is a modern phenomenon, the connotation is not new. Tool-making precedes thinking, and Marx did write a lot about the machinery of production for his time. Batteau (2010) traces the development of technology in cultural evolution and lists three core components of technology: instrumentality, social circulation, and engineering knowledge (e.g., instructions and standards). An object of local ingenuity, like a digging stick, embodies instrumentality, but it is not considered technology until after its entrance into social circulation. He further explains: "*Tools* are merely implements, innocent of the purposes to which they are put. When a tool enters social circulation as a technology, it picks up the values, social projects, and ultimate purposes of those who introduced them, giving those values and purposes a shape and sturdiness they would otherwise lack" (p. 21, emphasis as it is). This distinction clearly marks the boundaries of "technology," which prevents a loose use of the term in the discourse of technology design.

The process of social circulation manifests *the rhetoric of technology*, which is "the rhetoric that accompanies technology and makes it possible—the rhetoric that makes technology fit in the world and makes the world fit with technology" (Bazerman, 1998, p. 385). For Edison's invention of the incandescent light bulb to become a household technology (see Bazerman, 1999; Hughes, 1999), it went through a process of "enlisting supports of numerous publics (financial, legal, corporate, public, technical)" and "arguing for value in terms of business, law, government, the public, and consumers" (Bazerman, 1998, p. 384).

The core of technology also indicates that, for a technology, being usable—derived from its *instrumentality*—goes hand in hand with being meaningful on a cultural circuit with its engendered meaning through *social circulation*. The third element of engineering knowledge is actually the external demonstration and stabilization of instrumentality in social circulation.

Design matters profoundly in a technological culture. It is "basic to all human activity" (Papanek, 1972, as cited in Julier, 2008, p. 40), and it is "the crucial anvil on which the human environment, in all its detail, is shaped and constructed for the betterment and delight of all" (Heskett, 2005, p. 1). The notion of design encompasses contested meanings in contemporary society as well. Describing design as "a highly entrepreneurial profession," "a maturing academic discipline," and "a global phenomenon" (p. 1), Julier (2008) defines design as "a culturally specific practice which is driven almost entirely by strategies of differentiation" (p. 3). I argue that, with a technology as design outcome, *technology design* embodies a constellation of design processes, design communication, standards and regulations, manufactured products and deliverables, and production and consumption that aims to transform our lives and surrounding contexts. In addition, I would clarify that, while the approaches explored and discussed in this book apply to cross-cultural design issues for a vast range of technologies, I primarily look at interactive technologies or information and communication technologies pervasive in everyday life.

To understand how technology design functions on a complex cultural circuit, let us look at a real case occurring in a remote Indian village (Prabhu, 2007). Designers noticed that every day, young women had to walk one hour's distance from the village to a well to carry water for the whole family; designers built an electric-pumped well inside the village to help those women. However, the newly built well suffered an incident shortly after it was completed: It was buried with big stones and could not be used. Assuming it was a mischievous act from naughty kids, designers removed the stones and fixed the well. To their dismay, the well had another incident a few days later; this time the electric pump was damaged. After some covert investigation, they found the damages done to the well did not come from naughty children as they had believed, but from the target users who they expected would most benefit from this well—young women of the village.

Why did some young women want to damage a well that would save them time and labor? It turned out that, in an Indian village, married young women have the lowest status in a big family and they must listen to the orders of their mothers-in-law. Walking one hour to carry water was tedious and laborious; however, that was the only time in the day they could enjoy friends' company and have some time for themselves. When the well was built, they did not have an excuse to leave the house for an extended time period during the day and thus were deprived of quality time that was important and meaningful to them. The repercussions for these young women were similar to the riotous acts of destroying machines that German overworked wage-workers engaged in during the 19th century, even though the well's designers might defend that their goals were different (they were not trying to make profits by increasing work efficiency like the capitalist owners of the German plants): The well was introduced to make users' lives easier. Yet in a globalization age, designers might not realize that a design solution of goodwill could seem insensitive and sometimes rude to local users.

This kind of unintended, negative side effect that a technology could introduce to a local ecology can be termed "the water hyacinth effect." Water hyacinth is a beautiful, fragrant flower that has plagued the Lake Victoria area in Africa (Impiö, 2010; "Water hyacinth," 2010). It was brought from Brazil and planted in private ponds in Nairobi in the 1980s by a British gardener who had a naïve idea of decorating gardens. Far away from its natural rivals at home, this invasive weed grows like a virus on its new continent, occupies a large freshwater area, and negatively impacts local ecology by blocking boat access, sticking to the feet of water birds, and cultivating mosquitoes and other insects that carry and spread diseases. Determining how to eradicate this plant is a big headache for local governments.

The water hyacinth effect alerts designers about possible dark sides of a seemingly goodwill technology. For example, when social activists acclaim the democratic progress brought by the new technology of short messaging service (SMS) in countries like the Philippines,[7] conscientious designers should also be concerned about the possibility of introducing more uproar between tribes in countries such as Kenya and Nigeria, where text messaging and social media make spreading hateful rumors much easier. Impiö points out that "the lack of cultural understanding" and "stubbornly pushing Western ideals and operating models to African countries" (p. 25) are two main factors resulting in these unintended negative effects. To do no harm, technology designers from a Western culture should reconsider their commitments to the values that they assume are important—such as individualism, privacy, equality, autonomy, creativity, and liberation—in the countries where the designed technology would be distributed (Flanagan, Howe, & Nissenbaum, 2008).

Indeed, designers should be aware that they are in the "consequence business," as design practice is characterized as "an unequivocally interconnected, global, and consequence-creating endeavor" (Chochinov, 2009, p. 8). With an increasing consensus among designers on the values a technology embodies and the consequences it could hold to a local culture, more and more people take part in the movement of "design for social good" in the field of industrial design (e.g., Chochinov, 2007; IDEO, 2008; Pilloton, 2009; Smith, 2007; Thackara, 2005). In the field of computer systems design, the teams of "Value Sensitive Design" (e.g., Friedman 1996, 1997; Nissenbaum, 2005) and the Group of Computer Professionals for Social Responsibility (CPSR) are making bold efforts to bring sociological sensibility and humanistic values such as dignity, justice, and welfare into technology design practices.

Among these myriad efforts to achieve culturally sensitive design, culture has become a more integral part of the design process and has been advocated as a usability goal,[8] as a design tool, and as a research methodology. The practice of advancing culture as a design tool is popular in the field of instructional design, and various frameworks and tools have been put forward. For example, Lee (2003) proposes the "Cultural Modeling Framework" in instructional design to address student populations of color and those living in poverty. Likewise, Eglash, Bennett, O'Donnell, Jennings, and Clintorino (2006) suggest "Culturally Situated Design Tools," web-based software applications, to help Native American and African American students grasp mathematical principles, as part of their ethno-computing movement. As to culture as a research methodology, more and more social science theories and cultural theories are being introduced to guide technology design processes. Examples include using cultural theories to design mobile phone prototypes (Satchell, 2008), regarding "current design practices as a form of social research" in an approach of "culturally embedded computing" where the design choices and resulting implications are more important than the actual design (Sengers et al., 2004), and applying interpretive analysis as a framework of "interaction criticism" to examine design practices in HCI (Bardzell & Bardzell, 2008).

To conclude, technology design is a cultural practice—"the cultural production of new forms of practice" (Suchman, Blomberg, Orr, & Trigg, 1999, p. 404). Numerous case studies from the field of science and technology studies have demonstrated that technological artifacts are culturally constructed (e.g., MacKenzie & Wajcman, 1999; Pinch & Bijker, 1987). The role of technology design in a technological culture could be further contextualized with a deep understanding of a critical theory of technology (Feenberg, 1999, 2002). Criticizing a determinist view of technology, Feenberg believes that, on the one hand, technology embodies cultural values that influence our ways of using it, shape our lives, and eventually integrate us through interaction; on the other hand, the view of technology constituted as a cultural system offers opportunities for alternative modernity and social transformation through "a politics of technological transformation" (2002, p. 13). He combines philosophical substantive theory that regards technology as a form of domination and control with social constructivism that sees social values and interests constructed in the development of technology. In this regard, Value Sensitive Design and other participative design movements benefit from the intellectual contribution Feenberg made: "Most fundamentally, democratization of technology is about finding new ways of privileging these excluded values and realizing them in the new technical arrangements. I call this process 'democratic rationalization' because it translates public demands into technically rational advances in design" (2004).

Clearly, the possibility of developing culture-sensitive technology designs will not truly loom if a singular model of modernity in technological development has not been challenged and falsified. A mindful cross-cultural design that values cultural diversity is fundamentally founded on a philosophy of technology that believes in "cultural variety in the reception and appropriation of modernity" (Feenberg, 1999, p. 183). In contrast, a singular version of modern civilization "gradually homogenizes every other difference as it obliterates geography and subverts all traditional values" (Feenberg, 2002, p. 15). Therefore, cross-cultural design is valuable for democratic rationalization. Furthermore, opposing a determinist attitude to technology, the position of "constraining and enabling" is crucial in Feenberg's theory of technology to develop a proposal for alternative modernity based on different paths of technological development. It is a recurrent theme in cross-cultural design as a technology interacts with local culture, and we will see more discussion about this in later chapters.

Last, I want to emphasize that it presents a noteworthy stance as an author when I decided to interpret and investigate computer system design, software development, and IT implementation as technology design in this book. This stance signifies a shift in design philosophy that considers developing computing applications in a broader sociocultural horizon, and a focus on humanistic values and commonalities for technological artifacts. In this sense, while factors such as efficiency, effectiveness, and error-free are still highlighted in design practices, designers do not think only of "the object of instrumentality"—using Batteau's term—to develop a tool for augmenting a user's work and life, but also begin to explore the position and meanings of this object in the user's life and surrounding contexts, i.e., social circulation. It is a technology, more or less, with a sociological sensibility. It is not value-free: It comes from a particular sociocultural context and will shape and change the sociocultural contexts in which it will be introduced.

Advocating a Dialogic View of Local Culture for Technology Design

The case of the Indian well shows the sophistication and intricacy of capturing local culture in the process of social circulation. Representing local culture in the design process seemed pretty straightforward when local technological and economic conditions were considered; however, the local user culture was more complicated than it looked on the surface. Even though DOs and DON'Ts, value-oriented cultural dimensions, and structured fieldwork methods could offer insights into the actual design of the electric-pumped well for this particular user group, none of them would be able to anticipate the negative impact on the lives of the targeted users as the well altered their lifestyles. Culture here is mainly treated as a usability goal in the design process without a full inquiry into the role that culture plays in this process. Therefore, the three views of culture are incomplete. Indeed, the three approaches of capturing local culture function as "requirements gathering" in the design process, also called "requirements analysis," which is a beginning step in software development to determine the needs and goals of users. Due to this instrumental orientation on representing local culture, it is easy to miss the fact that the technologies being developed are also making culture, influencing and altering local culture, and becoming part of the local culture.

Going back to the iceberg model to look at local culture, we need to be aware that the iceberg does not stay statically in the water (i.e., the outside world, more specifically, global culture) but is growing itself and interacting dynamically with the surrounding waters. The inside of the iceberg constantly changes as time passes. Moreover, some part of the iceberg might be melting while in contact with the surrounding waters. In the age of globalization, culture is a dynamic process in which meanings, objects, and identities flow across institutions, nations, and generations (G. Marcus, 1995; Sassen, 1998). Local culture is concretely an open, back-and-forth dialogue of insiders and outsiders, of the local and the global, of diverse factions. It is hard to separate local culture from global culture. Both local culture and global culture are so closely intertwined that the former is actually one part of the latter.

For that reason, we need to have a dynamic and open-ended view of culture to tackle local cultural issues more effectively in cross-cultural technology design. This view treats culture as emergent, becoming, practiced, temporal, and thus contested (Myers & Tan, 2002; Slack & Wise, 2005; Weisinger & Salipante, 2000). The most provocative characteristic is culture in the making. Based on Giddens' structuration theory (1984) that structure and action constrain each other recursively, Weisinger and Salipante describe culture as "a socially enacted, dynamic process involving the reproduction and revision of practices," and they believe this view "captures a much richer conceptualization of the construct, recognizing the simultaneity of (a) similarities and stabilities and (b) contestation and change" (p. 384).

Therefore, I argue for a dialogic[9] view of culture that is both robust and flexible to study local culture and offer a more complete vision of culture for technology design. Here, culture is dialogic as an open set of practices and as an energetic process with meanings, objects, and identities flowing across sites in diffuse time–space. It is concerned with the production and the exchange of meanings between the members of a society or a group. Meanings are produced and circulated through several different key processes, including representation, identity, production, consumption, and regulation of the cultural circuit within a technological society (S. Hall, 1997).

According to du Gay, Hall, Janes, Mackay, and Negus (1997), "[the] two meanings of the word 'culture'—culture as 'whole way of life' and culture as 'the production and circulation of meaning'—constitute a recurrent theme" (p. 13) in defining what culture is. To me, these two aspects are not either/or options in an articulation for culture, but constitute a more complete reality of culture. In technology design and use, we seek to understand the "whole way of life" of local culture and articulate it into the design process (i.e., a social circulation process of "the production and circulation of meaning"). As design extends to use, the newly built tool becomes a new addition to a way of life, participates in and contributes to the meaning production and circulation in a local context, and becomes a technology.

The dialogic view of culture can be complemented by the characterization of culture as "a semantic space" by John and Jean Comaroff (1992):

> [W]e take culture to be *the semantic space, the field of signs and practices, in which human beings construct and represent themselves and others, and hence their societies and histories.* It is not merely an abstract order of signs, or relations among signs. Nor is it just the sum of habitual practices. Neither pure langue nor pure parole, it never constitutes a closed, entirely coherent system. Quite the contrary: Culture always contains within it polyvalent, potentially contestable messages, images, and actions. It is, in short, *a historically situated, historically unfolding ensemble of signifiers-in-action, signifiers at once material and symbolic, social and aesthetic.* (p. 27, emphasis added)

Here, practices and meanings are constituted in "a semantic space" where the collective meets the individual and where implementation (instrumental aspect) interacts with interpretation (social aspect) in a dialogic manner. In this sense, *local culture is both a site of the dynamic, ever-changing nexus of contextual interactions, and an assemblage of myriad articulations as a semantic space consisting of meanings and practices.*

Regarding culture as a semantic space constituted dialogically can help us form a more complex picture of cultural realities in cross-cultural design. This social practice view of culture places rich user activities on center stage and thus embodies vivid meanings. Compared to the other views of culture surveyed earlier, this view of culture is in the same camp as a hermeneutic approach. However, a dialogical view looks further and is deeply situated in local practices with a recursive process of structuration between structure and agent, between the context and the individual. This lens recognizes the merits of cultural dimensions models and structured fieldwork methods, and treats them as part of the dynamic interactions when the patterns from cultural models or fieldwork methods are articulated into a semantic space. So far I have primarily looked at the conceptual value of the dialogic view of culture; its methodological implications are reserved for further discussion in Chapter 4.

Conclusion

The central question of this chapter is how to approach local culture for cross-cultural technology design in a technological culture. Because of the disconnect between action and meaning in technology design, a sound solution needs to integrate both and capture local culture as dynamic and emergent. To develop that, I study three ways of representing local culture as "requirements gathering" in technology design and assess their methodological weaknesses in terms of action and meaning. Through a comparison of the three, I reveal that these narrow representations overlook rich activities in local culture and leave out dynamic meanings in technology design. Therefore, I argue for a dialogic vision of culture as a semantic space for technology design that addresses both implementation and interpretation.

A full grasp of this dialogic view of culture depends on a critical understanding of the complex relationships between technology, culture, and design in a contemporary society. Cross-cultural design is never neutral or instrumental. It is a site of becoming, and "a scene of struggle" (Feenberg, 2002, p. 15). Four pairs of dialogic relations emerge out of the discussion: (1) a view of culture that integrates practices and meanings, (2) a position for technology that is enabling and constraining, (3) an approach to technology design that aims for both instrumentality and social circulation (i.e., both the tool aspect and social aspect), (4) and a motive for cross-cultural technology design that should be both usable and meaningful. They are the key terms that form the scaffold of the design methodology of CLUE, and these dialogic relations will be constantly revisited and investigated in later chapters.

My goal for the first four chapters is to lay the groundwork for *Culturally Localized User Experience*. I chose to focus on the conceptual construction of *local culture* in Chapter 1, reserve the theory-building of *user experience* for Chapters 2 and 3, and explore the methodological implications of a construct that integrates both—*culturally localized user experience*—in the context of the comparative study of mobile text messaging use in Chapter 4. After that, we will move into an intriguing collective case study of mobile messaging uses in two cultural contexts.

In the next chapter, we will look at cross-cultural design from the angle of usability and user experience research, and work on developing a design and research framework that brings together action and meaning in cross-cultural design. While Chapter 1 examines the narrow representation of local culture, Chapter 2 examines the narrow conceptualization of usability in design practices. The former sees the meaning aspect but ignores action; the latter addresses only action, and thus it necessitates a holistic approach to user experience.

Notes

1. After LISA's insolvency in February, 2011, other international organizations such as the Translation Automation User Society (TAUS) and the Globalization and Localization Association (GALA) continue to develop industry standards for the field.
2. Globalization is a concept with complex political, economical, and cultural implications. In most parts of this book, globalization is used to provide a backdrop to the discussion of cross-cultural technology design and refers to business decisions and practices. A more theory-informed discussion of globalization can be found in Chapter 11.
3. This dimension was not added until the second edition of *Culture's Consequences* (2001). It was developed based on Confucian philosophy.
4. For a similar argument about the positivist paradigm, please see Ford, Connelly, & Meister (2003).
5. For a more detailed clarification of the difference between an activity and action, please see the section on activity theory in Chapter 3.
6. A cultural studies view of articulation refers to the contingent connections embodied in an entity when forming its unity. For a more in-depth discussion of articulation, please see the section on British cultural studies in Chapter 3.
7. SMS played a significant role in organizing massive protests rapidly to end the dictatorship of President Estrada in the Philippines in 2001 (Rheingold, 2002).
8. I will further elaborate on how culture is advanced and incorporated as a usability goal in the next chapter.
9. For an in-depth discussion of dialogicality, please see Chapter 11.

2

User Experience in Global Context

In the previous chapter, I reviewed the narrow representations of culture in cross-cultural design practices and looked at the resulting decontextualization. However, to make a fair judgment, this problem must be examined against a wide background. It not only occurs in cross-cultural design practices, but it commonly appears in current IT product design and development as well. Since traditional usability research tends to regard usability as an isolated quality, it ignores the sociocultural context surrounding the artifact, and technology use is often decontextualized (Adler & Winograd, 1992; Brown & Duguid, 1994; Spinuzzi, 1999b). Unsurprisingly, cross-cultural design—a sub-field of technology design and development—experiences the same problem, a disconnect between action and meaning.

When issues of sociocultural contexts are overlooked in design practices, as often happens, lower-level tasks are modeled in design rather than higher-order processes and more meaningful activities (Adler & Winograd, 1992; Mirel, 2004); design generally aims toward one preferred interpretation (Sengers & Gaver, 2006) based on one mental model representing those lower-level tasks, wherever the user is situated. To successfully reach culturally diverse users, cross-cultural design needs to articulate the single preferred interpretation into multiple ones that are meaningful to local users. This is currently achieved by introducing localization work to customize interface features for targeted users after the functions are specified. However, top-level interface features are closely connected to the user model and its derived functionalities on the bottom level, and thus it is doubtful how effectively all the interface adaptations, coming from the same—possibly problematic—mental model, could lead to multiple interpretations. The reality is that miscommunication would occur on various levels, ranging from a small icon that brings about unexpected interpretations to a simple task that might not make any sense to users who do not share the same mental model, as what we have seen from the case of the file folder icon at the opening of the book.

A narrow understanding of local culture complicates this situation. As discussed in Chapter 1, missing the actual practice of social activities is a big problem in cross-cultural design work. It is true that interpretation is a central issue in cross-cultural technology design because designing for culturally diverse users is "a problem of communicating the intended meaning of representations" (Bourges-Waldegg & Scrivener, 1998, p. 299). However, being a widely held belief in the cross-cultural design community, it speaks only half of the truth. While the completion of design goals depends on whether local users are able to interpret meanings mediated by a technology in their own contexts, the goal of communication is not just about transmitting a meaning the sender intends to in a postmodern age. On some occasions, a communication transaction expects that the receiver will be contributing to the meaning-making process by adding new meanings. So designing for culturally diverse users is more than *conveying* the intended meaning.

To address the problems surveyed above, we need to develop a deep understanding of how interpretation and interaction should be integrated and synced smoothly in cross-cultural design. I argue for a holistic, integrated vision of user experience that takes user experience as both situated action and constructed meaning. To make a clear case, I use the "why, how, and what" questions to develop the argument: This chapter explains *why* it is necessary and important to have a holistic vision of user experience, and the next chapter explores *how* the holistic approach forms and *what* it embodies. Here I first examine the usability concept and review the conceptual movement from usability to user experience. Then I review cross-cultural usability research and practices and probe into the disconnect between action and meaning in technology design.

Expanding the Narrow Scope of Usability

To understand the necessity and importance of having an integrated vision of user experience that connects action and meaning in cross-cultural technology design, we need to be clear about what user experience means and connotes, which should begin with a review of the history and status quo of usability studies.

Originating from the fields of cognitive science and computer engineering, usability studies started with an engineering perspective interested in measurable qualities of a product. Later, various social science perspectives were introduced to bring cultural consideration into usability studies and to expand the scope of usability.

Usability Engineering

The engineering approach of usability has dominated the field of HCI for the past few decades, and it remains influential today. It regards usability as a measurable quality of an artifact. One of the most cited definitions comes from Jakob Nielsen (1993), who describes usability with five metrics: learnability (easy to learn), efficiency (efficient to use), memorability (easy to remember for reuse later), errors (a low error rate), and satisfaction (pleasant to use). Nielsen stresses: "Only by defining the abstract concept of 'usability' in terms of these more precise and measurable components can we arrive at an engineering discipline where usability is not just argued about but is systematically approached, improved, and evaluated (possibly measured)" (p. 26–27).

Striving for accuracy and measurable results is an advantage of this approach, and researchers and practitioners of this school, mostly from the fields of computer science, psychology, human factors, and information systems, have made substantial contributions to the development of usability criteria, testing measures, design heuristics, rules, and guidelines for computing artifacts and interface design (e.g., Dumas & Redish, 1993; Keeker 1997; Norman, 1988; Nielsen, 1994; Rubin, 1994; Shneiderman, 1998). There are two types of usability evaluation methods (Gray & Salzman, 1998): analytic methods that examine product features to identify possible problems of usability (i.e., from features to problems), such as heuristic evaluation, cognitive walkthrough, and guidelines; and empirical methods that study the problems arising from use and then link them to product features for improvement (i.e., from problems to features), such as laboratory testing. For some researchers, scientific measures are the hallmark of usability research. They claim that the ultimate success of usability engineering will depend on the development of a new field of usability science—a marriage of cognitive and perceptual psychology and usability engineering (see Gillan & Bias, 2001).

With a focus on product features, the engineering approach sees usability as a component within a larger system. Nielsen (1993) maps usability as "a *narrow* concern compared to the larger issue of system acceptability" (p. 24, emphasis added). In his model (see Figure 2.1), system acceptability denotes "whether the system is good enough to satisfy all the needs and requirements of the users and other potential stakeholders" (ibid), consisting of social acceptability and practical acceptability. Usability is identified as a factor three levels down from system acceptability, via the branch of practical acceptability, and then through the branch of usefulness. Usefulness here refers to the system's ability to accomplish desired goals, and it is composed of utility and usability: Utility deals with system functionality while usability examines "how well users can use that functionality" (p. 25). This mapping confines usability to a corner of the whole system acceptability, away from sociocultural and contextual factors. As part of the concern for usefulness, usability attends to the desired goals of local users based only on product functionality.

As a result, the sociocultural context surrounding the product is often ignored in research and practice, which causes the following

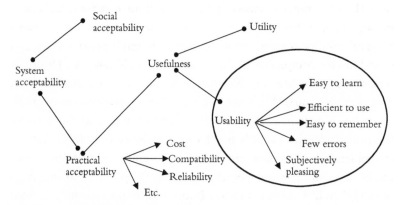

FIGURE 2.1   Usability as a Product Quality (Nielsen, 1993, p. 25. Used with permission from © 1993 Elsevier.)

problems in design practice (Adler & Winograd, 1992; Johnson-Eilola, 1996; Mirel, 2002):

- Users are treated as test subjects from a mechanical view.
- Only lower-level actions are attended to.
- Each usability metric becomes a separate design goal without being integrated as a holistic usability benchmark, and some measures, such as efficiency and learnability, are prioritized while a measure like satisfaction is ignored.
- Usability is not introduced to the design process until a late stage.
- Usability studies are reduced to usability testing, and only the decontextualized uses of technology are studied.
- The whole design process is regarded as a means instead of an end.

To expand the scope of usability research and incorporate cultural consideration into usability studies, a variety of social science and humanities perspectives have been utilized to study usability beyond measurable product qualities. Four design shifts have occurred, including from product quality to context quality, from user representation to user participation, from use to consumption, and from developer localization to user localization.

From Product Quality to Context Quality

A technological product is not used in a vacuum, but in a real context. The surrounding sociocultural contexts provide a setting for interactions, influence user decisions, and are ultimately immersed into user experience. The context is a part of the whole in which users interact with a technology and deems to be an important part of usability concern.

Situating usability study at the forefront of multidisciplinary fields such as HCI, psychology, sociology, anthropology, marketing, and technical communication, Sullivan (1989) was among the first who advanced a broader vision of usability (see R. Johnson, Salvo, & Zoetewey, 2007). She argues that usability research "includes the work of people who design systems, test them, develop educational materials, and study users" (p. 256). The subject matter should consist of users who would learn to use products and then actually use these products in various contexts, informed by different research methodologies from a variety of disciplines. Instead of usability testing, usability evaluations should be regarded as both problem solving and theory building, introduced into usability research, and inserted at an earlier phase of product development.

As more people recognized the importance of sociocultural contexts in usability research, "context of use" was mandated as part of the ISO 9241-11 definition of usability a decade later (ISO 9241, 1998). The standard defines "quality of use" as "the extent to which a product can be used by specified users to achieve specified goals with *effectiveness, efficiency,* and *satisfaction* in a specified *context of use*" (p. 2, emphasis added). Here "context of use" refers to characteristics of the users, tasks, and the organizational and physical environments.

In situations of complex problem solving, helping users to accomplish their goals is more than ease of use. Mirel (2002, 2004) thus advocates "designing for usefulness." Rather than being a product characteristic, usefulness is an experience coming from the context—"the structural arrangements and relations between people, resources, and contextual conditions for a given task or problem" (2002, p. 182). She calls a design shift "moving from task- and even user-centered designing to designs centered on use-in-context" (p. 167) and asks designers to consider both procedural support and structural support in technology design. For example, a bar code medication technology based only on a task sequence model runs well when a patient case is textbook perfect; however, it could cause a lot of hassle at a time when a nurse needs to override dose specifications to serve a patient who is too sick to take the prescribed doses.

With heightened attention to the use context, the view of usability as product quality becomes questionable. The use model of technologies such as wireless phones and mobile messaging makes the single-agent model of usability obsolete and calls for a system-wide view of usability. Wireless phone and mobile text messaging technologies require more than just a handset to instantiate practice. To get those technologies to work, the hardware, software, and service technologies must cooperate. For instance, the usability of wireless phones lies beyond the handset (Palen & Salzman, 2002a): The technological system of a wireless phone is made up of four socio-technical components: the hardware, software, netware (the network technology for mobile telephony including phone services, calling plan features, and calling coverage), and bizware (policy from wireless carriers).

Even for mundane technologies besides wireless ones, usability should be better explored as quality of the context rather than quality of a product. Tuomi (2002) declares that technologies are "social arti-facts that become usable only in a context of social practice" (p. 22). In analyzing why many early artificial intelligence and expert systems for medical diagnosis remained in laboratories, he finds that the use success of those systems "requires changes in current laws and terms of insurance policies, as well as guarantees from electricity suppliers that the power does not go off in the middle of a critical diagnos-tic task" (p. 28). Here "social activity system" and "institutions that embed social relations" play a vital role in product usability. In another case, Spinuzzi (1999a, b, 2003) proposes a distributed model to inves-tigate user activities based on the fieldwork of how workers use maps, reports, handwritten notes, and paperweights to assist a computer application for analyzing traffic accidents. He maintains that usability is a quality of the entire activity network and is distributed across the network (1999a, p. 77). According to this distributed model, usability is not located in a single artifact but distributed across various actors, tools, and goals. People use an interrelated group of tools to jointly mediate their activities.

To conclude, the problem of decontextualized technology use may be attributed to the problematic concept of usability itself: "[I]t projects the qualities of an activity system into one of its components, a tool" during a transformation process (Virkkunen & Engeström, 2001, see Figure 3.1). Accordingly, usability explorations usually stop at lower-level tasks and ignore higher-order processes.

From User Representation to User Participation

A network-wide view of usability implies and initiates a shift from product-oriented design to process-oriented design. In a process-oriented approach, user contributions are valued, their roles are ele-vated, and the whole design process is regarded as a communicative process rather than as an engineering process. This is what the par-ticipatory design approach advocates (see Ehn, 1993). Emerging from

Scandinavian working and political conditions, this approach is being embraced quickly by researchers and practitioners. Instead of treating user involvement as a means to an end, participatory design considers user participation as the end itself (Iivari, 2006). Technology use is thus regarded as an active process of "articulation work" in which users work with designers and producers as both actors and constructors to co-construct the whole practice in an "enabling and empowering" system (Hales, 1994). Participatory design aims for two types of user empowerment: functional empowerment—accomplishing jobs effectively and efficiently; and democratic empowerment—participating in the decision-making process (Clement, 1994).

The contribution of user knowledge to the design process is regarded highly in this movement. One approach to empower users in a technological order is to reclaim the value of user knowledge from the classical rhetorical tradition (R. Johnson, 1998). While *techne*, the procedural or productive knowledge related to technology use, has been historically placed much lower than scientific knowledge on the epistemological order since the Enlightenment (Sullivan & Porter, 1997), a close reading of Aristotle's definition of *techne* shows that *techne* "involve[s] a true course of reasoning," and thus it is "a generative source of knowledge that gives users the potential for a significant degree of involvement and power regarding technology" (R. Johnson, 1998, p. 52). This understanding elevates the status of users in the design process. Offering *techne*, users are not "idiots," but contributors to the design knowledge. They assume three important roles in design practices: "as practitioners" who use tools, "as producers" who are involved in the design process, and "as citizens" who serve as both active participants in the larger technological order and as equally responsible members of the technology enterprises of our culture (p. 46).

To increase users' involvement in the design process, a dialogic relationship between technology producers and users becomes more critical (see McCarthy & Wright, 2004; Wright & McCarthy, 2010; Spinuzzi, 2008). For example, Salvo (2001) proposes developing an ethic of dialogue for usability, based on the work of Bakhtin and Levinas. Dialogic ethics could help designers to counteract the ethic of expediency associated with the engineering model of usability and incorporate diverse local interests, "assuring full user-participation rather than mere user-representation in the design process" (p. 275). It also signals a focus shift in usability studies "from evaluation of user actions to engagement with users" (p. 273).

For some researchers and practitioners, the engagement with users through a communicative and collaborative process should not be the final end. An activist vision would aim for emancipatory potential and social changes—as argued in Feenberg's work (1999, 2002), which might include, for example, designing meaningful technologies for people living at "the Bottom of the Pyramid" (Prahalad, 2006). The Bottom of the Pyramid accounts for an estimated four billion people who live on less than US$1,500 per year and are eager to use technologies to improve their daily lives. Researchers propose to view these users "not as passive victims, but as active consumers, capable of identifying opportunities and creating innovative solutions" and to help them "become active participants in the movement towards improving their own lives and well-being in addition to advancing in the economic pyramid" (Aykin, Chavan, Dray, & Prabhu, 2007, p. 3), similar to the movement of "design for social good" reviewed in Chapter 1. Examples of such designs include the One Laptop per Child (OLPC) program, which designs low-cost laptops for poor children in the world, and Project Masiluleke, which uses mobile phones to fight HIV/AIDS and TB in South Africa.

From Use to Consumption

As today's computing technologies become mundane objects in users' daily lives, consumer culture plays an increasingly important role in technology use. Users adopt a technology more for its social values rather than its instrumental convenience. Particularly since the introduction of mobile phones in the 1990s, a new type of user has emerged (Kuutti, 2001). Unlike the users who were "a cog in a rational machine," "a source of error," and "partners in social interactions" in early decades and with whom designers have been familiar, these new users are consumers who have "emotions and needs for pleasure and self-expression." As consumers, users are not only interested in how to use a technology to complete a task but also looking for ways to integrate the technology into their everyday life according to their lifestyles—to paraphrase Descartes, "I use, therefore I am."

In this context, established usability methods with a focus only on ease of use are "ill-suited," particularly for emerging technologies and applications (Thomas & Macredie, 2002). A new vision of usability is called for to study consumer experience. In the case of mobile messaging, there is a strong tendency for integrating technologies into a user's everyday life, socially and emotionally. Several concepts have been proposed to examine the phenomenon beyond technology use. Mante and Heres (2003) put forward the term "technology integration." They point out that, rather than mere use, there are three aspects of technology integration in the case of mobile technology: the adoption of technology by the individual and the diffusion of the innovation on the societal level; the integration of technology to make it fit into one's daily life; and the positioning of technology among other daily technologies by considering life values, moral economy, and so on.

Clearly, the social aspect of technology integration is highlighted in this line of research. Carroll and her colleagues (2002) use the term "appropriation"[1] to describe "the way in which technology or technological artifacts are adopted, shaped and then used" with a "technology appropriation model." Based on their case study of Australian young people, they maintain that users are adopting not just a technology, but rather a lifestyle. During the appropriation process, the "technology-as-designed" is transformed into the "technology-in-use." They recommend that researchers focus on the psychosocial dimensions and socio-technical interactions in use. In another case, Haddon (2003) describes the integration process as "domestication" by applying the domestication model he and Silverstone (1996) developed from their TV studies. Here "domestication" looks at the *taming* of innovation by the individual, the process that integrates personal technology into everyday domestic life, leading to the real adoption of a technology. Derived originally from British studies on consumption, the concept of domestication emphasizes consumption rather than mere use. The three distinct dimensions of consumption—commodification, appropriation, and conversion—are also three moments in domestication.

Behind the phenomenon of integrating technologies into daily life, a process of cultural consumption is emerging when a user consumes the technology for his or her lifestyle and transforms a material user experience into a subjective and symbolic one. According to French thinker Michel de Certeau (1984), this type of consumption is itself production because consumers employ creative strategies to define their identities and thus have become producers on a cultural circuit. The interaction and overlap of production and consumption have been well documented in assorted cases of cultural studies (see Mackay, 1997), and consumers who innovatively consume cultural artifacts are called "prosumers" (Toffler, 1980), a combination of *producers* and con*sumers*.

The shift from use to consumption is influential to usability research and practice, when designers do not associate consumption with a passive consumer for technology use.[2] We see the use horizon expanding beyond the adoption stage, and the following design directions have appeared to meet new user needs. There are mounting efforts to design sensible services beyond a product to keep users as loyal consumers (e.g., Saffer, 2007; Merholz, Wilkens, Schauer, & Verba, 2008); to search for design solutions to meet user's emotional, aesthetic, and leisure needs rather than task needs (e.g., Blythe, Over-beeke, Monk, & Wright, 2004; Hassenzahl, 2008; Sutcliffe, 2010); to conduct usability evaluation for a full spectrum of qualities such as pleasure, humor, emotion, trust, identity, loyalty, and engagement, rather than functional qualities (e.g., Fogg, 2003; Green & Jordan, 2002; Norman, 2004); and to design for social computing (e.g., Porter, 2008; Crumlish & Malone, 2009). Furthermore, consumers tend to "produce" individually toward the better use of a technology in the active form of consumption; the shift from use to consumption also signals a turn to the individual in technology design. This turn brings subjectiveness and individual creativity to the center stage of design, and it is crucial in understanding how to design for local users in the era of participatory culture.

From Developer Localization to User Localization

In technology design, we tend to think a product with poor usability will not gain popularity. The case of mobile text messaging seems to be an exception. With inherent usability weaknesses at the time of the introduction, such as small display and keypad, poor input methods, and limits on message length, nobody expected that users would use wireless phones for composing and reading text messages. In fact, text messaging was originally introduced as a voicemail alert service in the UK in the early 1990s (Hill, 2004), but few people remembered that. It was not until a few years later, when a young generation in the UK and other Western European countries decided to take up this difficult technology as their own communication channel, different from their parents' and teachers' (MobileSMS, 2004), that the value of mobile messaging technology was recognized. In this case, creative users rescued a technology.[3] Their enthusiasm, wisdom, and efforts have turned a hard-to-use technology into a huge use success. Of course, text messaging is not the first technology in history that surprised its designers. The evolutionary histories of the telephone, the Internet, the World Wide Web, email, and the Linux operating system celebrate user success in a similar way (Tuomi, 2002).

I call these energetic user efforts of using a technology within meaningful social practices and incorporating the technology into one's life *user localization*. It differs from *developer localization*—the localization work occurring at the developer's site that we commonly refer to when thinking of localization. The endeavors of user localization continue from developer localization and occur in the context of local users through technology use. They often determine the market success or failure of a technological product. In the mobile text messaging case, users adopted this technology for instrumental convenience that other technologies were unable to offer (e.g., communicating silently and discreetly) for their daily routines. They have been building a new communication mode and a new form of social relations through use. Therefore, this technology has acquired its meaning and gained significance in users' everyday practice.

The term "user localization" implies two layers of connotations. On the first layer, as I wrote elsewhere (Sun, 2009b), user localization refers to integrating a technology "into a user's everyday life after adoption, socially and emotionally" (p. 249). This represents a methodological move of investigating beyond mere technology use for technology design, which explores the possibility of how to make a technology both usable and meaningful.

It is "artful integration" in technology design (Suchman, 2002), in which "[d]esign success rests on the extent and efficacy of one's analysis of specific environments of devices and work practices, finding a place for one's own technology within them." At this level, user localization shares some similarities with the concepts that study the post-adoption phenomenon of mobile communication, at a stage moving from use to consumption, such as "technology integration" (Mante & Heres, 2003), "appropriation" (Carroll, Howard, Vetere, Peck, & Murphy, 2002), and "domestication" (Haddon, 2003), reviewed in the previous section. However, an in-depth comparison of these concepts to "user localization" shows that user localization has a conceptual advantage of framing a user's interaction with a technology and the following integration in a locale, and thus it can give sufficient attention to the differences of local cultures and the dynamic interactions between situated uses and the surrounding cultural contexts. Accordingly, the integration process is twofold: It is a complex interplay among a mobile technology and its surrounding social, cultural, technological, and economic conditions, and an articulation work of self and locale involving concrete use activities surrounding the user's identity and self, both enclosed in a particular locale.

On the second layer, user localization emphasizes the contributions users have made to a technology's design process in participatory culture. As I have argued earlier (see Sun, 2006), the idea of user localization pushes the agenda of usability research toward considering localization as designing technology for local audiences with a full appreciation of their culture, and thus espousing a rhetoric of designing and evaluating technology at the user's site. Indeed, it epitomizes a way of culturally achieving usability goals. This line of thinking is aligned with what von Hippel (2005) advocates for: "end-user innovation." He finds that between 10% and 40% of users are developing or modifying the products they use. Compared to manufacturers who have more "solution expertise" in their specialized areas, users have more "need expertise" about local needs and context of use than manufacturers do. Therefore, he believes that the innovations from users informed by their need expertise, combined with manufacturers' solution expertise, will eventually help manufacturers to create better designs more quickly and less expensively.

This type of "'downstream innovation,' i.e. the innovative capability of the user community," is often the bottleneck of whether an innovative product is accepted by users or not, as pointed out by Tuomi (2005, p. 31). The technologies that function as "killer applications" in terms of technology innovation usually "have empowered the users to articulate and achieve goals that were difficult or impossible to achieve before. Often such 'killer applications' also enable many different types of use and multiple interpretations of the meaning of the provided functionality" (p. 29). Apparently, text messaging technology can be named as such a "killer application," with its flexibility of initiating and nurturing a huge variety of local uses.

It is noteworthy that although "user localization" shares the same interest in investing in user contribution in the design and use process as "end-user innovation" and "downstream innovation" do, the former examines *diverse* user efforts from an angle of technology design to create for a better user experience in a local context while the latter two look for *innovative* contributions in order to convert the innovation into new business opportunities. This heterogeneous characteristic of user localization also distinguishes it from the Technology Acceptance Model (TAM) (Davis, 1989), which is widely adopted in information systems research to study technological innovations (for examples of multi-cultural studies, see Meso, Musa, & Mbarika; 2005; Straub, 1994). TAM is interested in assessing individual user attitudes for technology adoption with the assumption of causality, but this linear model does not seem to account for complex cultural conditions in multi-cultural studies (see Straub, Keil, & Brenner, 1997; McCoy, Galletta, & Ring, 2007). In comparison, user localization looks at the co-constitutive interaction between technology and users beyond the adoption stage in a global context. The ultimate goal of user localization is to link design and use. Therefore, this dialogical nature of user localization makes it possible to incorporate complex subjectiveness into the objective design process and to develop a dynamic and co-constructive relationship between designers and users.

To sum up, all these new shifts and emerging developments in the field point in one direction: How can we make technology both usable and meaningful for users? How should we support users' meaningful activities in their local contexts?

Beyond Usability: User Experience

More and more researchers have come to realize that the problem of usability research scope is related to the concept itself, which has an inherent limitation (Jordan, 2000; Virkkunen & Engeström, 2001). A more robust and expandable construct is needed to address increasingly complex issues of technology use in a broader sociocultural context. The term "user experience" seems to be such a candidate concerning people's expectations. Appearing as early as the 1970s in an article about an interactive graphics application (Edwards & Kasik, 1974), the term was reclaimed and embraced by design practitioners and researchers since the later 1990s. Below are two definitions from well-established user experience professional groups:

> "'User experience' encompasses all aspects of the end-user's interaction with the company, its services, and its products." (Nielsen Norman Group, 2008)

> "User Experience is the quality of experience a person has when interacting with a specific design. This can range from a specific artifact, such as a cup, toy or website, up to larger, integrated experiences such as a museum or an airport." (User Experience Network, 2008)

User experience represents the changes for which people want to advocate in the design and use of information technology. In the case of IBM's "total user experience" (Vredenburg, 2002), user experience signifies an expanded scope of technology use in terms of the timeline and the range of services, and thus practitioners are able to work on a time span from when potential customers see an advertisement for the product or service to the point at which they consider upgrading that product or service. User experience also brings more design considerations to the table, including branding, identity, emotions, and pleasure. Web designers and information architects found that user experience provided a way of describing various design factors. User experience is described as consisting of three skills—information architecture, interaction design, and identity design (Kuniavsky, 2003)—as being made up of five planes of content areas including user needs, function specification, interaction design, interface design, and visual design (Garrett, 2003), and as presenting seven facets of the characteristics "useful, usable, desirable, findable, accessible, credible, valuable" (Morville, 2004).

The ascendancy of user experience is a natural outcome of a few converging forces: We are in a new era of *experience economy* (Pine & Gilmore, 1999). In addition to commodities, goods, and services, experiences are the fourth economic offering and the new source of value, which will provide most of the business values. Successful businesses excel in offering personalized, memorable experiences for their customers with techniques such as mass-customization. In the new field of experience design, designers work on staging the best consumer experience, and managers and strategists search for ways of connecting with customers at every touchpoint and yielding the most positive customer experience informed by the new knowledge domain of *customer experience management* (Schmitt, 2003; Watson, 2008).

Though a natural move, it is legitimate for us to wonder whether user experience is just a buzzword, an updated version of usability in a new age, or indeed a better solution to the problematic usability construct. In the fad of naming current design and evaluation practice with user experience without further conceptual investment of the term itself, there is a tendency to quantify user experience, as shown in some of the examples discussed above. This reductive approach reduces concrete lived experience into measurable and predefined elements and falls into the trap of a mechanical view of usability again. This view of user experience might help us to address some consumer culture concerns, but it still treats user experience work as product quality and does not support full engagement with users in the design process.

If we truly want to go beyond the scope of usability, we need to find a better way of theorizing the concept of user experience. User experience not only connotes a broader horizon of technology use but also introduces a new way of thinking for technology design and evaluation, and it has a great potential to attend to the wider issues of technology use in context. In contrast with a reductive approach, some researchers have been using a holistic approach to better understand technology use and user experience by returning to philosophical traditions: phenomenology and pragmatism. They believe experience is a key term that helps us see the connection and fusion between action and meaning in technology use, which will illuminate our technology design practices.

Hermeneutic and phenomenological philosophy was first introduced to the computing world by Winograd and Flores (1986) to advocate an alternative design ontology and methodology to the dominant view of rationalism at that time. In search of design heuristics for emerging trends of tangible and social computing, Dourish (2001) investigates the essential feature of everyday experience: embodiment, defined as "a form of participative status" (p. 18). Through a careful review, he finds that embodiment has been a common theme behind major schools of phenomenological thought. He maintains that embodiment is "the property of our engagement with the world that allows us to make it meaningful" (p. 126) and "a property of interaction" (p. 189). In this sense, embodiment is the nature of our everyday experience, as it is "being grounded in and emerging out of everyday, mundane experience" (p. 125). Based on this, Dourish developed a framework of *embodied interaction* to grapple with "everyday, mundane experience" in technology design.

Though Dourish never labels his work as user experience research, his key concept of embodiment elucidates the essence of user experience, and his design solution of "embodied interaction," which argues for "the creation, manipulation, and sharing of meaning through engaged interactions with artifacts," applies to both tangible computing and social computing, as well as general user experience design practices. Furthermore, another major contribution of Dourish's work is that it accentuates the importance of designing for meaningful activity, as he declares that "the relationship between action and meaning" is "a central concern" for interaction design (p. 184).

According to Coyne (1995), pragmatism should be regarded as a guiding philosophy for computer system design. The engagement with human action from pragmatic thinkers such as Dewey would introduce "a pragmatist orientation" to the computing world that is "primarily concerned with the way the computer system will be used" to understand "how the technology fits within the day-to-day practical *activity* of people" (p. 31, emphasis added). For McCarthy and Wright (2004), the values of Dewey's pragmatic thoughts go beyond that.

Though starting with human action, Dewey's pragmatism attends to both action and meaning of experience. Along with his focus on the practicality and materiality of human action, Dewey is also interested in studying the relationship between self and object, examining how creative action emerges and unfolds in an "open, unfinalized, and unfinalizable" world through "a dynamic process of becoming" (p. 69), and discovering how the meaningful action forms everyday experience and continues through aesthetic experience.

McCarthy and Wright believe these pragmatic insights align well with Bakhtin's dialogic world view and his exploration of everyday meaning-making experience through individuals, and thus can be combined together to bring back "the livedness and feltness" and sense-making to user experience research, and serve as "an enlivening antidote to the means-to-ends instrumentalism" (p. 52) of those reductive models. They maintain that "experience is essentially holistic, situated and constructed" (Wright, McCarthy, & Meekison, 2003, p. 46) and argue for a holistic approach to experience that is a "lived, felt experience as prosaic, open, and unfinalizable, situated in the creativity of action and the dialogicality of meaning making, engaged in the potential of each moment at the same time as being responsive to the personal stories of self and others, sensual, emergent, and answerable" (McCarthy & Wright, 2004, p. 184). Thus they developed a view of user experience that is both material and interpretive. In this view, subjectivity has gained ascendancy, and searching for the subjectivity in the dialogic process of becoming turns into an important design goal (Wright & McCarthy, 2010).

It is not coincidental that phenomenology and pragmatism are chosen to explore the notion of user experience in the above two cases. They share many traits: Both are interested in everyday experience and focus on practice; both investigate the relationship between action and meaning; and both hold a participative stance to engender changes for transformation. Clearly, a holistic approach regards user experience as the relationship unfolding in practice as both interaction and interpretation, aiming for change and improvement.

It should also be noted that both treatments of user experience share a theoretical emphasis on the meaning of user experience, which traditional usability research and practice tend to lack. Sense-making has taken on an increasingly important role in design practices as the scholars of science and technology studies have successfully shown that technology fosters different ways of interpretation among various user groups with myriad cases (e.g., Krippendorff, 2006; MacKenzie & Wajcman, 1999; Pinch & Bijker, 1987; Verbeek; 2005). Sengers and Gaver (2006) claim that "[i]nterpretation is a central issue for HCI" (p. 99). Experience is meaning-construction (Hassenzahl, 2010; Vyas & van de Veer, 2006). It is "a dynamic process and an emergent product that is a contextually and socially constructed in the lived environment" (Vyas & van de Veer, 2006, p. 84), and it is the user who completes the final meaning of this construction process. Seeing "a user's experience with an interactive system as the meanings he/she establishes about the system" will help designers understand how a user interprets a technology in a sociocultural surrounding and will be beneficial for design. Therefore, it is necessary to allow multiple, potentially competing interpretations to coexist in design. And one of our design challenges is how to "incorporate and balance multiple, perhaps conflicting interpretations and processes of interpretation in design and evaluation" (Sengers & Gaver, 2006, p. 101).

Cultural Usability Research

From the review of the development of usability and user experience research, it is clear that meaning and interpretation have gained heightened attention in technology design and have become the central themes. The endeavor of designing for meaningful technology becomes more challenging in the arena of cross-cultural design during a globalization age when the technology is expected to fit with a local user context, usually distant from the context where the technology is conceived, designed, and implemented. The growing competition in global markets and the increasing interest in social computing have resulted in the need for studies that explore a deep relationship between usability and culture. Since the end of the 1990s, the term "cultural usability" has gained academic currency.

Nowadays, cultural usability stands for cross-cultural usability to most people. However, it originally represented two camps of thought depending on their take on culture: cross-cultural usability or critical cultural usability. For cross-cultural usability, culture is primarily interpreted as ethnic culture, often in a positivist manner, and thus cultural usability is a study of national or regional cultural effects on technology product design. When working on cultural markers for website localization, as reviewed in Chapter 1, Barber and Bader (1998) state that "usability issues must take on a cultural context" and coined the term "culturability" as "the merging of culture and usability." They define culture as "a means of distinguishing among the different countries and their respective web-sites" and regard culturability as a quality that can be added at a certain stage of the design process. Pushed by industry need, plenty of empirical research findings have been gathered about cross-cultural interface design elements (Aykin & Milewski, 2004; Badre, 2002; Choi, Lee, & Kim, 2006; Horton, 2004; A. Marcus & Gould, 2000; Singh & Pereira, 2005; Yli-Jokipii, 2001), information architecture (Woods, 2004; McCool, 2006), cross-cultural user profiles (Faiola, 2002), and usability testing methods (Clemmensen & Plocher, 2007; Dray & Mrazek, 1996; Schumacher, 2010).

Critical cultural usability interprets culture in the sense of cultural studies. It regards culture as practices and meanings shared in a society or group, involving issues of representation, identity, and power. Tarkka and Tikka (2001) propose cultural usability as a search for a design approach that "situates the practices of technology within its cultural and social contexts"—a critical design sensibility. It is a combination of culture and technology with interpretation and implementation. They focus on the design practices from the discursive angle and the influences of consumer culture in HCI design.

Both approaches are plausible, considering the robustness and versatility of the concept of culture itself; however, each tells only half of the story. For example, studies of cross-cultural design usually stop at the level of ethnic cultural preferences and fail to explore the dynamic relationship between cultural preference and underlying structuring forces, while studies of critical cultural usability fail to realize that ideology frameworks vary in different cultures. In my early work (2002a, 2004, 2006), I discussed ways of combining two approaches to develop a broader vision of cultural usability, which is further developed into the framework of CLUE that will be discussed later in the book.

Since more research energy has been poured into the line of cross-cultural usability rather than critical cultural usability, cultural usability has become a de facto name for cross-cultural usability at recent conferences and lately in publications (e.g., Choi, Lee, & Kim, 2006; Clemmensen & Plocher, 2007). Acquiring a general name for a particular entity is a sign of remarkable development in the area of cross-cultural technology design during the past decade, but it also constantly reminds us of the narrow vision of culture in cross-cultural design and research practices.

This line of cultural usability research is interested in how to conduct cross-cultural usability research in an instrumental way. It is influenced by the dominant methodology of the field, the technical/engineering approach. For example, "[f]or the purpose of designing cultural usability, we will keep the definition [of culture] simple and operational" (Badre, 2002, p. 214). This view fails to see cross-cultural technology design as a cultural practice itself. Its limitations are also due to this mindset. As discussed in Chapter 1, culture is approached statically and monolithically; the dynamic cultural contexts have not received enough attention; and the interaction between local culture and global culture is often ignored. Therefore, researchers and practitioners seek measurable patterns for describing and designing for different cultures.

Think about a case of designing websites for users from a collectivist culture, such as Vietnam, who prefer to act in groups. We can find the following design suggestions to emphasize group-oriented values (Marcus & Krishnamurthi, 2009; Singh & Pereira, 2005): For corporate websites, designers should implement web features such as clubs and chat rooms, have family-themed pictures, develop content for community relations and loyalty programs, and use symbols of national identity and traditions; for social networking websites, designers might want to avoid displaying individual profile pictures on the homepage to nonmembers. While these design suggestions certainly stand to some degree, they neglect other group-oriented use activities. Fieldwork research found that people share computers and cell phones in Vietnam. Multiple family members would sit side by side and browse websites together on one computer, sharing the same login ID and screen name (Hsieh, Hausman, Titus, & Miller, 2008). Apparently the design suggestions do not apply to this scenario of group use—a manifestation of collectivism—because they imply a user model of individualism: An individual user from a collectivist culture is using a computer to reach out to virtual group members. This case shows that this line of cultural usability research remains at a stage at which usability is narrowly interpreted as product quality without full contextual consideration or much user participation.

While the whole field evolves and aims to support a full spectrum of user experience, cross-cultural design research and practice need to make corresponding moves and search for ways to make technologies both usable for and meaningful to local users. In this age of globalization, which values user participation, many design challenges arise. For example, how can we design a technological artifact that appeals to users in different corners of the world and lets them feel at home? How can we balance the objectivity of IT modeling and implementation with the subjectivity of local users? How can we grapple with the messiness of local culture and value "the vividness and feltness" of user experience?

Action and Meaning in Cross-Cultural Design: Disconnect and Breakdowns

Indeed, the interplay between action and meaning is more complicated in cross-cultural design. As many people have noticed, meaning has been a weak area in technology design. Design tends to prioritize interaction over interpretation, and thus designing for the mediation of action usually precedes designing for the mediation of meaning in practice. This often leads to use breakdowns when only tasks, usually lower-level, are modeled in design without considering other social and cultural factors in use contexts. When users and designers share a similar sociocultural context, often users are still able to implicitly interpret and use the artifact even though the meaning might not have been adequately considered during design. In the example of the file folder icon, an American user would unconsciously associate the manila folder icon with common filing activity. However, designers do not have this luck when designing for users in another culture. If meaning and cultural factors are not carefully studied and attended to in design, serious breakdowns will occur.

Because of the tendency to represent lower-level tasks in technology design (Adler & Winograd, 1992; Albrechtsen, Andersen, Bødker, & Pejtersen, 2001; Mirel, 2002; Virkkunen & Engeström, 2001), generally lower-level tasks from a particular cultural context (typically an American culture) are represented and modeled in cross-cultural design. This causes two problems. First, the designed technology supports only lower-level actions, likely taken from the cultural context of designers, rather than higher-order activity that would make sense to users. Second, lower-level actions that are packaged in cultural metaphors originating from the cultural context of designers are confusing or even unrecognizable to users who live in another culture and are unfamiliar with the cultural practices associated with the metaphors. Cognitive anthropologist Hutchins (1995) believes in "an integrated view of human cognition" (p. 354) and maintains that "culture is a cognitive process...and cognition is a cultural process." In this regard, lower-level actions inevitably represent the cultural ways of doing certain daily tasks in one cultural context, and these everyday practices might be vastly different from what users in other cultural contexts would perceive.

For example, research shows that Americans prefer to see things or phenomena in parts rather than in wholes, whereas Chinese people would prefer to do the reverse (Yang, 1986). In the case of a simple application such as an address book, though it is very common and natural for American users to group contacts in categories of work vs. family vs. friends, some Chinese users might find it uncomfortable to classify their contacts in this way. Their contacts usually form a big and complex *guanxi,* or network, and it is hard to separate contacts into family, work, and friends because some relatives might work for their family business and play golf together after work. Similarly, while the yellow file folder icon of the Windows system is explicit for American users who use manila folders to organize files in their daily lives and who prefer to divide things in parts through a hierarchical file structure, it causes confusion for users in another culture who have not used or seen a manila folder before and are not used to taxonomical thinking for filing.

The disconnect between action and meaning on lower-level tasks can be compared to the structural differences across cultures in a writing genre such as business letters. Though aiming for the same goal of reaching a potential customer, an American business letter would get to the main topic right away, while a letter from East Asia would establish a long-term relationship first and then refer to the business opportunity toward the end. If we believe that an effective business letter to a Japanese customer should follow the rhetorical moves of Japanese business letters, why do designers keep designing technologies for users in other cultures by following the rhetorical moves of their own culture? If we trace it back to its philosophical roots, this disconnect between action and meaning represents an instrumental view of technology. This view of technology considers it a neutral tool that is indifferent to the variety of ends it serves and the surrounding social, cultural, economic, political, and technical conditions. It has been criticized by many critical theorists (e.g., Feenberg, 2002; Slack & Wise, 2005; Winner, 1980).

Two types of breakdowns occur due to the disconnect. First, there is an incompatibility between user expectation of the higher-order activity and lower-level actions represented by functions. Duncker (2002) discusses how the seemingly universal and simple library classification systems originated from Western cultures are incomprehensible to Maori users in New Zealand. The collectivist Maori culture values shared knowledge among group members and approaches information and knowledge in its unity. When Western library classification systems divided the higher-order activity of learning about a Maori tribe's genealogy by searching for a related book into the lower-level actions of locating the book's subject heading, publication format, volume, and issue number, Maori users got lost in a digital library. Second, there is a conflict between the meaning conveyed through lower-level program functions and the local meaning. In the file folder icon example, a yellow file folder icon does not suggest the filing practice to a user in some European countries but instead appears only as a yellow rectangle. Furthermore, depending on target users, the "local" here does not stop at the nation/state level. In some cases, the local would go to the community and even the individual level for a sub-culture. However, many times local meanings are plagued by discourse hegemony that lacks respect for individual subjectivity, which makes the breakdown of local meaning even worse.

To fix use breakdowns, some might argue that it would not be difficult to replace an American file folder icon with a European cardboard box, a Chinese file pocket, or another cultural metaphor meaningful to a local culture. But do these different icons suggest the same filing practice represented by program functions? For example, it is technically possible to place one manila folder inside another to imply the practice of using subfolders, but it is not possible to put a same-size Chinese file pocket into another one. Put this way, what about making task representations meaningful to local users, like the Maori digital library users who are unfamiliar with Western library practices?

While it is important to convey the intended meaning to local users, we have to admit that it seems that the generation of meaning has been neglected for too long in cross-cultural design. Wertsch (1991) describes two types of meaning-making practices with Lotman's "functional dualism." Lotman (1988) believes that texts fulfill two basic functions: "to convey meanings adequately, and to generate new meanings" (as cited in Werstch, 1991, p. 73). These two functions work with two different communication models separately: a transmission model and a dialogic model. The transmission model holds on univocality and emphasizes "the transmission of meaning," and the dialogic model aims for multivoicedness and focuses on "the generation of meaning." Wertsch observes that "when a text is serving a dialogic function, it cannot be adequately understood in terms of the transmission model of communication" (p. 75). The same rationale applies to technology design. The online digital library for a Maori user should not be regarded just as a place for knowledge transfer, but as a communal space for sharing and preserving the oral tradition that is meaningful to the Maori culture as well. A digital library based on the dialogic model of communication would let the user find his tribe history in a way that makes sense to him, and encourage him to participate in the making of his tradition and heritage by contributing stories and songs.

The chance will be slim to get multiple, local interpretations right based on just one user model if localization work is introduced only near the end of the design and on the surface level. As Hutchins (1995) already eloquently showed in his field observations on the use and developmental history of navigational artifacts, culture, context, and history "cannot be comfortably integrated" (p. 354) into a material model of cognition because they have been "simply omitted" from the model for easy operation and synthesis since the first day of cognitive science. In this regard, technology internationalization and localization should not be considered as just the processes of "removing" and "infusing" cultural contexts.

Conclusion

This chapter continues to review the unintegrated situation of cross-cultural technology design from the angle of usability and user experience started in Chapter 1. I have investigated the problem of what hinders us from designing meaningful technology across cultures—the disconnect between action and meaning. I maintain that the narrow conceptualization of usability in technology design focuses only on action in technology design practices, complicated by the narrow representations of culture that just reflect static meaning but ignore action.

If the disconnect between action and meaning continues as is, no matter how hard the design community works on the central issue of cross-cultural design—i.e., interpretation—to improve user experience, the beautiful "Tower of Babel" being built is founded on drifting sands. Action and meaning are more intertwined in cross-cultural design, and we need to look for better ways to fuse the material and the discursive, as well as integrate implementation and interpretation in local uses.

Notes

1. Appropriation is often used to describe technology integration in various settings. For other examples of technology appropriation, see DeSanctis and Poole (1994), Dourish (2003), and du Gay et al. (1997).
2. The active form of consumption is explored in Chapter 10.
3. This can be regarded as a dramatic case of what Pinch and Bijker (1989) have called the "interpretive flexibility" of technology (pp. 40–41).

3

Integrating Action and Meaning into Cross-Cultural Design

In addition to the disconnect between action and meaning that causes poor user experience culturally, cross-cultural design faces a dilemma of how to strike a balance between local cultural ethos and individual subjectivity. Designing for a local culture might fall into a pitfall of stereotyping the culture; therefore, it is always an issue of how local a design should go within the culture. Should it go to the country, the society, the community, the subgroup, or the individual level? How feasible or manageable is the business of designing for the real local for an average IT company that wants to value its local users but possesses limited resources? In this rising participatory culture, users are eager to participate in shaping their own use journeys. This raises an intriguing and more fundamental question: How can we design an IT artifact for culturally diverse users while letting it touch each individual? We need to have an effective approach to designing appropriately localized products that meet the cultural expectations of local users and support their complex activities in concrete contexts.

In this chapter, I advocate a holistic, integrated vision that takes user experience as both situated action and constructed meaning, and explore how action and meaning are integrated and interwoven through a dual mediation process of technology use—a mediation of action and a mediation of meaning. Based on this holistic vision, I advance a methodology for analysis and design in cross-cultural design, Culturally Localized User Experience (CLUE). This approach highlights the praxis of use, i.e., user localization that makes a usable technology meaningful to an individual. Therefore it seeks to tie local cultural ethos with individual subjectivity and searches for innovative ways of initiating and facilitating local interpretations in cross-cultural design and research practices.

This chapter answers the questions *how* and *what* in developing a holistic view of user experience. I focus on explaining how this holistic view of user experience forms and functions by bringing in three strands of intellectual traditions—activity theory, British cultural studies, and genre theory—to investigate a dual mediation process in technology use and to study affordances emerging through use. This dual mediation process is an important feature that characterizes the CLUE framework as sketched later. Finally, I outline what the framework of CLUE is. This chapter lays the foundation for the presentation of use cases and the development of the CLUE framework in later chapters.

Studying Action and Meaning of Local Uses

A holistic approach regards user experience as the relationship unfolding in practice as both interaction and interpretation, aiming for change and improvement. It is both *situated* activity and *constructed* meaning,[1] and thus inherently related to its surrounding contexts, including the immediate context (i.e., the material) and the sociocultural contexts (i.e., the discursive). To explore the dual mediation process of a technology during use, in this section I will review and compare three strands of practice theories—activity theory, British cultural studies, and genre theory—that help us study both the instrumental and the social aspect of human action. Each of them provides a different angle to integrate action and meaning in local uses and complements the other two intellectual traditions.

Here activity theory helps to examine contextual factors at the community level with a focus on action, while British cultural studies helps at the individual level and the society level with a focus on meaning, and then genre theory integrates levels of individual, community, and society and connects both action and meaning through instantiation and enactment.

Activity Theory: Examining Use Activities in Local Contexts

Being the first strand of practice theory introduced and reviewed, activity theory is regarded as the theoretical foundation to inform and develop an integrated perspective in cross-cultural technology design. As I have argued before, current cross-cultural design practices focus on interpretations and ignore concrete activities, leading to unsatisfying user experience in local contexts. To solve this problem, activity theory helps define the integrated framework I am proposing as an activity approach that places concrete use activities on center stage in cross-cultural design, different from other design methodologies. In this subsection, I will review key concepts from activity theory that influenced the CLUE methodology and then discuss the value of activity theory and its limitation for cross-cultural technology design.

As a cultural–historical approach, activity theory claims that people's activities are an object-oriented and tool-mediated process in which actions are mediated through the use of artifacts (including tools and languages) to achieve a transformative objective. Activity theory is significant for the field of HCI in order to explore contextual issues by bringing the following valuable concepts and principles to practice and research.

First, a focus on the tool (or artifact) on the basis of activities from activity theory helps us see how a technology is interpreted as an object that is used by people to perform activities in context. A tool becomes a tool only through use. Therefore, a tool needs to be studied in its use setting; it is not meaningful to study a tool in isolation. As Bannon and Bødker (1991) explain, "a human activity approach to analysis of artifacts must include the actual praxis of use, as well as the specific material, social, and historical setting of that use."

Furthermore, a tool (or artifact) represents materialized activity. It has been "created and transformed during the development of the activity itself and carr[ies] with [it] a particular culture—a historical residue of that development" (Kuuti, 1996, p. 26). In fact, the role of a tool (artifact) is so important for a cultural–historical theory, like activity theory, that activity theorists compare it to biology's focus on the gene: "the *artifact* is to cultural evolution what the *gene* is to biological evolution" (Wartofsky, 1979, as cited in Engoström, 1999, p. 29, emphasis as it is). One could trace archaeological and cultural accounts for every mundane artifact from a pencil (see Petroski, 1989) to a cell phone (see Goggin, 2006).

Second, the idea of mediation is key to understanding the use of artifacts, human activity, and human experience. An activity theory view of mediation believes that human activity is mediated by either external tools (like a hammer) or internal tools (like concepts or heuristics) (Kaptelinin, 1996), and the instrumental mediation and communicative mediation of human action shape our experience (Nardi, 1996a). This view of mediation puts forward a holistic vision of experience in which the individual mind is integrated with the culture and the society (Engoström, 1999).

According to Vygotsky, mediation is the control of our activity and experience "from the outside"—through artifacts (see Engoström, 1999), and thus it shows that the ways in which people use artifacts are socially, culturally, and historically formed. For instance, the design of a dining table mediates an egalitarian or authoritarian meal culture the host chooses to honor (Verbeek, 2005). This observation is significant for cross-cultural technology design because different designs mediate different cultural expectations in different cultural contexts. And the emphasis of activity theory on the mediation process, on the transformational objective that is connected with the mediation process, and on the activity network suggests a process-oriented view of technology design rather than a product-oriented view.

Third, activity theory uses an activity as the unit of analysis to study human activity and tool mediation, which brings the vision of contexts into the object of inquiry. The activity network includes "a minimal meaningful context." In this "minimal meaningful context," history, development, meanings, community, rules, and even culture are constituted into a unified framework (see Figure 3.1), which makes

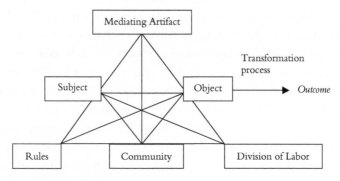

FIGURE 3.1   Activity Triangle

context consideration an inherent feature of activity-theory-based HCI design and research. As Nardi (1996b) describes:

> Activity theory...proposes a very specific notion of context: the activity itself is the context.... Context is constituted through the enactment of an activity involving people and artifacts.... [T]he specific transformative relationship between people and artifacts...is at the heart of any definition of context, or activity. (p. 76)

This inherent consideration of context in an activity unit allows for a design model built on activity theory to include culture and history from the beginning. Therefore it will avoid the problem Hutchins (1995) observes from technology design based on the traditional cognitive model: If cultural and contextual factors are omitted in a cognitive model, then it would be very hard to integrate them back "comfortably" later.

Fourth, the three-level structure of activity (see Table 3.1) makes it possible to distinguish and describe contextual factors as associated with the instrumental or social aspect of an activity. According to Leont'ev (1978), the unit of activity is hierarchically structured on three functional levels. A concrete *activity* is always motivated by general objectives acknowledged and recognized in the local community and in the sociocultural context. It is composed of a sequence of *actions*, which are goal-directed in an immediate context (e.g., at the workplace or at home) and are usually conscious. It should be noted that actions are similar to the "tasks" we often talk about in interface design. An action is realized by conditions in a use situation (i.e., a material setting), achieved by *operations*. Operations are usually non-conscious routine processes and automatically performed. For example, a concrete *activity* involves a user who wants to maintain regular contact with an

TABLE 3.1   Levels of Activity

Levels of Activity	Governed by	About
Activity	Motive	Why
Action	Goal	What
Operation	Conditions	How

old college friend by occasionally sending messages of greetings. As she does not want to disturb her friend, who might be busy at that moment, she chooses text messaging for communication. The act of sending a text message to the friend is the *action* here. *Operation* refers to the mundane details when the user interacts with the cell phone's keypad and text messaging application. In all, the three-level structure is not static but rather fluid depending on the use situation.

For cross-cultural technology design, the implication of activity theory is that it places on center stage the actual practices of use activities in local contexts rather than technological artifacts (Kaptelinin & Nardi, 2006), which are often absent in current localization literature and practice. As discussed in Chapter 1, a common approach in cross-cultural design is to treat cultural considerations as "international variables" to guide processes of internationalization and localization (see Hoft, 1995), in the form of design heuristics and localization guidelines (e.g., Aykin, 2004; Baumgartner, 2003; Ess & Sudweeks, 2005; Singh & Pereira, 2005). Built on well-developed intercultural communication theories from established scholars such as Hofstede, E. Hall, and Victor, these design instruments categorize cultural differences into comparable measures. However, most of these variables are value-oriented. They do not come from field studies of use activities in context, and they tend to be static and abstract. Accordingly, the guided localization work usually ends up on the interface and appearance level, though the ultimate goal here is to support user activities in their local contexts.

Indeed, meaning is a central issue in cross-cultural design and is usually where use breakdowns occur, but the attention to meaning in design cannot be separated from the attention to action. The local interpretations will be inaccurate if the interactions on which they are based are problematic. When cultural factors are operationalized into abstract dimensions separated from concrete user activities in the localization process, the mediated meaning by a technology will be out of context and incomprehensible for users. Activity theory provides a possibility to enrich taxonomical cross-cultural design guidelines from the action angle.

Of course, activity theory is the foundation of the CLUE framework not only because of its action bent; other action-oriented theories would also offer insights to cross-cultural design practices on this aspect. The advantage of activity theory is that it presents a robust framework to study contextual factors on an activity basis, and it shows us the complexities and fluidity of activities in context. However, we should admit that the scope of context and culture here is still limited, and it does not give us a complete picture of contextual factors, even though it is a much better picture than those offered by other theories. For example, activity theory is good at the interpretation of tool-mediated production but weak at sign-mediated communication (Engeström, 1999; Spinuzzi, 1999b). On a contextual spectrum from individual to community to broader sociocultural contexts, activity theory is positioned at the middle point, near the anchor of community. Activity theory starts with individual consciousness, but these individual concerns are later mapped to a set of models that emphasize groups, communities, organizations, and institutions—particularly through Engeström's work—and thus contextual factors within an activity network are primarily immediate and do not attend to subjectivity or broader sociocultural factors. In this way, a contextual view informed by activity theory "has system without experience" (McCarthy & Wright, 2004, p. 45), and "the richness and the messiness of experience" (p. 46) is lost. In the case of mobile text messaging, activity theory can illustrate why a user chooses text messaging based on instrumental convenience, but it lacks the vocabulary to investigate how this use act helps that user maintain her multiple identities in her daily communication.

As Kaptelinin (1996) says, activity theory has an advantage in its "potential for integration with other conceptual frameworks" (p. 64). To overcome these limitations, I am combining concepts from British cultural studies and genre theory to investigate use situations in a broader cultural arena. These two theoretical constructs are strong in sign-mediated communication. Specifically, British cultural studies offers a lens on the subjectivity situated in a broader sociocultural context in an age of globalization, and genre theory helps us look at the end of broader sociocultural contexts and link two mediation processes together. Facing the dilemma of how to make a design appealing to a local context without stereotyping the local culture in an essentialist fashion, both theories bring important strengths for cross-cultural design in the era of participatory culture.

British Cultural Studies: Articulating Local Uses
as Cultural Consumption

After activity theory exemplifies local technology uses as mediated action, British cultural studies is introduced next to illuminate the other side of coin, the mediation of meaning in technology use.

In British cultural studies, culture describes "a way of living within an industrial society that encompasses all the meanings of that social experience" (Fiske, 1987, p. 284). It shares a similar interest in everyday life as phenomenology and pragmatism, the two philosophical traditions that help construct our understanding of user experience. This school of thought is concerned with "the generation and circulation of meanings in industrial societies" or, more accurately, in technological societies, since technology is regarded as the center of our experience in the contemporary situation (Slack & Wise, 2005). Its emphasis on popular culture and daily life practices helps us to understand technology use in everyday life and the influence of consumer culture on IT product design and use.

I have extensively discussed the integral and complex relationship between culture, technology, and design in Chapter 1 and argued that technology design is a cultural practice, using some of the key concepts from cultural studies already. Then what else could British cultural studies contribute to further our understanding of cross-cultural user experience with its focus on culture? Here I'd like to focus on the articulation model (Slack, 1989; Slack, Miller, & Doak, 1993; Slack, 1996) and its application, the circuit of culture (du Gay et al., 1997; S. Hall, 1997). I believe both complement activity theory by bringing signifying practices and a developmental perspective into the articulation of local user experience as cultural consumption in a globalization age.

Articulation refers to "the *contingent* connection of different elements that, when connected in a particular way, form a specific unity" (Slack & Wise, 2005, p. 127, emphasis added). It looks at nonfixed, nonnecessary relations among practices, representations, experiences, affects, and material objects. For example, the unity of a train in a certain culture articulates an engine, cars, railway, passengers, a method of travel, the state policy of transportation, and so on. Articulation is an ongoing process. Some articulations are tenacious and are difficult to disarticulate. For example, a disarticulation of the engine from the train would make the train lose its entity, but the disarticulation between the train and local transportation policy would not change the entity of the train.

According to Slack (1996), articulation as a methodology maps the context "not in the sense of situating a phenomenon *in a context*, but in mapping a context, mapping the very identity that brings the context into focus" (p.125, emphasis as it is). Thus "identities, practices, and effects generally *constitute* the very context within which they are practices, identities or effects." This nonreductionist (or holistic in this discussion) view of context is a process of creating connections between various contextual elements (including both conceptual and material things) and between practices and meanings. Grossberg (1992) describes the process as follows:

> Articulation is the production of identity on top of differences, of unities out of fragments, of structures across practices. Articulation links this practice to that effect, this text to that meaning, this meaning to that reality, this experience to those politics. And these links are themselves articulated into larger structures, etc. (p. 54)

To describe how the articulations are structured as a whole, Slack and Wise (2005) later call context the *assemblage*—the web of heterogeneous "corresponding, noncorresponding, and contradictory articulations" (p. 113). The notion of assemblage is influenced by Latour's actor-network theory (2005) and Deleuze and Guattari's work (1987). An assemblage constitutes "singularities and traits" deducted from the articulations but does not reduce complex connections and relationships of a network (or a structure) to an essence or a critical factor. Different levels of tenacity of the associations between elements help to differentiate the articulations in an assemblage. Therefore, while an assemblage in an articulation model may look symmetrical to a web, it is different from the symmetrical connections between humans and nonhuman objects that come from the assemblage of the actor-network—the latter is criticized by activity theorists as lacking stability (Spinuzzi, 2008). The articulation view of assemblage recognizes the unequal distribution of agency and power in networks through the tenacity of the connection (Slack & Wise, 2005). The agency and the structure are thus integrated, and identity comes from the contingent articulations. Clearly, the articulation model explores contextual factors from a discursive angle more robustly, highlights the mediation of meanings on the social aspect of human action—which activity theory does not—and offers another lens through which to analyze the structure of the context.

As an instance of such assemblage, the circuit of culture (see Figure 3.2) examines five key processes in the development cycle of an artifact: (1) how the artifact is represented, (2) what social identities are associated with it, (3) how it is produced, (4) how it is consumed, (5) and what mechanisms regulate its distribution and use. In the real world, these five elements continually overlap and intertwine in complex and contingent ways. Furthermore, the cultural circuit illustrates how meanings are mediated by an artifact and suggests that a study of the whole circuit of culture is needed to examine a cultural artifact completely.

The cultural circuit view regards technology use as cultural consumption[2] (Storey, 1999), which happens when a user consumes a technology for his or her lifestyle and transforms a material user experience into a subjective and symbolic one. This is the articulation work of constructing the subjective experiences according to a user's lifestyle and identities. It links the instrumental aspect of the mere use process to the subjective user experience situated in a particular cultural context. It directs our attention to the signifying practices and "identity values" of daily technology use. Applying the circuit of culture to

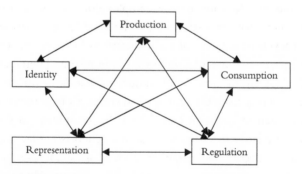

FIGURE 3.2   Circuit of Culture (Adapted from S. Hall, 1997, with permission of SAGE publications.)

technology design can show how other elements (representation, identity, production, and regulation) interact with and contribute to the "consumption" element in the whole life cycle (Churchill & Wakeford, 2001). This expands the usability research focus from an organizational context to an individual context and moves our attention to the total user experience. While subjective experience has gained more attention here with elements such as *identity* and *representation* than has individual consciousness from activity theory, the circuit of culture construct also explores broad cultural patterns in a use context. In the case study of the Sony Walkman (du Gay et al., 1997), the cultural circuit shows that nowadays text and technology, hardware and software, and product and use are dependent upon one another and are interrelated; technology companies like Sony are not simply hardware or software companies but part of a culture industry. The successes of iPod and iPhone from Apple tell a similar story.

The broader sociocultural factors informed by the lens of British cultural studies are "neither aesthetic nor humanist in emphasis but instead political" (Fiske, 1987, p. 284). S. Hall also comments in an interview (Chen, 1995), "cultural studies is always about the articulation between culture and power" (p. 395). This political bent is set against the backdrop of the globalization process from the beginning. British cultural studies originated from a search for "Britishness" inside British society, but it was later found that "the question of 'Britishness' can only even be framed in relation to its 'others' within the global cultural system" (p. 399), and thus local questions are inevitably pushed toward answering global ones. The local–global interaction positions a local design as part of the globalization process with the implication of a power struggle behind technology discourse. And a local design is always situated in the context of a global one. The cross-cultural design community should be aware of this and make accountable design decisions.

Applying articulation theory to study cross-cultural design can help us see that the design practice is a process of articulation, disarticulation, and re-articulation. A technological artifact with certain design features is an assemblage of articulations between user goals and tasks, between technical functions and cultural meanings, between work efficiency and lifestyle choice, between design and production, between designer's culture and user's culture, and so on. Some of the articulations embodied in the artifact are more tenacious across cultures, but some are not and can be easily disarticulated and could cause confusion in another cultural context, for example, the articulation between a manila folder icon and a filing practice. Therefore, a re-articulation process will be needed.

Genre Theory: Tracing Social Actions through Stabilized Articulations

While activity theory illuminates the mediation of action during local use and British cultural studies examines the mediation of meaning, genre theory links the two mediation processes together. To achieve it, genre theory explores how action is solidified in meaning-carrying generic features through a structuration process with its enlightening view of non-literary genres:

> A genre is a patterning of communication created by a combination of the individual (cognitive), social, and technical forces implicit in a recurring communicative situation. A genre structures communication by creating shared expectations about the form and content of the interaction, thus easing the burden of production and interpretation. (Erickson, 1999, p. 2–3)

This view demonstrates that while genres are usually classified by their distinctive textual features, genre theory is more interested in the functions genres serve and in the interactions between functions and texts. Indeed, social practices represented by generic features are what attract many researchers to study genres. For them, a genre is "a collection of practices that finds its nexus in the recurrent, dynamic activities in which users engage" (Spinuzzi, 1999a, p. 37). A closer examination of genre patterns could tell "many things about the institutional and social setting, the activities being proposed, the roles available to writer and reader, the motives, ideas, ideology, and expected content of the document, and where this all might fit in our life" (Bazerman, 2000, p. 16). In this sense, a genre is also a gene in cultural evolution, like an artifact as discussed earlier. As genre theory brings a peculiar lens to typified human activities, it has been widely adopted in the fields of HCI, technical communication, information studies, and information systems. For example, user studies in library and information studies are recommended to be regarded as genre studies (Andersen, 2008).

Clearly, the notion of genre can help us better understand technological artifacts in a social and historical context. In HCI research, genres do not have to be textual ones, and "designed, communicative artifacts" can be broadly interpreted as genres, as suggested by Brown and Duguid (1994, p. 10). They explicate that genres are "socially constructed interpretive conventions" that connect designers who "try to invoke a particular genre, to establish the conventions they are putting into play," with users who "try to recognize what has been invoked, what conventions are in play so that they might respond appropriately"; for example, a library reading room is interpreted differently from a dining hall by visitors who adjust their behaviors to different places. An expanded view of genre[3] is beneficial in studying how the connection of design and use is dynamically settled in different interface features by inquiring about rules and habits related to genres (e.g., Brown & Duguid, 1994, 1996; Spinuzzi, 2003; Yates & Orlikowski, 1992). For example, a hierarchical layout on a German website and vibrant colors on a Brazilian website reveal different local reading habits and visual preferences through their generic features.

Genre theory provides a foundation for interpreting actions from a social angle through the meaning-laden format of a genre. According to C. R. Miller (1984), genres are social actions in response to recurrent situations with social motives. Dias, Freedman, Medway, and Pare (1999) explain that, for C. R. Miller, "[s]ocial motive means not a motive about the social or a motive shared by the group but a motive that is socially recognized and allowed for" (p. 20). At the same time, an effort of genre participation will not be successful if the user is not well versed in local culture, for social motives are bound by the context, and they take the form of "local purposes"—"the social motives that prevail in that setting" (p. 22). Here local purposes act as a filter for the most effective communication out of the options suitable for the same social motive. A funding proposal will be rejected if a writer fails to connect the project benefits with the mission of the sponsoring organization. A text alert message of school closing on a snow day is chosen over an email message because it can reach a larger portion of its audience faster due to the accessibility and portability of a mobile phone.

Social motives in the form of local purposes, or localized social motives, are similar to the objectives on the activity level in activity theory. In this way, genre theory is akin to activity theory, as genres are "specific human activities" (p. 24) and "enactments of recognized social motives" (p. 25). Therefore genres are purposive. This emphasis on functionality leads to attention to tasks and actions, but this attention is investigated through forms. Therefore, both action and meaning in local uses are blended together. In this sense, genre theory reflects activity theory in that technology use is socially and culturally formed, and thus generic features of a technology carry meanings and enhance culturally situated actions and local practices. For example, laundry practices vary greatly across the globe: How to take care of 18-foot-long saris made of fine cotton or silk is a big concern for Indian housewives, while Brazilian housewives believe a pre-soaking is important to achieve a clean wash. Thus a popular washing machine in India has a specially designed agitator that does not tangle saris, and a Brazilian model includes a soak cycle to accommodate local preferences (Heskett, 2005).

Genre is not only a behavioral construct but a structural construct as well. The fusion of action and meaning is instantiated through a structuration process. Influenced by Giddens' structuration theory, C. R. Miller (1994) suggests that genres are capable of reproducing social structures with their recurrent nature in situated communication. Within organizational contexts genres are produced, reproduced, and modified by individuals through a process of structuring (Yates & Orlikowski, 1992). It should be noted that Giddens' view of structure (i.e., "the set of rules and resources") is never material, but virtual, according to Orlikowski (2000, p. 406). Therefore, social structures are not *embodied* in technological genres, but instead *emergent* from those genres as a result of being "instantiated in recurrent social practice" (ibid). In that regard, recursive interaction with a technology "produces and reproduces a particular structure of technology use"—enacting an emergent structure of technology use. To put it simply, "in their recurrent practices, users shape the technology structure that shapes their use." Orlikowski calls this process *technology enactment* and sees the enactment which is "a situated and recursive process of constitution" (p. 409), as both constraining and enabling: For constraining, it can "invoke intended activities or replicate familiar uses"; for enabling, it would "ignore...conventional uses or invent new ones." The outcomes of constraining and/or enabling provided by genres for enactment depend on how closely the social motives allowed by the genre (using the words of Dias and his colleagues), or the inscribed rules and resources instantiated in recurrent technology use practices (using Orlikowski's phrase), match with our own motives, agendas, and identities.

This process of genre enactment as constituting structures is a process of articulation, in relation to British cultural studies. Borrowing Schryer's (1994) characterization of genre, "stabilized-for-now," I describe a genre as a stabilized assemblage of articulations, for the time being, in an ongoing process of structuration. Regarding the notion of genre as both behavioral and structural helps reconcile the difference between activity theory and British cultural studies in mapping the context: While activity theory positions contextual factors squarely in a schematic triangle of activity, British cultural studies sees context as the movement and the flows of relationships with no hierarchical structure or center. A genre construct with its "stability-with-flexibility" characteristic could help "frame the stability/instability dialogue more productively," as Spinuzzi (2008, p. 23) recommends. Furthermore, the robustness of stability/instability from the genre notion will help the design community avoid the essentialist position brought by the cultural dimensions model in cross-cultural design.

The structuration process is dialogical,[4] which indicates that a technology-in-use is a response to local conditions, and that the practice of technology use is a dialogue between the user and the technology, the technology and local conditions, and the present and the past. For example, when creating structured layouts of corporate websites for German users as mentioned earlier, a genre lens would not just conclude distinctive design features as cultural patterns, but rather would further explore how these cultural patterns represent particular communicative situations and activities for a given task, and follow how they would evolve as situations change. At the time when the Internet was still a novelty for many users, who used it primarily for seeking information, I found that German users preferred the links of a navigation panel placed in alphabetical order for easy search in a cross-cultural web usability project (Sun, 2001). As the Internet becomes more entertainment-oriented and its users become more sophisticated, an alphabetical-order list of links is less important than before in web design for German users. As a matter of fact, many German corporate websites do not place the links in alphabetical order any more.

It should be pointed out that the structuration process impacts design on different levels: from individual through community and then through the society level. A decision to adopt and use a technological genre is not only an individual decision based on the user's identity, lifestyle, subjective experience, and other individual factors, but is also related to a discourse community where people share similar interpretive conventions about a particular genre and a particular communication activity. Moreover, the values of that society will be reinforced in this adoption process. In this way, a genre view connects various levels of contexts in an ecology of different genres, or an assemblage of genres. Spinuzzi (2003) finds that the cross-scope flexibility of genre has made the genre concept suitable to be "an integrated-scope of unit of analysis" (p. 47) that examines typified actions across microscopic, mesoscopic, and macroscopic levels, which is useful for studying a full spectrum of user experience.

Comparison of the Three Approaches

Table 3.2 illustrates how the three approaches could work together to explore contextual issues in cross-cultural design and investigate dual mediation process in technology use.

It is important to note that the three theoretical approaches presented above are not randomly chosen, but rather are specifically outlined because of their shared core values: With an in-depth probe into contextual factors, they are heavily invested in studying the process of mediation in which they regard either activity or meaning as a dynamic process with a dialogic angle. Therefore, they are able to complement and enrich each other to inform an integrated cross-cultural design approach. As "post-cognitivist theories," which appreciate "the vital role of technology in human life" (Kaptelinin & Nardi, 2006, location 2136), these three theories are used to "remedy perceived shortcomings of cognitivist theory" (location 2128) in technology design, particularly in cross-cultural technology design.

TABLE 3.2   Comparison of Three Approaches to Understanding Technology Use

Theories	Activity Theory	British Cultural Studies	Genre Theory
Lens of Focus	action	meaning	technological genre (stability vs. instability)
Methodology of Studying Contexts	activity as a unit of analysis	articulation model	genre as social action in the sense of both a cultural artifact and a structuring force
Methodological Strength on Different Mediations	mediation of action (tool-mediated production) at the community level	mediation of meaning (sign-mediated communication) at the society and individual level	mediation of action (tool-mediated production) via mediation of meaning (sign-mediated communication) at the society level
Ways of Situating Artifacts in Context	an artifact-practice dyad[a]	artifact on a cultural circuit	an artifact-rule dyad[a]
Types of Contexts Mostly Studied	organizational context	individual context	organizational context

[a] Source: Spinuzzi (1999a).

Examining Affordances out of Dialogic Interactions

To design a technology that affords meaningful activities to local users, the technology should provide clues to local users and facilitate effective communication between the technology and users for smooth and fluent interaction. I review technology design's common problem in Chapter 2: Technology is designed for lower-level tasks rather than higher-order processes, and thus the cultural context is omitted from design. This problem becomes much worse in cross-cultural design because meaning is a central issue, but users and designers do not share the same cultural contexts, making communication less transparent. Therefore, how to enhance a technology to successfully mediate both action and meaning becomes a fundamental issue in design.

This section continues discussing *how* action and meaning are interconnected in technology use by inspecting technology affordances. Affordances describe the action possibilities posed by an artifact in use and associate the artifact with practices. They emerge as the material and the discursive are fused together during technology use. I am interested in exploring how an understanding of affordance as dialogic interaction helps us to better design a technology for local users. In this section, I review the origin of the notion "affordance"; recast it as the outcome of dialogic relation between technology, user, and activity with a focus on social interactions; and depict affordance as a three-level, activity-based structure.

Origin of Affordances

Affordance is an important term in Gibson's ecological psychology (1979), which "refers to both the environment and the animal in a way that no existing term does. It implies the complementarity of the animal and the environment" (p. 127). He asserts that an affordance is "equally a fact of the environment and a fact of behavior. It is both physical and psychical, yet neither. An affordance points both ways, to the environment, and to the observer" (p. 129). Gibson's explanation clearly shows that, in the beginning, affordances were considered as only emerging from the context of material encounters between actors and objects. It is a three-way relationship between the environment, the organism, and an activity (Dourish, 2001; Baerentsen & Trettvik, 2002). Considering that Gibson's goal for advancing ecological psychology was to counter the dualism in modern psychology, Costall (1995) comments that Gibson's theory of affordances "attempts to put meaning back into the world, first by relating meaning to action, and then by addressing the neglected dualism of agent and world" (p. 468). Therefore affordance as relationship was mapped "within a frame of being and acting" (Dourish, 2001, p. 118).

Norman adopts the term affordance from Gibson and introduces it in his book *The Design of Everyday Things* (1988). He defines affordances as "the perceived and actual properties of the thing, primarily those fundamental properties that determine just how the thing could possibly be used" (p. 9). Since then, "affordance" has become a popular concept in the HCI field. This term helps designers to describe the features and functionalities of the artifact on which they are working and to examine the implicit and explicit interaction cues their designs provide to users with artifacts. However, to Norman, affordances cannot be used to describe every HCI design. He states that affordances should be physical affordances only; for example, the computer screen affords only viewing but not pointing and clicking. Pointing and clicking are only "perceived affordances," not real "physical affordances" (1999). For Gaver (1991), Norman's student, pointing and clicking are affordances, but are "perceptible affordances." He distinguishes perceptible affordances from hidden and false affordances: "when affordances are perceptible, they offer a link between perception and action; hidden and false affordances lead to mistakes" (p. 79). Practitioners today generally use this definition when referring to "affordances."

This view of affordances implies a focus on artifacts as tools mediating between users and the context of use, but it has two weak spots. First, affordances are regarded as technology properties that derive from an artifact. Affordances are about "the relationship between form and function in design" (Dourish, 2001, p. 119). This is a one-dimensional relationship centering only on an artifact. Albrechtsen and his colleagues (2001) posit that affordances in this view are short-term and do not take the developmental aspect of an artifact into account; thus affordances are "more or less static surface phenomena" (p. 10). Second, this vision of affordances fails to address issues of sociocultural contexts. As Norman's affordance is based on a matching of two models (user's model and system's model), it lacks cultural considerations and places sociocultural contexts "outside the confines of the system's domain... relegat[ing] affordances to a kind of no-man's land" (Albrechtsen et al, 2001, p. 10). Because of that, HCI design has mostly been focused on lower-level interaction modalities.

To solve these two problems, Baerentsen and Trettvik (2002) declare that the field of HCI must throw away their belief that affordances are "magical qualities of objects in isolation." Instead, "artifacts, technologies, and their knowledgeable users are seen in their actual interdependency and co-existence in processes of activity, ultimately as abstract moments in societal forms of praxis" (p. 59). Two lines of inquiries have been undertaken to enrich the notion of affordances.

Affordances as Dialogic Relation

The first move is to bring the dialogicality back to the nature of affordance. Informed by activity theory, Baerentsen and Trettvik place the concept of affordances in an activity-based framework by asserting that "[a]ffordances are not properties of objects in isolation, but of objects related to subjects in (possible) activities" (p. 59). They approach affordances from a cultural–historical angle and distinguish between two types of affordances: natural affordances for animals and cultural–historical affordances that "originate from adaptation of (objects in) the environment to suit the satisfaction of human needs, and are nested in cultural-historical *forms of societal praxis*" (p. 57, emphasis as it is). The latter are "produced intentionally and are specifically designed for inclusion in cultural–historical forms of practice. The cultural–historical artifacts and forms of practice are artificial habitats." In simpler terms, affordances emerge "as activity-relationship between actors and objects" (p. 59). Their theorizing of affordances introduces the sociocultural context from the beginning.

Following this line of inquiry, researchers explore how affordances arise from interactions (Sun, 2004; Vyas, Chisalita, & van de Veer, 2006) and serve as the property of interaction. Particularly, the move to user experience research mandates affordance as interaction quality. Affordances are realized not only by the artifact in use, but also by other parts in a technological system. In the case of mobile text messaging, the whole system consists of the artifact (both software and hardware), the services received from carriers, and the network technology. We cannot simply locate the usability issue in the handset or in one component. The emerging trend of service design clearly validates this too.

Dialogicality is a key feature here, as affordance comes from the milieu of the artifact, user, and activity. According to genre theory, a rule–tool relationship surfaces from the structuration process when structuring forces and social habits (i.e., rules) are clustered and instantiated in a technological genre (i.e., tool), then are solidified as generic features. A genre view of technological artifacts is essential to technology affordances because it helps interpret an artifact's use in context by providing socially constructed interpretive conventions. In arguing for a blend of procedural and structural support in software design for complex tasks, Mirel (2002) associates "a genre of performance" (p. 177) with her structural representation of social actions. She describes contextual and structural support as capturing functional relationships and typified actions in local contexts, and suggests that structural representations should organize performance instead of breaking down actions into steps. For her, structural representations "call forth shared performance goals for a given context and circumstance" and "reveal possibilities for action and offer performers ample latitude in specific behaviors based on their roles, arrangements of labor, infrastructure constraints, and the like" (p. 177). Indeed, technology affordance unfolds in this praxis of use and develops as a result of the interplay of habituated uses and sociocultural factors. For example, a Korean refrigerator's multifunctionality reflects local sociocultural factors. It not only refrigerates and freezes food, but also ferments kimchee, a pickled cabbage staple on Korea's dining tables.

The characteristic of dialogicality sheds light on how cultural dimensions affect a particular technology design and use. The emergent feature of affordance manifests in cross-cultural design. Affordances that arise from design features come out of multiple articulations between user needs, commercial interests, client expectations, cultural constraints, and so on. The same technology could enact different technologies-in-use in different local contexts in the process of articulating multiple interpretations, and thus we need to design corresponding affordances for them. For example, upon discovering that mobile text messaging was used to conduct long conversations in one culture and for small talk in another culture (as discussed in later chapters), we would want to design different interface features to support these different user tasks.

Understanding the dynamism of the technology enactment process shows the possibility of avoiding the pitfall of stereotyping local culture in cross-cultural design. If cultural patterns are utilized in a dynamic fashion to explore the enactment process, then we will be able to stay away from reducing concrete culture into static patterns. To design a technology is to immerse oneself in a local context and understand the socially and historically developed, typified activities related to that technology. The issue here is how we could develop a dialogic rhetoric to facilitate conversation between the local and the global and between designers and users, to initiate and sustain multiple interpretations.

Affordances for Social Interactions

The second move is to study the sociocultural milieu from which affordances come. In the psychology field, Costall (1995) believes that the nature of affordances is social since "[n]ature has *become* artificial and social" (p. 471, emphasis as it is). The trend of incorporating social dimensions into affordances in HCI started in the mid-1990s, when the community of Computer Supported Collaborative Work (CSCW) began to loosely use the term "social affordance" to describe opportunities of technology that afforded social behaviors.

Bradner (2001) defines social affordance as "the relationship between the properties of an object and the social characteristics of a given group that enable particular kinds of interaction among members of that group" (p. 132). For example, a wireless phone affords friends the opportunity to stay in touch anytime and anywhere. She argues that social affordances indicate how members of a social group might interact with one another when interaction is mediated by technology. Accordingly, a study of social affordances of a given technology must study both the social context of human–human interaction and the features of technology used during the mediation. As to the relationship of social affordances with physical affordances, she suggests that "social affordances arise out of the physical properties of an object when considered in the context of the social interaction that the object mediates" (p. 133).

In addition, Bradner compares the verbs *afford*, *support*, and *enable*, suggesting that the distinction comes from the German root *aufforderung-scharakter* for *afford*, meaning demand or invitation. "Both these words connote something compelling, i.e., an object is present that is compelling human action" (p. 135). Therefore, the social affordance of a technology comes from the fact that there is something inherent in the technology that *compels* certain social interactions among other similar technologies. For example, in a comparison between calling people and texting people, both technologies *support* and *enable* communication, but texting might *afford* "keeping in touch" better than calling because texting is an unobtrusive communication mode that does not disturb the other party. Clearly, this "compelling" feature is closely related to local culture—"local purpose" as genre theory suggests—and it could be very appealing to a culture that values an implicit communication style. In their discussion of the development of personal blogs for the past decade, C. R. Miller and Shepherd (2009) refer to this compelling feature as "a suasory aspect" of affordances. It connects the material and the symbolic in technology use by motivating users to take the rhetorical action of blogging.

Bradner's contribution helps to distinguish social affordances from physical affordances (the affordances we typically talk about in HCI design). However, her view of social affordances fails to explain how these physical affordances and social affordances are interconnected and interact during a user activity. Other than claiming that social affordances arise out of physical affordances, she does not tell us where the social affordance is located and precisely what relationship exists between the two types. Her scope of social affordance is also limited. She admits looking only at social interactions on the level of dyads and small groups, and she does not consider interactions at the level of society and culture.

From the stance of social constructivism, Hutchby (2001) explores "communicative affordances" in technology-mediated conversations with the methodology of conversation analysis. In his view, communicative affordances provide both "constraints and unique possibilities" in social interactions. Though he does not approach affordance from a design angle, he treats technology affordances as technology properties, and his primary interest in assigning this term is to propose a middle position between radical constructivism and technological determinism to study technological discourse so that the biases of the two could be avoided; his sharp observation on "constraints and unique possibilities" of affordance deserves a further probe when both the social orientation and dialogic angle are connected in the notion of affordance here. Following the discussion of examining affordance informed by rhetorical genre theory from the previous section, the enabling and constraining feature of technology affordances are similar to what Orlikowski (1992) describes as the "duality" of technology use: Technology use is both an active process of socially constructed interpretation, where new meanings and practices are explored, but is also a "passive" structuring process where norms and traditions are strengthened. This enabling and constraining feature of technology affordance, reminiscent of the form aspect of a genre, plays an important role in cross-cultural design. I will discuss this in vivid detail in Lili's case in Chapter 6 and further examine its role and function in the section on "Local Uptakes" in the last chapter.

Structured Affordances

The activity theory approach makes it possible to develop a structured construct of affordances (Albrechtsen et al., 2001), and Baerentsen and Trettvik (2002) build a three-level structure of affordances enlightened by activity theory. Because affordances are realized in interactions as activity-relationships between actors and objects, they argue that the concept of affordance should be treated as a generic concept that distinguishes affordance from "operational affordance" on the operation level, "instrumental affordance" on the action level, and "need-related affordance" on the activity level.

Based on the work of Baerentsen and Trettvik and informed by genre theory and British cultural studies, I further develop a three-level structure of affordance here. Affordance consists of operational, instrumental, and social affordance. In the example discussed in the section on activity theory, a user wants to maintain regular contact with an old college friend and sends messages of greetings occasionally. As she does not want to disturb her friend, who might be busy at that moment, she chooses text messaging for communication. Here, the touch and feel of a phone pad is "operational affordance," communicating unobtrusively is "instrumental affordance" on the action level, and staying in contact with college friends is "social affordance" on the activity level.

The following changes were made on Baerentsen and Trettvik's model. First, I changed "need-related affordance" on the activity level to "social affordance." This change incorporates and expands on some of Bradner's insights. Here, "social" refers to social interactions on various levels including the individual, the community, and the society and cultural level as related to the discursive aspect of human action. Second, different levels of affordances interact and evolve through the process of technology enactment in the milieu of technology, user, and activity. Social affordances arise out of instrumental affordances through users' interactions in local contexts, and thus the same instrumental affordance (the text messaging features of being quick, quiet, and discreet) might lead to different social affordances and support different social uses (for sharing emotional support or for staying in contact) when affordances are realized in different contexts. Furthermore, different local cultures will nurture different social affordances.

The robust, three-level framework allows the study of affordances in context by showing connections between different levels of affordances. With this structure, it is clear to see which levels of affordances have been designed as well as realized in practice. This way it will help the design community to locate user needs and prioritize design goals in the design process. Current HCI design is not good at higher levels of affordances because it spends too much time developing operational affordances.

For the five individual cases of mobile messaging uses in Part II of this book, I distinguish technology affordances from the three-level structure into two types: instrumental affordances and social affordances. Instrumental affordances will refer to affordances on the levels of both operation and action by combining operational affordance and instrumental affordance. These are affordances emerging from use interactions in the material context. Social affordances are the affordances on the activity level that emerge from use interactions in the sociocultural and historical context. For example, the instrumental affordances of mobile text messaging include silent communication, convenient use, discreet action, and so on. Its social affordances include staying in contact, having fun, etc. I made this distinction because I am focusing on examining the higher-level interactions of situated use and cultural contexts in this project without probing into the interactions on the micro-action level. It is not meaningful to describe operational affordances without an in-depth understanding of operations and conditions. Therefore I treat these two levels of affordances in a general manner; however, I recognize that the instrumental affordances I am discussing in this book come from both levels of actions and operations, and I do not want to suggest that operational affordance can be ignored in research.

It should also be noted that the distinction between instrumental and social affordances corresponds to the instrumental aspect and social aspect of human actions, the dual mediation process (mediation of action and mediation of meaning) of technology use, and the two core components of technology—instrumentality and social circulation. This distinction helps me to better address how affordances are designed, realized, and articulated to support the two aspects of actions through technology mediation.

Intended Use and Possible Uses

The activity-based construct of affordances explains how affordances are realized in use. There is a gap between intended and possible uses, and between design and use. As people often find in IT product designs, though certain types of affordances are designed into an artifact, they might not be recognized or appreciated by users as intended by designers. In fact, quite often other uses develop through use beyond the designers' intentions. These uses are the local uses, or technology enactment in Orlikowski's sense.

The phenomenon of unintended use appears because affordances actually cannot be designed in advance. As I discuss above, affordances emerge only during interactions through use, and they are "abstract moments" of "the concrete user activity" (Baerentsen & Trettvik, 2002, p. 60). Thus, "[t]he task of design is in many cases not to eliminate the possible uses, but rather make sure that the intended use is visible for the user" (p. 59). Sengers and Gaver (2005) recommend "taking user interpretation seriously," and claim that "the role of designers must shift from determining the meaning of a system to encouraging, shaping and occasionally disrupting users' processes of meaning-making."

Toward a Methodology of Culturally Localized User Experience (CLUE)

After I discuss *how* action and meaning interact and are synced in technology use through a dual mediation process, in this section I outline *what* an integrated approach looks like in cross-cultural design. Here I propose a new analytical and design approach of Culturally Localized User Experience (CLUE)[5] that integrates action and meaning in order to design for a holistic user experience for culturally diverse users. The mission of CLUE is to craft appropriately localized IT products to meet the cultural expectations of local users as well as support their complex activities in concrete contexts.

Presented below are the defining features of the CLUE framework, which I hope readers will keep in mind as we begin to look at the user case histories in Part II of this book. Because this framework will be further developed, enriched, and illustrated through user case histories, a more detailed discussion of these features will follow in Chapters 10 and 11 after the user cases.

1. The CLUE approach highlights the praxis of use.

   Integrating key concepts and methods from activity theory, British cultural studies, and genre theory, the CLUE approach places on center stage the actual practices of use activities in local contexts, which are often missing in current localization literature and practice. The praxis of use is shaped by myriad articulations of practices and meanings on a cultural circuit. Technology affordances unfold in this praxis of use and develop as a result of the interplay of habituated uses and sociocultural conditions. At the same time, the praxis of use is cultural consumption itself in which a user actively localizes the technology for his or her lifestyle and transforms a material user experience into a subjective and symbolic one. The praxis lens here helps capture the livedness and messiness of local culture and avoids the problem of stereotyping.

2. Local culture constitutes the dynamic nexus of contextual interactions and manifests numerous articulations of practices and meanings.

   The CLUE framework is based on a dialogic view of culture, which regards culture as an open set of practices and as an energetic process with meanings, objects, and identities flowing across sites in diffuse time–space in an age of globalization. Local culture is constantly in the making. It is both a site of the dynamic, ever-changing nexus of contextual interactions and an assemblage of myriad articulations as a semantic space consisting of meanings and practices.

3. User experience is both situated and constructed.

In the CLUE framework, I define user experience as the complex relations between users and technology. It consists of a material interaction with the artifact and its surrounding context and an interpretation process of this activity. Experience is regarded as both situated activity and constructed meaning. In this way, user experience is both situated and constructed in a local cultural context, and thus action and meaning are blended smoothly.

4. Technology use is a dual mediation process.

I argue that a technology creating a culturally localized user experience mediates not only instrumental practices but also social meanings. User experience is founded on and originates from the process of mediation. In simpler terms, user experience is a mediation process that includes tool-mediated production and sign-mediated communication. Only with this dual mediation process in mind can we successfully design technologies that work in local contexts.

5. Structured affordance comes from dialogic interactions.

The CLUE approach asserts that affordance cannot be designed but must be enacted through use. Affordance is the outcome of dialogic interactions between technology, user, and activity. It is described as a three-level activity-based structure consisting of operational, instrumental, and social affordances. This structure distinguishes different levels of affordances with a focus on social interaction. It can help designers to locate user needs and prioritize design goals in the design process.

6. Culturally localized user experience respects use practices of individual local users and values their efforts at user localization.

The CLUE approach begins with an exploration of user activity in context for design inspirations, and continues and circulates in a cycle as users localize a technology according to their lifestyles. Users play a vital role in bringing something to the experience and in co-constructing the experience. Because user experience would not be meaningful without the involvement of users, user participation, interpretation, and contribution are important elements in the whole experience cycle. This stance toward local users, even individual local users, and its appreciation of user localization efforts show possibilities for finding a balance in cross-cultural design between diverse user groups and individual subjectivity.

7. Design is both problem solving and engaged conversation.

One of the major goals of the CLUE approach for cross-cultural design is to foster an ongoing conversation between technology and users, technology and its surrounding local conditions, the local and the global, and designers and users. Technology use occurs on a cultural circuit against the backdrop of globalization. It is a continuous cycle that gains momentum with constant interactions and ongoing dialogues. A dialogic methodology is essential to help create meaningful technology use experience. A CLUE perspective asks us to extend our view of design from problem solving to engaged conversation in this era of participatory culture.

Conclusion

For the disconnect between action and meaning and the design conflict between local cultural ethos and individual subjectivity, my solution is to develop a holistic, integrated vision of user experience for cross-cultural technology design. In this chapter, I illustrate *how* action and meaning are connected by exploring ways of studying a dual mediation process in technology use and bringing together key ideas and methods from activity theory, British cultural studies, and genre theory. I also develop a robust structure of affordance that regards affordance as the property of interaction and accounts for social interactions. In the end, I describe *what* this approach entails and present the framework of Culturally Localized User Experience (CLUE).

A simple scenario demonstrates why it is essential and critical for us to integrate action and meaning in cross-cultural design for satisfying user experience: In traditional technology engineering and design practices built on cognitive science, meaning is often omitted at the time when the cognitive model is conceived (Hutchins, 1995), and only action is considered in design, in terms of its cognitive modules and program functions. Meaning is usually integrated at a later stage of design, though in an unsatisfying way. If this design has a market potential for users from other cultures, a localization professional is brought in to add local meaning to the design. The localization practitioner focuses only on the meaning aspect of the design and usually has no say about action; it would be too late to shape the design of action at that time. Obviously the disconnect between action and meaning occurs in two places: when the design is conceived, and when the design is localized. Since the second disconnect builds on the first disconnect, the user breakdowns in cross-cultural design can be disastrous.

To fix the two disconnecting points, an activity model that includes a cultural context in its entirety from conception is brought in from activity theory to improve our understanding of the mediation of action; an articulation model and a cultural circuit from British cultural studies that investigate everyday practices are used for the mediation of meaning; and a genre notion informed by genre theory's structuring process is introduced to link the two mediation processes together. This is how the integrated perspective is developed.

Notes

1. McCarthy and Wright (2004) also describe user experience as "holistic, situated and constructed" based on their careful and convincing integration of Dewey's and Bakhtin's works. While I strongly agree with their precise characterization of user experience, we see how the holistic experience is developed in different ways with different focuses. Their work centers on "the livedness and feltness" of experience and constructs it with four threads (sensual, emotional, compositional, and spatio-temporal). In comparison, the holistic view of user experience I advance in this book is built on a dual mediation process that integrates action and meaning, which I see as one of the central issues of cross-cultural design.

2. Consumption is interpreted as an active form rather than a passive behavior. A more detailed discussion of this can be found in Chapter 10.

3. Of course, a view that regards artifacts as genres can be slippery in theory. In this book, I focus on technological artifacts rather than general artifacts. Technological artifacts, as technologies themselves, are defined by the core components of technology—instrumentality and social circulation (see Chapter 1). In this sense, the socially recognized interpretive conventions are a part of a technological artifact, while a general artifact (e.g., an object of local ingenuity) does not necessarily have that.

4. An in-depth discussion of the dialogical characteristic of the CLUE framework is presented in Chapter 11.

5. The CLUE approach was formerly named cultural usability. However, cultural usability has been a widely used term that describes cross-cultural design within the confines of usability, which does not fully represent the scope of this framework.

4

CLUE as a Framework for Cross-Cultural User Experience Research

After building a theoretical understanding of the Culturally Localized User Experience approach, I am moving to the case of this book, a cross-cultural study of mobile messaging uses in American and Chinese contexts, to exemplify and expand upon the CLUE approach in a dialogic interaction between theory and practice, and between a framework for analysis and design and a concrete problem. I have two goals with this case. First, I want to illustrate, develop, enrich, and interrogate the CLUE framework through individual case stories and a consolidated discussion that follows. Second, I am interested in exploring the methodological potentials and consequences of the CLUE approach for cross-cultural user experience research.

My stance of research is "praxis"—"a set of critical and reflective practices" as Sullivan and Porter (1997, p. ix) advocate in their critical practices view of research. This position regards research as a dialogic design activity. It appreciates the "rhetorical situatedness" of research design and sees methodology as local, contingent, dynamic, and negotiable in research practices. Methods that are used to approach problems and accomplish research results are not just neutral instruments but have ethical and political implications in local contexts as well. More careful planning and execution is needed for research conducted in multicultural contexts.

In this chapter, I first review the phenomenon of mobile messaging use in a larger context and explore what challenges and implications this case has brought to the practices and research of cross-cultural design. Then I discuss the analytical value of the CLUE framework for cross-cultural user experience research, like this study.

Challenges of Mobile Text Messaging
for Cross-Cultural Design

The case of mobile text messaging is compelling and valuable here because its success and popularity challenge our assumptions about technology design and use: How could a technology originally considered useless by its service providers, difficult to use by novice users, and marketed in a wrong direction achieve a phenomenal use success across diverse cultures?

From a design point, mobile text messaging is a hard-to-use technology with inherent limitations (e.g., small display, poor inputting methods, and moving environments). From a localization point, the technology of text messaging involves only minimal work at the developer's site—during the localization process phone manufacturers mainly translate the interface and menu into local languages for operational affordances. However, the following phenomena surprised the mobile industry: A hard-to-use technology with inherent limitations enjoys a huge market success; a technology originally designed and marketed as a business application has been adopted primarily for personal use; a technology whose only value at its inception was its instrumental convenience has now introduced a completely new social world because of that convenience; a technology that is adopted and used by enthusiastic users is also integrated and localized to fit their daily lifestyles.

Gap between Design and Use

Mobile text messaging refers to the Short Message Service (SMS) available on most digital wireless phones that allows sending and receiving short text messages (or more colloquially "texts" or "txts") between wireless phones and other handheld devices. Originally designed as part of the GSM (Global Systems for Mobile Communication) mobile phone standard, it is supported also on digital wireless networks such as CDMA (Code Division Multiple Access) and iDEN (Integrated Digital Enhanced Network). The message can contain alphanumeric characters with a maximum length of 160 characters for Latin alphabets, including English, and 70 characters for non-Latin alphabets, such as Chinese

(Mallick, 2003). The first text message was sent by British engineer Neil Papworth to colleagues at Vodafone, a UK mobile phone giant, on December 3, 1992: "MERRY CHRISTMAS" ("Texting," 2004).

There is a huge gap between design and use in the case of text messaging. Designers and telecommunication companies were at a loss about its utility before this "object of local ingenuity" entered into "social circulation." In a book published to celebrate the 25th anniversary of SMS standardization,[1] the engineer who developed the technology recollected the early days below:

> In 1991, the skepticism about SMS was summed up by the
> director of one mobile network operator in the words: "Why
> would anybody want to send one of these messages when they
> can talk to them?" It is fair to say that, in 1992, when the first short
> message was sent, nobody foresaw that SMS would become the
> most important revenue earner next to speech for the following
> 18 years and perhaps beyond. A message service that was limited
> to 160 characters and that has to be keyed in on a mobile phone
> keypad using fingers and thumbs, and whose message delivery
> could not be guaranteed, was hardly likely to attract much
> attention. (Hillebrand, 2010, p. 126)

SMS thus embarked on an interesting journey of socialization on the cultural circuit. Some companies decided to market the technology as a voicemail alert service—a simple mechanism to inform subscribers about the arrival of a new voicemail (Hill, 2004). Others left it in the telecommunication network as it was without charging for it, seeing it as a useless technology (Hillebrand, 2010). Due to poor radio coverage, interoperability problems between networks, and the limitations of one-way messaging, the potential for mobile text messaging was not realized until a few years later when teenagers in some Western European countries took up this technology for communication purposes among peers. It has been widely popular in those countries since 1997 (Nieminen-Sundell & Vaananen-Vainio-Mattila, 2003).

Watching the revenue pulling in from young people using the service for personal chat, telecommunication companies began to market the technology zealously, not as voicemail alerts any more, but still for business use. For example, a typical text messaging ad in 2003 would tout the convenience of using text messaging like this: Two employees secretly exchange work-related messages during a business meeting so that they could give the boss the information he needs right away. However, it is estimated that close to 80% of SMS messages sent were consumer-oriented by that time (Mallick, 2003), despite the fact that the design did not effectively support the use of exchanging messages in personal life spheres, and that the interface was poor (Hillebrand, 2010; Sun, 2006). Indeed, unlike other emerging technologies, which are constantly refined and upgraded, the design of SMS technology has remained the same since its inception, "as if the industry turned its back on text messaging" (Jenson, 2005, p. 305).

No wonder the European Telecommunications Standards Institute (ETSI) comments on SMS technology this way: "SMS has become a phenomenal success that has been a surprise to many both inside and outside the communications industry" (2010).

For the initial novice users, mobile text messaging was a technology difficult to use. Now, almost two decades later, that difficulty is hard to imagine because mobile text messaging has become part of our everyday lives with its *easy* access and *convenient* use. Apparently, wireless phones were designed with little expectation that people would use them for composing and reading text messages: Typing a short mobile message on a mobile phone was described as "a difficult and tedious task" (Schneider-Hufschmidt, 2005, p. 223) or "an odd construction" (Ling, 2004, p. 147) for most mobile phone users at that time. In fact, the early adoption of mobile text messaging among Western European teenagers happened *because* it was difficult for beginners to use. Since one needs some practice to become a proficient texter, those teenagers used that learning curve to create and protect their own communication channel, hoping to block their parents and teachers (MobileSMS, 2004).

The use difficulty is evident in the phone's small display and keypad, poor input methods, and limits on message length. When text messaging was first introduced, most phones' screens would display only three to eight lines of text (unless the phone was a PDA-based smart phone). Though the message length limit is 160 characters for Latin alphabets and 70 characters for non-Latin alphabets, it was not convenient to input or read a long message on a cell phone's small display.

The text entry mechanism greatly impacts the usability of messaging technology on mobile phones (e.g., Cox, Cairns, Walton, & Lee, 2008; Liu & Räihä, 2010; Schneider-Hufschmidt, 2005; Silfverberg, MacKenzie, & Korhonen, 2000). There are four options available, keypad input, pen-based input (or handwriting input), keyboard input, and voice input; among these, keypad input has been the most prevalent (Liu & Räihä, 2010; Mallick, 2003). This might be due to the fact that phones with keypad inputting are cheaper and easier to hold due to their compact size than phones with other input technology. On a 12-digit keypad, each button represents three letters; for example, the button "2" corresponds to the letters "a," "b," and "c." A user needs to press the associated key a specific number of times to get to the desired letter. In this case, a user must press the "2" key twice to get the letter "b," pausing between each key press. This method is referred to as "multi-tap."

Predictive typing technology was developed to make entering text messages easier. This technology preloads the cell phone with a database of thousands of words, emoticons, and punctuation, and can then automatically scan possible variations to determine the correct word as a user types it. This allows the user to simply press each key once for the letter she/he wants and then advance to the next letter without pausing—just as people would on a computer keyboard—watching as the screen displays what the cell phone assumes that the user wanted to type. Some smart predictive typing can also do word completion. In this case, after the user types "lu," the technology will automatically complete the word with whatever word the user has typed most often (e.g., "lunch"), and thus the user does not need to type out the full word each time. The three predictive typing technologies—T9, eZi, and iTap—that were popular at the time of the study support multiple languages, including English and Chinese (SJInfo, 2003; Yesky, 2003).

The text entry methods of Chinese are divided into two input modes: sound-based input (e.g., Pinyin mode or Bopomofo mode) and shape-based input (e.g., stroke mode). The sound-based input mode is built on Pinyin, the standard notation for the Romanization of the Chinese simplified character set. In the Pinyin mode, a user spells the character phonetically using Pinyin. In the stroke mode, the technology divides the Chinese character into a few basic strokes with each

key representing one stroke, such as dot (✦), dash (➖), perpendic-
ular downstroke (|), downstroke to the left (⸗), wavelike stroke
(╲), hook (⌋), upstroke to the right (╱), and bend (➔).

If comparing only text entry speeds of English and Chinese with
predictive typing methods on a phone keypad, entering Chinese texts
is not as difficult as entering English texts due to the linguistic brevity
of a character language: A phrase is the smallest meaning unit in the
Chinese language, consisting of one or two characters. For a phrase
of two characters, it usually takes two or three taps to locate the first
character with the Pinyin mode, and then takes another one or two
taps to choose the second one from a list of recommended characters predicted based on phrase relevancy. A shape-based input method
could locate the same character even faster. However, Chinese inputting has its own challenges. For sound-based input, since Pinyin was
not introduced until the 1970s by the Chinese government, older generations are not good at it. Thus text entry is a big barrier for users over
50 who want to adopt text messaging technology. Furthermore, there
are many dialects in China that pronounce dramatically differently,
but Mandarin (the official spoken language of China) is based only
on one type of dialect: the Northern dialect. Many southern Chinese
(e.g., Cantonese) have strong accents, causing them to have problems
pronouncing Mandarin properly.

It should be noted that mobile phone usability has been improving,
as more phones with bigger screens and keyboards have been introduced
on the market to address users' texting needs. However, for many novice users, particularly the elderly, mobile messaging technology is still
a hard-to-use technology with the barrier of text entry (Weilenmann,
2010). In contrast, expert users who have practiced text messaging for
some time can send a text within seconds, even while multitasking.
Meanwhile, different inputting technologies offer different affordances.
For example, one of my participants resisted predictive typing because
she had to watch the screen while typing in order to see when the correct letter was displayed, and thus she could not text in secret or while
multitasking. In a similar way, the virtual full alphabetic keyboard of an
iPhone does not offer the tactile feel of a traditional-styled keypad.

The technology of text messaging is particularly intriguing because,
as an emerging technology, it has bypassed the usability barrier and

become a huge success even though the industry refused to refine it. It is "the triumph of the consumer—a grassroots revolution that the mobile industry had next to nothing to do with and repeatedly reacted to" (MobileSMS, 2004). When mobile text messaging was first introduced as a voicemail alert service, nobody imagined the great impact it would have on our culture and communication practices: Mobile messaging has been a popular communication mode in Asia-Pacific, Europe, Africa, Australia, and other parts of the world, and displays interesting local use patterns (e.g., Baron, 2008; Donner, 2008; Glotz, Bertschi, & Locke, 2005; Goggin, 2006; Harper, Palen, & Taylor, 2005; Hjorth, 2009; Ito, Okabe, & Matsuda, 2006; Ling, 2004). With the phenomenal success of mobile text messaging, we have a generation named after this technology, "Generation Txt" (Rheingold, 2002, p. 20). The word "text" is not just used as a noun any more but also as a verb, a practice that I follow in this book.

A Contrasting Phenomenon of Local Uses

From the localization perspective, the phenomenon of mobile text messaging is striking. The technology of text messaging involves only basic localization work from the engineering side, the language translation of the interface and menu (Sun, 2006). And as discussed in the previous section, the overall design of a wireless phone itself is not sufficient (actually poor in some situations) to support the messaging task; however, a large number of users love texting, and we see the growth of SMS traffic globally. What happened and is happening behind these huge numbers of text messages exchanged on wireless phones? Why is mobile text messaging so popular even though mobile phones are not a good tool for writing? How do users "localize" a hard-to-use technology into their everyday life to augment work and life? Fascinated by this phenomenon, I chose two distinctively different cultural contexts to study local messaging practices between 2003 and 2006, an interesting moment when text messaging began to fly and was flying at both sites.

The technology of mobile messaging diffused from Europe to China and America almost at the same time. In China (CN), text messaging service was officially released by China Mobile in the second half of 2000, and text messages could be exchanged across wireless carriers since May 1, 2002 (Xinhua News, 2002). Similarly, the United States (US) began a two-way text messaging service in May 2000 (Wireless Telecommunications Bureau of the U.S. [WTB], 2003), and all American wireless carriers were interconnected by the end of 2002 (3GAmericas, 2004).

Table 4.1 and Figure 4.1 show the remarkable development of SMS use in the two countries between 2001 and 2009.[2] Clearly the use traffic of text messaging had significant increases in both countries after the inter-carrier interoperability of text messaging was available; however, these two countries have experienced different development trajectories since then. Text messaging quickly took off as both a huge business and cultural phenomenon in China and has grown steadily. Between 2001 and 2009, the annual SMS traffic volume rose from 18.9 billion to 771.3 billion (Jiang, 2007; Ministry of Industry and Information Technology of the People's Republic of China [MIIT], 2010). It is widely used by users from diverse age groups, social classes, and economic statuses.

TABLE 4.1   SMS Traffic Volumes in Two Countries (unit: billions)

	US Monthly (June)	US Annually	CN Annually
2001	0.03	n/a	18.9
2002	1	1.2	90
2003	1.2	14.4[*]	137
2004	2.8	49.4[**]	218
2005	7.2	81	305
2006	12.1	158	429
2007	28.8	362	592
2008	75	1000	699.6
2009	152.7[***]	1560	771.3

Sources: US CTIA (2010); US WTB Annual CMRS Competition Reports (2002–2010); CN MIIT Monthly Reports of December (2008–2010); Figliola (2008); Jiang (2007).
[*] This is a rough estimate, calculated by multiplying the traffic volume of June 2003 by 12. The official tracking of SMS annual volume in the U.S. was not available until 2005, which speaks something about the development of SMS in the U.S.
[**] A rough estimate again, calculated by doubling the total traffic volume of July through December in 2004.
[***] This is the monthly SMS volume for December 2009; I was not able to locate the number for June 2009.

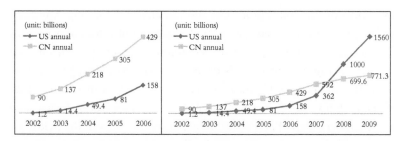

FIGURE 4.1   Chinese SMS Use Grows Steadily while American Use Lags at First
Left: Comparison for the study period. Right: Comparison over years.
(Note: Both the close-up view and the general view are provided to eliminate
"scaling effects" for this type of time series line chart (Klass, 2008). A same-size
unit measure is used for the horizontal axis.)

Nielsen's report (Stewart & Quick, 2009) shows that China had an 80%
penetration rate of text messaging by the first quarter of 2009, a bit
higher than the UK (77%), where mobile text messaging originated.

In comparison, the Unites States is well known for its initially
lagging use of mobile messaging: For a long time, text messaging was
not popular among American mobile phone users. Researchers have
wondered what happened in the U.S. that turned Americans away from
text messaging (e.g., Ling, 2004; Rheingold, 2002). Americans slowly
caught up with the rest of the world over the years; the monthly volume
of text messaging rose from 30 million to 152.7 billion between June
2001[3] and December 2009 (Richtel, 2004; CTIA-The Wireless Asso-
ciation® [CTIA], 2010). The turning point came in 2008, as Nielsen
reported that in the second quarter of 2008 U.S. mobile subscribers
exchanged more text messages than phone calls monthly, primarily
attributable to the heavily texting age group of 13–17-year-olds (Covey,
2008). Sixty-six percent of American 12–17-year-olds used text messaging in September 2009, and one in three sent more than 100 messages
a day (Lenhart, Ling, Campbell, & Purcell, 2010). The overall penetration rate of text messaging across ages was 58% by the first quarter of
2009, according to Nielsen (Stewart & Quick, 2009).

While the numbers above provide sketches of different local use patterns, my fieldwork highlights that two distinct types of uses resonating
with local cultures have been developed by users, even with minimal
localization work from developers: Text messaging was primarily used

as a form of fun communication and for small talk among American participants to express emotions and feelings about informal occasions. In contrast, text messaging was used among Chinese participants as a way of staying in contact with friends in order to exchange information. It was deeply embedded in the everyday lives of Chinese participants who texted about numerous topics, about both formal and informal occasions. The variety of local uses found from the fieldwork illuminates how complex uses were formed around situated activities in local cultures rather than abstract cultural dimensions, contrary to what cross-cultural designers commonly assume in design and localization practices.

These vivid and lively differences of development trajectories and use patterns between the two sites need to be understood in a holistic fashion. They cannot be simply explained with dimensional cultural factors. For example, if we make a claim that East Asian people are more inclined to the implicit communication mode of text messaging, how could we explain the instant popularity of text messaging in the UK, a culture that appreciates more direct communication? Similarly, I found that the frameworks, such as the Technology Acceptance Model and Innovation Diffusion, were also unable to account for the rich scenarios of local uses that unfolded in the field.

One popular answer is that the cost has played an important role here. For example, the low cost of text messaging services in China helped the messaging use in that locale soar (see Figure 4.1 left). While a low cost makes texting attractive for new users, the significance of cost for the SMS adoption and use should be examined with the perception of constant users about whether they consider SMS as a mode of communication that can be replaced by other means. If so, a lower cost will make users stay; otherwise they will switch to other even-lower-cost communication technologies or choose nothing in order to save money. In fact, after they adopt the technology, users tend to send many more text messages than they thought they would and send text messages on occasions they would not have taken any communicative actions before, and they end up spending more money. And it is constant users, not new users, who primarily contribute to the SMS traffic. Neither can the cost factor convincingly explain the popularity of mobile messaging among a group of American participants found from the fieldwork. There is more going on than cost in the articulations that make up the text messaging phenomenon on the cultural circuit.

When a technology with an inherent usability weakness still enjoys a great use success, this implies that there is more happening in the complex sociotechnical ecosystem than what we realized. Indeed, more is going on locally. Therefore I develop a rich understanding of local uses, based on the integrated approach of CLUE, to figure out these use differences.

Cross-Cultural User Experience Research as Praxis

As a holistic perspective, the CLUE framework has methodological consequences to advance research practice in cross-cultural user experience research. As I said earlier, research is "praxis"—"a set of critical and reflective practices." I agree with Sullivan and Porter (1993) that the study of writing technologies (in other words, technology-mediated communication research) is "a design activity involving the construction of a method worked out from the intersection of theory and situation, which leads not to knowledge (in the sense of total truth), but toward understanding, the basis for future rhetorical judgment" (p. 237). In this sense, a search for a culture-sensitive and ethical design approach and a convincing and coherent theoretical perspective that integrates action and meaning in cross-cultural design by combining and braiding multiple intellectual traditions together is also a process of designing the appropriate methodology for studying phenomenon in this area. As a result, the CLUE framework worked as a research methodology in shaping the research design of the case studies I will be presenting in the next five chapters.

The comparative user experience study was conducted between 2003 and 2006, which was an interesting moment for text messaging because it reached a point of being widely adopted by a larger population of users in many places of the world, including the two cultural contexts studied in this book (see Figure 4.1). We see instances of early adopters and early majority (Rogers, 1995). Text messaging became a seamless part of many users' lives and was used in different ways according to their lifestyles. I looked at the messaging practices of frequent users at that time to study their post-adoption experience and understand why they developed, stayed with, or changed their particular ways of using the technology. Drawing up the insights gained from the fieldwork, I saw user localization happening at users' sites, which is valuable for culturally situated design research and practices.

Of course, the phenomenon of mobile messaging use has always been evolving, and the local culture contexts are in flux too. Why is it worthwhile and important for us to look at the cases of user localization that happened *then*?

First, what happened then is still relevant and thought-provoking for users who are adopting and localizing mobile messaging technology now. To use the American context as the example, the Pew study of American teens and mobile phone uses released in 2010 (Lenhart et al.) reports that this new cohort of heavy messaging users was engaging in similar modes of uses with text messaging in 2009 as those enthusiastic early adopters described in the book: texting primarily to "just say hello or chat," texting to connect with close friends, texting to avoid confrontation, texting in class, exchanging hundreds of messages daily, texting while driving, texting under the table when talking with researchers/teachers, displaying gender differences about texting, and so on. By no means have I suggested that my findings are complete by comparing them to more recent data; I believe triangulating the findings with previous or later research in mobile messaging could reveal the fullness and richness of the phenomenon and situate it in a global context dialogically—it is a critical reflective practice. I also think the constant popularity of text messaging among teens should be studied with a new research lens (e.g., Ling, 2010). However, the similarities between use patterns across time and user groups do demonstrate the necessity of learning those concrete uses behind the numbers, trend charts, and interview quotes, through thick interpretation, for people who want to gain a deep understanding of technology adoption and use and listen to those individual voices of local users, as speaking from the case histories presented in the book.

Second, the design challenges and usability problems faced by the mobile messaging technology are faced and will be faced by other emerging technologies too. How can we design a technology that will let local users adopt, stay, localize, and resonate with it? And how can we make a technology both usable and meaningful? In the case of mobile messaging technology, as I have argued elsewhere (Sun, 2006), "users have rescued not only themselves, but also the technology" (p. 458). Their enthusiasm, wisdom, efforts, and knowledge have turned a hard-to-use technology into a huge use success. I believe the answers to the questions raised can be found in vivid use cases, which will be beneficial for the cross-cultural design community as we develop other emerging technologies.

Even for mobile messaging technology itself, industry experts and market researchers predict that mobile messaging still has "enormous" potential for traffic growth, considering SMS is mainly adopted by young people, particularly in the U.S. (Hillebrand, 2010; Entner, 2010). As text messaging is expanded to other user groups, such as parents and grandparents who are enticed to stay in contact with their children and grandchildren via text messaging, the lessons learned and insights gained from these user cases will help this technology reach more diverse users.

Research Sites

The fieldwork was primarily conducted in two sites: the capital region (Albany) of New York State and the capital area (Hangzhou) of Zhejiang province. Both are middle-sized cities in well-developed regions of the two selected countries and are representative of the typical user base for mobile telephony in each country. All major national wireless carriers can be found in these two cities. As a researcher, I am familiar with both areas and local cultures, which is important for a study on contexts of use. I was living in the Albany area for my PhD study at that time, and Hangzhou is my hometown.

Table 4.2, based on a report released by Morgan Stanley (2004), describes demographics and technology usage in the U.S. and China in 2002, a year before the comparative study began. I also include the data of mobile communication in 2007, after the study ended, for comparison. At that time, the U.S. and China contrasted with each other interestingly in their IT use profiles. With 162 million Internet users and 198.5 million PCs in 2002, the U.S. was the top market for personal

TABLE 4.2   IT Use Profiles of Two Countries in Year 2002

Categories	USA	China
Population (millions)	280.6	1,284.3
GDP per Capita (US$)	37,231	963
Installed PCs (millions)	198.5	29.2
PC Penetration	71%	2%
Internet Users (millions)	162.1	59
Internet User Penetration	58%	5%
Telephone Lines (millions)	177	214
Telephone Line Penetration	63%	17%
Mobile Phones (millions)	140.8 (vs. 263 in 2007)	206.6 (vs. 547.3 in 2007)
Mobile Phone Penetration	50% (vs. 86% in 2007)	16% (vs. 42% in 2007)
Mobile Phone to Internet User ratio	0.9:1	3.5:1

Sources: China Internet Report (Morgan Stanley, 2004); US WTB 13th Annual CMRS Competition Report (2009); CN MIIT Monthly Report of December 2007 (2008).

computing and e-business; however, American users seemed to be very reluctant to use mobile content services such as mobile text messaging. Compared to the U.S., China boasted the second-largest Internet and PC user base, though the penetration rates of PC and Internet users were still very low due to the country's large population and the cost of these technologies.

Among other available ITs, mobile phones stand out as a "revolutionizing force." The penetration rate of mobile phones in China in 2002 was eight times larger than PCs, and more than three times the number of Internet users.[4] In contrast, the rate of mobile phones in the U.S. was 71% of the rate of PCs, and 86% of that of Internet users. Morgan Stanley states that "[n]o major market comes close to China's 2003 ratio of 3.5 mobile users for every one Internet user...Simply based on volume, interest and momentum, it is likely that China will possess increasing scale advantages in mobile phone and Internet connectivity/messaging" (p. 27).

At the American site, there were six national wireless carriers at the time of study: Verizon Wireless, Cingular Wireless, Sprint PCS,

Nextel, T-Mobile USA, and AT&T Wireless.[5] At the Chinese site, there was a tight competition between two national carriers: China Mobile and China Unicom.

American carriers offer two payment options: monthly plan packages and prepaid phone cards. Most customers select the former. Wireless plan packages often include monthly airtime minutes ranging from two hundred to thousands of minutes, unlimited nighttime and/or weekend minutes, free long distance, and other features such as voicemail, caller ID, call forwarding, call waiting, etc. At the time of study, a typical calling plan ranged from $30–$40 with 200–300 monthly airtime minutes in addition to free night and weekend minutes. Additional minutes beyond monthly airtime allowance were usually $0.40–$0.50 each. Text messaging was—and still is—typically a separate feature that American customers pay an additional monthly fee to get. Different carriers offered different choices. For example, customers could opt for a bundled text messaging plan, such as $2.99 for 100 text messages (e.g., Verizon Wireless); pay $10 for a "vision package" for text messaging and unlimited wireless Web access (e.g., Sprint PCS); or choose a bundled text and talk plan in which text messaging was included (e.g., T-Mobile). Occasionally text messages were free in some bundled text and talk plans. If customers did not choose a separate text messaging plan, they would pay $0.10 for a message sent and $0.02 for a message received.[6]

Like their American counterparts, Chinese customers also had two choices: monthly plans and prepaid cards. Individual customers often chose prepaid phone cards, as there were usually no discounted service packages available before 2002. As wireless competition became more intense and the wireless carriers introduced discounted monthly packages, an increasing number of customers opted for monthly plans. Compared to American calling plans, Chinese calling plans did not include features such as free long distance, voicemail, caller ID, and call forwarding. The monthly fee ranged from 20–50 yuan[7] with free incoming calls, a few hundred in-network and out-of-network local minutes, and a few hundred text messages. Additional minutes outside the network would have cost 0.55–0.60 yuan each, and those inside the network would have cost 0.35–0.40 yuan each. In most cases, text messages were bundled with phone calling plans. Customers paid 0.10 yuan for additional text

TABLE 4.3   Comparisons of Calling Plan Features between the Two Sites

Features	American Site	Chinese Site
Monthly airtime minutes	Included	Usually not included. If included, only for local in-network calls
Free night and/or weekend minutes	Usually included	Not included
Free long distance	Included	Not included
Voicemail	Included	Not included, an extra feature to order
Caller ID	Included	Included
Text messages	Not included, an extra feature to order	Included
Additional minutes	$0.40–$0.50 each (same price for both inside and outside the network)	0.55–0.60 yuan each for calls outside the network, 0.35–0.40 yuan each for calls inside the network
Additional text messages	$0.10 for a message sent and $0.02 for a message received	0.10 yuan each a message sent in-network, 0.15 out-of-network, free for messages received

message sent in-network, 0.15 or 0.20 yuan out-of-network, and incoming messages were free. As a result, cost-conscious customers watched closely where text messages came from and went to.[8]

Table 4.3 compares different features of typical calling plans at these two sites based on information found on carriers' websites at the time of study. It is clear that Chinese phone plans encouraged the use of mobile text messaging.

Because phone minutes and text rates were calculated differently at the two sites, sometimes it was cheaper to call than to text for American participants when they had enough phone minutes to use. For Chinese participants, most of them thought texting saved money, particularly when contacting long-distance friends or using text messaging to replace the function of voicemail.

Research Design

The CLUE methodology informed the methods of data gathering and analysis and guided the fieldwork for this project.

The comparative case studies were conducted through a dissertation project (Sun, 2004) and its follow-up study.[9] I selected multiple cases to describe ways of local uses. Each individual participant poses a peculiar and meaningful case (Stake, 1995). Cases were chosen based on the criteria of variety and diversity for understanding use practices from different angles. More specifically, I used measures to compare across cases and to interpret information in depth for some of the cases. Thus I picked a broad group that was stratified and as varied as possible by age, gender, profession, and wireless carrier for the first stage of study (questionnaire survey and text messaging diary). Here, wireless carrier was used as a measure because each carrier had its own service packages and special plans, which affected the affordance of the technology. At the second stage, cases with interesting patterns of use were selected to bear further exploration using methods of qualitative interview and/ or shadowing observation to see how the users used text messaging technology in context and to hear how they interpreted their uses. The follow-up study was implemented to watch the development of local uses over time by revisiting some of the unique cases identified previously and interviewing again those participants who were available.

Nineteen American users and 22 Chinese users were recruited from the two sites. They were selected based on the following criteria: high frequency of use, age, gender, profession, and wireless carrier. Participants were college students or young professionals (18 to 30 years old) who sent and received at least five text messages[10] per day (the more, the better) from different wireless carriers. A large number of participants exchanged more than 10 messages each day, and some reached 20 to 30 per day. I chose frequent users as participants because my goal was to study various successful adoption cases of mobile messaging technology and understand what factors would improve and sustain localization practices. Participants were offered payment for their contribution based on the local hourly rate. A few participants declined payment.

Two trends of user demographic characteristics deserve our attention. First, two-thirds of the participants are female, and female participants dominate at both sites. This pattern is related to research design: I did not arrange gender constraints for participant recruitment. As long as people met the criteria and helped me stratify the participant pool, they were accepted for research. Second, the number of participants from some wireless carriers (e.g., Sprint PCS, Nextel) is much smaller than the number of those from other carriers (e.g., Verizon Wireless, T-Mobile) at the American site. This situation was either caused by the size of the customer base in the Albany area or by their not-so-easy-to-use texting services.[11] In all, these participant patterns illustrate a general user scenario of mobile messaging use at the two fieldwork sites.

I collected data by stages with different foci on use patterns and mediation practices. At the first stage, my goal was to uncover various messaging practices related to assorted lifestyles. A questionnaire survey (see Appendix A) was used to gather participants' personal and technology background information. Use patterns of mobile messaging across sites were captured through the use of a text messaging diary (see Appendix B). Participants were asked to log text messages for four consecutive days, including workdays and non-workdays, and weekdays and weekend days.[12] Here the diary was used as "a middle-ground solution to the opposing limitations of laboratory studies and field studies" to "capture activities that occur in real environments vis-à-vis some kind of technology currently under investigation" (Palen & Salzman, 2002b, p. 87–88). It helped to record the mediation practices and sample the participant's typical patterns of an ad-hoc activity like mobile text messaging, which occurs in almost any context, sometimes very private, where a researcher is unable to study directly.

After message diaries were collected, a preliminary analysis of messaging activities was conducted to identify distinctive messaging patterns. Based on that, I selected a small group of participants for a follow-up interview(s) to explore their use practices and trace their use trajectories over a time period. As an exploratory study to investigate the interactions between mobile messaging technology and its surrounding cultural context, preferences were given to participants who presented interesting use patterns from the first stage. Special attention was also taken to keep a balanced variety of subjects. An interview usually lasted 45 to 75 minutes, all of which was audio-recorded. A few participants agreed to be shadowed. They were followed for one or two half-days as they went about their tasks in their cars, offices, and stores—popular places for messaging, according to their diary studies and interviews. In one case I had a contextual visit when shadowing observation was not applicable for that particular use pattern: texting late at night. Seven participants (four American and three Chinese) were interviewed once, nine (two Americans and seven Chinese) were interviewed twice, and one American was interviewed three times. For participants who had multiple interviews, the interviews were conducted between a span of five months or longer to see the development of local uses.

The qualitative interview, shadowing observation, and contextual visit were chosen to develop a rich understanding of the technology mediation practices of selected participants. Rooted in the philosophy of qualitative research, the qualitative interview is a field interviewing method to find out what participants feel and think about their worlds (Rubin & Rubin, 1995) by allowing the researcher to avoid imposing their worldview on the participants. The shadowing observation and contextual visit helped me to gain deep insights into a participant's messaging activity and his or her use contexts.

The integrated theoretical perspective guided data analysis as described below:

- To explore a concrete use activity situated at the intersection of various contexts, I used a simple 5W structure (Where, When, Who, What, and hoW) to examine patterns of use activities, such as where and when the text messaging practice occurred, who people texted to, and what they texted about, which emerged from the message diaries. The activity-based instrumental affordances and social affordances were brought in to understand the dynamic interactions between a user and a technological artifact, and between practice and context.
- To understand the mediation of meanings, I analyzed interview transcripts and observational notes and looked at the circuit of culture through which text messaging technology revolves to see how the social motives originating from broad cultural contexts affect the adoption, use, and consumption of this technology in daily life practices.

• To investigate recurrent use situations of mobile text messaging
in context and to search for structuring forces of this technology
in a broad sociocultural context, I drew from genre theory, linked
textual patterns of mobile messages to routinized use behaviors (Sun,
2004), and analyzed collected text messages with a verbal data analysis
method (Geisler, 2004). In that regard, I interpreted the technology
of mobile text messaging as a genre that mediates between social
motives and local goals with instrumental and social affordances in
context.

I saw the integrative theoretical vision as emerging and developing through fieldwork. For example, the coding scheme for verbal data analysis was informed by activity theory, genre theory, and
my fieldwork observation. A total of 2,474 text messages (including
813 American messages and 1,661 Chinese messages) were analyzed
with two dimensions of coding categories: rhetorical purposes and life
spheres[13] (see Appendix C). Here a rhetorical purpose is conceived as
both a user goal in terms of activity theory and a social motive in
terms of genre theory, which could be translated into design functionality in the future. Based on speech act theory (Cutting, 2002), conversation analysis (McLaughlin, 1984), previous research on instant and
mobile text messaging use (Issacs, Walendowski, Whittaker, Schiano,
& Kamm, 2002), and my observation, I coded text messages segmented
by a single rhetorical purpose[14] into seven categories: (1) informing,
(2) co-experiencing, (3) expressing, (4) instructing, (5) coordinating,
(6) switching, and (7) other. The dimension of life spheres (Wheeler,
1999), developed in a similar way, was used to explore how participants
used mobile text messaging to augment their work and life, including
five categories: (1) work, (2) school, (3) family, (4) personal leisure other
than with family, and (5) other.

A variety of procedures was followed to validate fieldwork findings.
At the data collection stage, the plan of data collection was shaped by
theoretical propositions. Pilot studies were conducted to test the sites,
examine research methodologies, and refine the research plan. Multiple
sources of data were used to achieve triangulation of data sources. At
the data analysis stage, an integrated perspective helped to better address

validity issues. The analysis was triangulated by different methods and different intellectual traditions, and I became more aware of alternative explanations and negative evidences emerging from the study.

In addition to the validity and rigor required for a cross-cultural qualitative study, I was also conscious of the suitability and ethical implications of my methods in local contexts, or "rhetorical situatedness," to use Sullivan and Porter's notion (1997). To conduct a culturally sensitive study of local technology use, the researcher does not do his or her homework well if he or she thinks only about the particular procedures of implementing methods. More issues need to be attended to. For example, will the methods I choose fit for both local contexts? What methods should I use if I want to encourage participants who come from a culture different than mine to feel comfortable about sharing their technology use experiences with me? How should I design a text message diary book that will both account for local differences and collect comparable data across sites?

In retrospect, I think my study benefited from the following factors: First, I was working with young people in two distinctive cultures. In this rapidly growing global economy, young people across cultures share more similarities than they do with older generations of their same culture (Victor, 1992). My young participants were not very sophisticated, and many of them seemed open and honest. For example, I allowed participants to self-remove private text messages they did not want me to see from the text message diary workbooks. To my surprise, I still got a few private messages from both sites concerning personal sex and pregnancy situations. And I did not see many behavioral differences between the two groups of participants when conducting interviews and shadowing. Second, the Albany area in the United States is more liberal than other regions in the United States, a multicultural society that is more equalitarian than many other countries. As a result, my ethnic background did not hinder my fieldwork at the American site. Third, the local articulations of mobile text messaging use are influenced mainly by popular culture rather than a particular organizational culture, where I either lived and was embedded (for the Albany case) or with which I was familiar and had access to as a member of the Chinese diasporas (for the Hangzhou case).

Conclusion

Using broad strokes to paint the backdrop of the study presented in the following chapters, I have introduced the case of this book, a comparative study of mobile messaging uses in two cultural contexts, and I have delved into its challenges and implications to cross-cultural technology design, framed in a discussion of the methodological potentials and values of the CLUE approach.

The comparative user localization cases of mobile text messaging are compelling here because they were conducted at an interesting moment, when text messaging had reached the point of being widely adopted by a larger population of users in many places of the world. It became a seamless part of many users' lives, and they used it in different ways according to their lifestyles. Unlike teenage users, who are commonly portrayed in many studies of text messaging (e.g., Baron, 2008; Eldridge & Grinter, 2001; Lenhart, Rainie, & Lewis, 2001; Ling 2008, 2010; Schiano et al., 2002; Taylor & Harper, 2001), I looked in particular at a group of college students and young professionals to see how they localized a hard-to-use technology into their everyday practices to augment work and life.

In the following five chapters of this book, I will illustrate the CLUE approach with user localization cases of mobile text messaging in two distinctly different cultural contexts—the U.S. and China. Out of the 41 participants with whom I worked, I have chosen these cases because each provides a distinctive angle for us to study complex local uses and gain insights for cross-cultural technology design. The five users came from different cultural backgrounds, held assorted professions, and led various lifestyles. However, they had one thing in common—they successfully localized a hard-to-use technology to fit their lifestyles. These user cases describe how each specific local use develops in a concrete activity situated at the intersection of multiple material, social, cultural, and technological contexts and how this local use echoes with both the subjectivity of the user and the ethos of the surrounding culture. In this way, they form an eloquent account of "situated and constructed" user experience.

My goals in writing Chapter 5 to Chapter 9 are to present rich and messy local user experiences as holistic, situated, and constructed, and to illustrate how an integrated view drawn from key concepts and methods of activity theory, British cultural studies, and genre theory (e.g., action, meaning, genre, and affordance) would inform cross-cultural design practices. Because of this, I will focus on key concepts and will deliberately not trace how the three practice theories influence each case. For me, this type of tracing does a disservice to an integrative approach like CLUE by decomposing and reducing it. To further clarify this, I also put forward a more detailed rationale in the Conclusion section of Chapter 10, after presenting a consolidated view of culturally localized user experience.

Notes

1. The GSM committee of Europe began to develop the technical standards of SMS in 1985 (European Telecommunications Standards Institute [ETSI], 2010).
2. The comparison of American and Chinese SMS volumes should serve as an approximate index. United States and China track the traffic volume of SMS differently. According to the 10th Annual Commercial Mobile Radio Services (CMRS) Competition Report (2005) released by the Wireless Telecommunications Bureau (WTB), the SMS traffic volume in the U.S. includes both mobile text messages and instant messages sent by phone, while only mobile text messages are counted in the Chinese data. WTB is one of the seven operating bureaus under the Federal Communications Commission (FCC) in the United States.
3. CTIA-The Wireless Association® is the organization that tracks the traffic volume of SMS in the United States, and their data are used by the WTB's Annual CMRS Competition Reports. Perhaps due to the slow development of SMS in the United States, initially CTIA tracked only the SMS volume in June and December of each year; starting on July 2004 it began to track a six-month volume. The annual volume amount was not available until 2005.
4. It should be noted that the penetration rates of Chinese IT refer to the rates of the whole country, which has a large rural population. As the research was conducted in well-developed urban areas, the penetration rates at the study site were much higher than the national average.
5. AT&T Wireless introduced their service to the Albany area after the recruiting of participants for the study ended. Therefore I did not have participants who used this service.
6. This price went up in 2006, first to $0.15 for a message sent and then to $0.20 (Reardon, 2008a). However, for heavy texters, if they choose an unlimited texting plan, the texting cost could be reduced to $0.01 per message in early 2010 (Entner, 2010).

7. In 2003, the currency exchange rate was 8.264 yuan per U.S. dollar, and the cost of living comparison between China and the U.S. was 0.214:1.000 (World Salaries, 2008).

8. Starting from 2009, all text messages sent in-network and out-of-network are 0.10 yuan.

9. The project was sequentially approved by the Institutional Review Board of Rensselaer Polytechnic Institute for human subject research and by that of Grand Valley State University.

10. The number of five messages was determined based on the pilot surveys conducted at both sites. It should be noted that this study began at the time when text messaging was not widely adopted and not many people would send hundreds of texts daily like American teenagers did in 2010. A daily volume of 20–30 messages was considered a high volume at that time.

11. At the time the study began, for example, Sprint PCS users needed to log in to the mobile web on their phones to send and receive text messages. There were lots of complaints about that design on the discussion forums of SprintUsers. com, and one user, William Frantz, even developed a J2ME application called SendNote in 2003 that allowed Sprint PCS users to send email and text messages directly to Sprint cell phones and any valid email address (Frantz, 2003), which I downloaded and enjoyed using.

12. This measure was included because phone minutes were charged differently on weekdays and weekends at the American site.

13. The simple agreement for the dimension of rhetorical purposes is 0.90 or 0.87, corrected by Cohen's Kappa, and the simple agreement for the dimension of life spheres is 0.98 or 0.96, corrected by Cohen's Kappa. The second coder tested 12.7% of message segments, including both American and Chinese.

14. There were a total of 2,866 message segments, with 942 from the American site and 1,924 from the Chinese site.

PART II

EXPERIENCES

5

Sophie's Story: New Chocolate at Work

"Mobile text messaging gives me more opportunity to communicate with people in creative ways."

Profile

"Sophie"[1] was a 30-year-old retail manager and an owner of a home-based interior design company at the American site when she joined the study. Eighteen months later, she left the retail business to focus on her own firm after moving from the East Coast to the Southeast with her husband. Shortly thereafter, they had their first baby. Sophie first participated in the diary study and had shadowing observation. She then took part in three follow-up interviews, one right after the diary study and observation, one in the second year, and one in the third year after she quit the retail job, relocated to a new place, and had the baby.

Sophie's daily communication technologies included a wireless phone, mobile messaging, email, walkie-talkie,[2] landline phone, fax, instant messaging, and letters. She used a wireless phone, mobile messaging, and email the most, typically for personal communication. She used her walkie-talkie, landline phone, and fax for business communication at work. She seldom used instant messaging.

Sophie started using a cell phone in 1997 and adopted text messaging technology in February 2002. She chose mobile text messaging to work out a communication constraint with her best friend Dana during working hours. Dana's boss did not allow employees to make personal phone calls during work. As a store manager, Sophie's work schedule was "hectic and erratic." She was either in the retail office holding conferences, completing paperwork, or on the sales floor serving clients and arranging merchandise. She was typically unable to check email during work. Mobile text messaging solved this problem: Dana was able to use the computer in her office to send short emails to Sophie's cell phone, and Sophie's reply could be quickly sent via text message. Using this method, they maintained close contact with each other without being noticed by the boss or other people. Later Sophie found text messaging to be "a whole other dimension." She texted to her husband and coworkers to "have fun."

Since Sophie worked in the design business, she was very sensitive to new technologies and fashion, and she would happily embrace new things. She remembered the days when email was first invented and her home computer was in black and white. It was fascinating for her to watch her younger coworkers use the phone and other new technologies. In some ways, she felt that texting helped her "stay young."

She changed a few cell phones as text messaging technology evolved. She first had the Kyocera KWC 2235, a phone with basic text messaging function that introduced her to texting. She upgraded her phone to a camera phone (LG VX6000) when she discovered the fun of picture messaging. After her baby was born, she purchased an LG VX8100 with a new video messaging function. Her newest phone was the iPhone.

Texting in Action

The case study shows that Sophie used text messaging in the workplace primarily to balance work and life over the study time period.

Patterns of Daily Use

In the four-day period of the diary study and the follow-up half-day of shadowing observation conducted at the beginning, Sophie sent 40 messages and received 27 pieces for a total of 67. Most of the messages were sent and received at her workplace where, according to her descriptions in the workbook, she spent the most time. She actually texted to only a small number of people. In the interview she said she usually texted to four to five people. There were three recipients logged in the diary study and observational study: her best friend Dana, her close coworker Ida, and Sophie's husband.[3]

It is striking that, though most messages were exchanged in the workplace, only 15% of these messages were work-related messages. All of the other messages were about her personal life (80%) and family life (5%). Examined against the overall pattern at the American site—76.2% for personal, 17.9% for work/school, and 3.5% for family—Sophie's message distribution shows a stronger inclination toward her personal life.

In the area of rhetorical purposes, compared to the overall distribution pattern of the American site (see Figure 5.1), 58.1% of Sophie's messages were exchanged for an expressing purpose (vs. 33.1% at the American site), 14.9% were for an informing purpose (26.2% at the American site), 14.9% were for a co-experiencing purpose (19.3% at the American site), and 9.5% were for an instructing purpose (11.9% at the American site). It's notable that more than half of her messages were sent for an expressing purpose considering the average for an expressing purpose at the American site was already 7% higher than the average at the Chinese site.

A closer look at those messages with an expressing purpose shows that Sophie employed different communication styles and vocabularies when she interacted with people of different ages. The messages sent to her best friend Dana and her husband (both of whom are her age) have a common colloquial style as illustrated below:

"City kitty:-D" (Greeting to Dana, who was taking a trip to New York City that day. Kitty is Dana's nickname.)

"Smart kitty…awesome opportunity for you..take it…i believe in you" (Encouraging Dana, who decides to go back to school.)

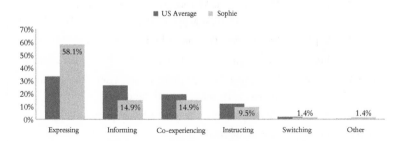

FIGURE 5.1   Sophie Sent More Texts for Expressing than the American Average

"Arrrgh" (A complaint to Dana.)

"Closer than my peeps u r to me..ba-be //[4] Closer than my friends you are to me..babe" (A love message to her husband.)

When communicating to Ida, a close friend and coworker in her early 20s, she used a lot of slang and phrases from TV comedies and talk shows such as Saturday Night Live. In the text snippet below, we find slang in almost every message. As described by themselves, these text messages here present a "jive talking" style. The conversation occurred on a weekday when Sophie was working in the store and Ida was off.

TEXT SNIPPET 5.1		
Time	Sender	Message Text
2:30 PM	Ida	jive from the dialectizer:-[
2:35 PM	Sophie	Woo doggie . . . u all up n everything // Woo doggie . . . you are all up? And how about everything?
2:36 PM	Ida	Im all up in that s★★t[5] yo! how do you feel about "m-kitty" im changing my name.//I'm all up. How about you? How do you feel about (my new name) "m-kitty"? I'm changing my name.
2:40 PM	Sophie	Jenna will have fun w (with) your new name
3:00 PM	Sophie	Do m-kitties roll on dubs? //Do m-kitties drive?
3:10 PM	Ida	Hells no g-funk (a nonsense word used as a compliment to a friend who is particularly savvy) //Yes, I am driving.
3:15 PM	Sophie	NOther (another)? . . . who is the coolest m-cat in the world? :-[//Another question . . . who is the coolest m-cat (another way of saying m-kitties) in the world?:-[
4:00 PM	Ida	Tonight on the M-Kitty Show: How to Fashizzle One's Nizzle with musical guest L-Doggie and The DawgPound[6]
4:10 PM	Sophie	Sounds like a fascinating dizzle ..i'll watch fojizzle (for sure)
5:00 PM	Ida	Big pimpin' (very cool) and spendin' cheese (very luxurious)
5:15 PM	Sophie	That cheez (Greatest thing in the world) is na-chos (not yours) . . . lay off the toastah (gun) yo
6:45 PM	Sophie	Youre (You're) my favorite schizzle (sure) m-kitty
7:00 PM	Ida	talk to you later

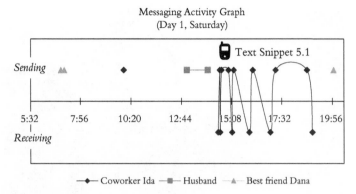

FIGURE 5.2   Sophie: When Did She Text?

Figure 5.2 provides a typical one-day interaction pattern of the text messaging practice emerging from Sophie's diary log with the above text snippet mapped. As shown from the graph, Sophie tended to send greeting messages in the morning to Dana, her best friend. Dana was unable to reply to her that day due to her day trip to New York City. In the afternoon, she sent two loving messages to her husband, realizing that he might not be able to answer her messages because of his busy schedule. Later she exchanged many fun messages with her close coworker Ida, who was off that day. Before she headed back home, Sophie sent another greeting message to Dana. She knew that they would be able to chat on the phone when she was home.

Texting at Work

A five-hour observation on a Saturday morning illustrates how mobile text messaging meshed with Sophie's work life.

It was a warm and sunny Saturday. At 7:30 a.m., Sophie left home early because she needed to do a routine blood test at the hospital on the way to work that day. While driving to the hospital, she sent three messages. Two were morning greetings to her best friend Dana. She used "meow" to greet Dana because Dana's nickname was Kitty. Sending morning greetings to Dana was her daily ritual, as shown in the message log:

Meow goodmorning //Meow good morning

Meowkipp..owwyoudoowin[7]? //Meow how are you doing?

FIGURE 5.3   Texting While Driving to Work in the Morning

In addition, she also sent a grocery-shopping reminder to her husband, who was still asleep.

After completing the blood test, she found that she still had time,
so she went to a grocery store and bought some chocolates, a bouquet
of flowers, and a vase to cheer up a coworker who was passed over for a
recent job promotion. She also made a phone call to Dana while waiting
for another associate to open the store where she worked. On the phone,
they updated each other on what had happened over the past week.

At 9 a.m., she entered the store and started her busy day. She began
with some paperwork in the office and then went to the bank in the mall
to deposit the previous day's earnings. On the way to the bank branch,
she got a text message from Dana. Dana had promised to take Sophie to
a butterfly sanctuary in Massachusetts on her birthday, but she changed
her mind and asked Sophie to go with her husband instead. Sophie was
very disappointed, and Dana felt sorry about it. That message started
their text conversations for the morning. They exchanged 17 messages
about this topic while Sophie was preparing to open the store, arranging new arrivals on the shelves, and serving customers during the early
hours when most customers had not yet arrived at the store.

After 11 a.m., many people came to the mall. Sophie was so busy
with her clients that she did not have time for texting.

FIGURE 5.4   Texting at Light Hours

FIGURE 5.5   Busy Hours: No Time for Texting

		TEXT SNIPPET 5.2
Time	Sender	Message Text
9:36 AM	Dana	Sigh
9:36 AM	Sophie	Big sigh…was looking forward to butterflies
9:54 AM	Dana	Go with mr //[You should] go with your husband
9:55 AM	Sophie	ON way to hos // [Are you] on the way to [your mom's] house and stress?[8]
10:00 AM	Dana	Goin with mr //Going with your husband
10:01 AM	Sophie	Dode enjoying the yard? //[Is your dog] Dode enjoying the yard?
10:13 AM	Dana	Small talk // (Dana suggests Sophie was doing small talk without answering her request)
10:15 AM	Sophie	Arrrgh
10:20 AM	Dana	What //What [did you "arrrgh" about]?
10:20 AM	Sophie	Small talk ref //[I went "arrrgh" about your message of] small talk
10:25 AM	Dana	Is yes Goin w mr ref //Is [the answer] yes for [the suggestion of] going with Mr?
10:29 AM	Sophie	Goin w mr ref // [I went arrrgh about your suggestions of] going with Mr
10:30 AM	Dana	Goin insane //Going insane
10:57 AM	Dana	There
10:57 AM	Dana	Cancel B4 U do //Cancel the plan before you do
10:58 AM	Sophie	Ok…thats fair bc of other times…but im looking forward to it…pbbbblt //Ok…that's fair because of other times [I cancelled our plans]…but I'm looking forward to it…Disappointed
11:10 AM	Dana	I suck

Figure 5.6 shows when and how often Sophie texted that morning. For example, she sent three messages while driving to work and exchanged many messages with Dana during the light hours. After 11 a.m., she had no time for texting.

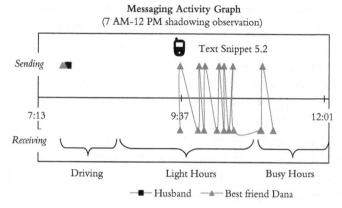

FIGURE 5.6   Texting at Work

Change over Time

The two follow-up interviews with Sophie conducted in the second year and third year confirmed that Sophie continued texting at work, though with changes to message numbers and the messaging format.

In the second year, Sophie reduced the use of text messaging as its newness wore off and the promotion of an unlimited messaging plan from Verizon Wireless ended. For a while, she sent just two or three messages a day because she opted for a messaging package of 100 messages a month. Meanwhile, she described her new fun with picture messaging. She found that the handy feature of picture messaging made her design consultation easier. It was very convenient to take quick pictures of fabrics and other accessories with the phone and send them to her own email for later reference when she was out shopping for her clients or visiting clients' homes. She was also excited about sending pictures of funny things to her friends right away: "It completely satisfies all the requirements of immediate gratification and it's a great way to digitally shout 'see what I'm looking at RIGHT NOW!!!!!' "

In the third year, Sophie experienced a lot of life changes. She moved to the Southeast and concentrated on her own design business. Later she started a new chapter of her life, becoming a mom of a little girl. The little girl brought so much joy to the family that she became the main theme of Sophie's messages. She reported that she sent more messages than she did in the first year and went back to an unlimited messaging plan. For example, she sent 30 messages and received 35 messages during the three days prior to the interview. Half of those messages were picture messages, and five were video messages. The majority of the picture messages and all the video messages were about her baby girl. When she spotted interesting episodes of her baby girl during the daytime, she would just grab the phone and send messages to her friends, mom, and brother-in-law, all of whom were interested in watching the little girl grow up. She always made sure that picture messages were sent to her husband at the same time so that he could put those photos of the baby on their Flickr page to be checked out by a broader network of family and friends. Juggling work and family life, she rediscovered the fun of mobile messaging.

Texting and Lifestyle

Patterns of use emerging from the diary log and the half-day shadowing study at her workplace painted a vivid picture of how Sophie used mobile text messaging in her immediate context (e.g., her workplace). The three qualitative interviews helped reveal how her use patterns were influenced by the surrounding broader cultural contexts. The dynamic interactions between these two levels of contexts show how well mobile messaging blended into her work life: She used mobile messaging, a form of unobtrusive communication, as an emotional support to stay in contact with her friends and loved ones in her hectic work schedule. Mobile messaging also allowed her to get away from her stressful work environment and maintain productivity.

Texting as Chocolate: Affordance in a Work Setting

Text messaging was originally designed and launched as a business application; however, Sophie localized it for personal use in her work setting. As unobtrusive communication, mobile text messaging fulfilled Sophie's emotional needs of staying in contact with friends and loved ones at work, whether she worked in a structured setting or at her home.

In a structured business setting, text messaging had important affordances for Sophie. On the instrumental level, text messaging afforded silent communication, convenient use, and discreet action. The phone was not noticeable when tucked into a pants pocket. By setting it to vibrate, only Sophie would know when a message arrived. In addition, she could take the phone with her while she moved around in the store helping clients. On a social affordance level, text messaging helped Sophie stay connected with her friends in an unobtrusive way.

Sophie described the importance of mobile text messaging to her as below:

> "Mobile text messaging is important to me because it gives me more opportunity to communicate with people in creative ways."

> "Especially at work, some time I could get pretty frustrated. So I would sneak a minute to go back to the office and text something funny…"

> "It's nice to just have that little [messaging] break. It's like you get a little greeting card in the mail every day. It's nice to know you thought of someone that made you laugh…"

In the non-traditional work setting of her home office, Sophie juggled her client projects, baby care, and housework and found that text messaging was "the perfect solution" for communication in that situation:

> "With a little, short message to let people know what's going on, or just sending a picture, it's a lot easier than sitting down and writing really lengthy emails."

> "This is an excellent way for me to communicate because I have short periods of time between her (the baby's) nap and other things when I can work, when I can be productive, and when I can communicate."

Indeed, text messaging was the "new chocolate" for Sophie (Lowe, 2003): "instead of dashing to the fridge in times of emotional fragility, girls are now grabbing their mobile phones and texting a support team of female friends." Sophie liked chocolate: She used to keep a big bucket of chocolates in her office that she ate during her breaks or shared with her coworkers when she was the store manager. She also liked chocolate in the form of text messages from friends, which let her know that she was being thought of.

This new chocolate actually made her daily communication with Dana easier. As shown in Text Snippet 5.2, Dana tended to change her plans with Sophie frequently, causing a lot of frustration for Sophie. Thus, she preferred to talk to Dana about changing plans via text messaging: She could just type bits of vital information to Dana and avoid complicated conversations. In some ways, text messaging let Sophie both stay in contact with her best friend and get away from her during the more frustrating moments of their friendship.

Enhancing Personal and Work Life with Text Messaging

At first sight, texting to friends and loved ones at work seemed to disrupt workflow and harm performance, but Sophie found that those short text messaging breaks indeed made her more productive in the work setting. The affordances of mobile text messaging were as sweet as chocolate, and she utilized them to creatively present and negotiate her identities of a good friend, a good mom, a good daughter, and a good boss in her life.

From the aspect of her personal identities, Sophie was very consciously establishing and maintaining an image as a close and approachable friend to her girlfriends. Friendship was such an important facet of her life that it constantly motivated her to stay in contact. We can see this point from her message log. She initiated conversations very often and sent more messages than she received.

For Sophie, texting provided innovative ways of constructing her identity. Being 30 is a very big deal to many young women, and Sophie refused to fixate on her age and wanted to stay younger. By identifying with younger people in her workplace, speaking their language, and using popular slang in her daily text messages, Sophie found a way to cure this anxiety about turning 30: "Whenever I can get my hand at any these types of new technologies, I will. That does keep me feeling younger as possible." As a new communication mode, text messaging made her "reconsider (her) tone and think of new ways to use humor."

Quite a few references from popular culture can be found in her text messages, such as the use of "fashizzle" and "-izzle" and her creative shorthand of "hos," which combines both "house" and "stress."

As a new mom, Sophie was excited about every little developmental step her daughter made and eager to share her joy within a broader network of family and friends. She would take spontaneous photos with her phone to record all those precious moments. Though she had a good-quality digital camera at home, mobile messaging made spreading of the joy and excitement much faster and easier. For example, she could take and then send pictures or videos directly from her phone to friends' phones and grandma's computer, and fresh images of the little angel could be uploaded to the Flickr website and posted right away. Sophie embraced the role change in her life and enjoyed being a mom by constantly working with her digital version of Mom's "brag book," her cell phone.

Texting also helped Sophie to negotiate her identities on her social network. For instance, text messaging "fundamentally" changed Sophie's relationship with her mother in terms of communication. Sophie described her mom Debbie as a loving but "overbearing" woman. In Debbie's eyes, her adult daughter was still that little girl who needed her mother to decide most things. In fact, Sophie had been afraid of confronting her mom since her childhood. Debbie worked in an office with her own computer. Though she did not have a cell phone, she enjoyed seeing her granddaughter's photos sent from Sophie's phone via text messages to her email account. And thus Debbie was on Sophie's text recipient list after the baby was born. On Sophie's first Mother's Day, Debbie wanted Sophie to bring the baby home, which was five hours from where Sophie lived. Sophie declined this request because she had been busy with work lately, but Sophie's refusal led to a burst of Debbie's harsh words, to which Sophie never knew how to respond. Since she had been communicating with her mom in loops of text messages and emails for a while, this time she decided not to back down and replied in a polite manner via text messages and emails to explain her situation and avoided talking to her mom directly. It worked! After one week of silence since Sophie's last message, Debbie apologized and invited Sophie to come home when she had time. From that time on, Debbie realized that Sophie was an adult and became more respectful in their communication. Sophie later commented, "I waited 33 years for that to happen."

From the perspective of her business identity, texting enhanced Sophie's leadership credibility. Text messaging was a popular practice in the store where she worked, and many people liked texting during off hours. By keeping up with popular trends and speaking her coworkers' language, Sophie developed a management style that encouraged her younger coworkers to ignore the generation gap between them and enjoy working for her.

As a store manager, Sophie was fully aware of her different identities. She marked clear boundaries for her different information technologies and used them differently. For example, her three most-used communication tools in the store were the office phone, a walkie-talkie, and a cell phone. The office phone was always placed on a noticeable area of her desk, and she would use it only for business communication with different stores. The walkie-talkie was clipped to her back, and she used it for in-store communication. Compared to the visible status of these two tools, her cell phone (tucked into her front pants pocket) was invisible to outsiders and primarily used for personal communication.

In addition to the differences in visibility of these technologies, Sophie's use of this messaging technology was actually regulated by two kinds of rules: rules for professional communication and rules for personal communication. Professional communication rules and etiquette told her that she should not text to clients because mobile messaging technology does not have a status of authority in American culture. She also knew that she could "only text at the break or when the work is slow . . . ." At the same time, her use of mobile text messaging was affected by personal communication rules. In her small circle of friends, everyone loved to text to each other; it was impolite not to text friends. This peer pressure explains her high volume[9] of messages from another angle.

Reflection Notes on Cross-Cultural Design

As the first case portrayed in this part of the book, I want to use Sophie's use story to uncover how action and meaning are seamlessly intertwined in an individual user experience as individual users negotiate their text messaging practices between immediate material contexts and broader sociocultural contexts. Here a wireless phone served as a genre mediating between local goals and social motives across different levels of contexts. In the immediate context, Sophie chose text messaging to accomplish tasks such as working out a communication constraint with her best friend in the workplace. She wanted to exchange quick, invisible messages in a mobile setting with friends and loved ones and get little breaks from a stressful working environment. From the sociocultural level, she wanted to stay in contact with the people important to her in a creative way. Overall, mobile text messaging provided both instrumental and social affordances for her different goals originating from various levels of contexts, allowing her to mediate between work and life and between business tasks and emotional needs. The fact that a mobile phone was used as an emotional device to mediate social networks and emotional support in contexts explains why Sophie was enthusiastic about using mobile text messaging.

This case also shows how Sophie constructed the meaning of a technology and negotiated her multiple identities through innovative ways of using the technology in the sociocultural contexts in which she was situated. Her ways of using text messaging were very Sophie, originating from her work environment, lifestyle, and personality. They also had been consistent with her life change and role change. At the same time, this messaging use pattern represented the general use patterns revealed from the fieldwork at the American site, where a higher percentage of text messages was sent to express feelings and share current experiences (Sun, 2004). In contrast, a larger percentage of text messages was sent to exchange information and initiate actions from the Chinese site.

It should be noted that this pattern of use conflicted with the original design of mobile text messaging. Mobile text messaging was designed as a business tool rather than an emotional device and did not fully consider how to better afford emotional communication. For example, Sophie found it extremely inconvenient to input the exclamation mark ("!") on one of her phones. There was no exclamation point on the first key for the punctuation, which was important to compose a cute, funny, and emotional message. To use such punctuation, she typically had to press a few keys to go several screens deep.

In Chapter 2, I introduced the concept of "artful integration" (Suchman, 2002) to look at user localization. Based on Haraway's argument that "[feminist] objectivity is about limited location and situated knowledge" (1991, as cited in Suchman, 2002), Suchman suggests that a successful design would work smoothly with its surrounding conditions and fit in the local context. This view of technology design can also be used to examine technology use. Indeed, technology use is a process of "animating and finding subjectivity in technical artifacts." The meaning of a technology is important to users who need to be able to relate to the technology. Subjectivity here is the essence of technology use. It defines whether a user can find part of herself in a technology and whether a user can envision how a technology might be located in her life. This is what I call "constructive subjectiveness" in this book. Though text messaging was initially designed for business communication, Sophie used it to extend her personal communication into her work sphere in a productive way. At a time when middle-class workers dread the invasion of work into personal lives introduced by advanced information and communication technologies, this use shows another direction of movement in this power struggle. It is an example of "tactics" advocated by Feenberg (2002) in his proposal for democratizing technology. When Sophie was actively integrating the mobile messaging technology into her work setting to enhance her work and personal life, she was challenging the homogeneity and dominance prescribed by the technology and participating in the practice of artful integration on a broader horizon. In this way, a hard-to-use technology was localized into a user's personal life through thoughtful articulation work of various cultural factors, and new meaning of the technology was constructed. Clearly the constructed "new meaning" of the technology comes from the use situated in a local context.

For the cross-cultural design community, the challenge revealed from this case is how we can help a user locate subjectivity through her own way of using a technology by constructing her meaning of this technology. And thus she would be able to negotiate a holistic user experience with the surrounding cultural context and make the technology both usable and meaningful.

Notes

1. All the names and places in this book are pseudonyms.
2. In this case it refers to a common walkie-talkie, not a feature on mobile phones.
3. A diary study of 60 households in Switzerland in 2005–2008 shows a similar pattern that participants tend to use various technologies to communicate with very few close ties (Broadbent & Bauwens, 2008).
4. This symbol suggests that the translation of the whole message will be followed.
5. Impolite words from text messages are modified by the author in this book.
6. -izzle: Coined by rapper Snoop Dogg who likes to add "-izzle" to words either for amusement or creating rhymes during interviews/shows. It has no meaning.
7. A New York pronunciation of "How are you doing," which came from a Budweiser TV commercial popular at that time.
8. Dana found going to her mother's house was an experience of stress. Sophie used "hos" to stand for "house and stress."
9. See Endnote 10 of Chapter 4.

6

Lili's Story: Pure Water in Social Network

"Sending text messages helps me realize 'the friendship between gentlemen appears indifferent but is pure like water" in a deeper way. It makes me feel good by texting and greeting to friends occasionally... It is a very beautiful thing to convey feelings this way."

Profile

"Lili" was 26, a teacher and student advisor for a local technical college at the Chinese site when she participated in the study. Lili first did the survey and diary study and was interviewed a few months later. She was interviewed again and shadowed for four hours in her workplace one year later. During the 20-month period of study, she married her long-time boyfriend and changed her job to a similar position at another local college.

Growing up in a small town one hour away, Lili had lived in Hangzhou since she obtained her college degree from another city. While a student, Lili was enthusiastic about school activities. She had been an anchor of the school radio station for three years and served as an officer for the undergraduate student government the entire time she was at college. Lili made many friends this way, but nowadays her childhood and college friends were scattered everywhere. At work, a big part of her job was advising students and organizing various student events, and she communicated with quite a few students each day.

Her daily communication technologies evolved over the time period. According to the survey at the beginning, her most-used technology was a wireless phone that she "always" used. The second one was text messaging, which she "usually" used. She did not have a landline phone at home and thus used the landline only at work. However, she got a Little Smart® wireless cityphone², which she used as a supplementary phone to her cell phone for long-distance phone calls and some local phone calls due to its cheap rate. When the study began, she noted that she rarely used the QQ[3] or MSN instant messengers for communication and seldom used email. Later, after getting a better Internet connection, she reported checking emails daily. By the end of the study, she had become a frequent QQ user.

Lili received her first cell phone (a Nokia model) as a gift from her future husband when she started work in September 2001. Before that cell phone, beginning in her sophomore year she had used a numeric pager to assist in daily communication with friends and colleagues. After Lili received the cell phone, she sent text messages right away to her friends who had cell phones, notifying them of her new communication status and her phone number. It was a natural move for her to adopt texting and join her texting circle. As she became familiar with the phone's features, she texted more and more. Soon it was "an indispensable means of communication" in her life that she found very useful.

The phone Lili used during the study was the Amoi A80, nicknamed the "Dancing Queen" by the local manufacturer Amoi in China. As a phone model popular among young women at that time, it had an elegant red color with a diamond-like flashing light on top, and included applications such as a menstrual cycle calendar and a biological clock, which Lili found handy. This phone was a replacement of the same phone, another phone gift from her fiancé, which was stolen shortly after she got it. She bought the current one herself, as she liked the chic design.

Texting in Action

The diary study and the observation illustrate that Lili used text messaging primarily to stay in contact with friends and relatives for the purpose of informing, that is, sharing information.

Patterns of Daily Use

In the four-day period of diary study at the first stage, Lili sent 28 messages and received 24 pieces, totaling 52 messages. Seven distinct locations can be established from her message log, including her home, office, meeting room, classroom, a park where she organized a student activity, the bus, or simply on the go. It shows that she texted primarily at two sites: at home (44%) and in the workplace (44%).

Lili texted to a total of 15 people in that period, among whom were four college friends, four colleagues, three childhood friends, two students, her fiancé, and her cousin. Additionally, she exchanged messages with her wireless carrier to check on her phone usage. More than 70% of these messages were sent to her college friends (42%) and childhood friends (31%). Most of these friends were not located in the same city where she lived. She initiated conversations most of the time, and sometimes her messages received no response because the person she was trying to contact was unavailable. When she was able to connect, they usually engaged in a conversation consisting of several message exchanges, as in the example below.

TEXT SNIPPET 6.1		
Time	Sender	Message Text
7:45 PM	Lili	Wei, zai wang shang kan dao ni ding hun de xiao xi, gong xi a! (Wei, I saw your news of engagement online, congratulations!)
7:50 PM	Wei	zai wang shang ma wo ye zai (Are you online me too[4])
7:51 PM	Wei	xie xie 2xxxx8 (Thanks 2xxxx8[5])
7:56 PM	Lili	wo mei zai wang shang, shi xia wu kan dao de. wo hen shao shang wang, jin tian wan shang you yong ren dan wei zai xue xiao zhao pin, wo zai zuo pei, hen wu liao a! (I'm not online, and I saw it this afternoon. I seldom go online, some company is having a job recruiting event at school, and I'm accompanying them, so boring!)
7:59 PM	Wei	o you kong lai Cixi Sandun de fang zi zen me yang wo ye xiang mai (Oh welcome to Cixi when you are free how is the real estate market in Sandun)
8:02 PM	Lili	wo mei mai san dun de fang zi, suo yi qing kuang bu tai shu xi. wo mai le xue xiao fu jin de fang zi, hai zai shi qu mai le tao xiao fang zi, mu qian ya li hen da a! (I didn't buy the condo in Sandun, so I'm not familiar with the real estate market there. I bought one near school, and also bought a small one in downtown. I have lots of pressure (to pay for two condos) now!)
		(Continued)

		TEXT SNIPPET 6.1 (Continued)
Time	Sender	Message Text
8:06 PM	Wei	hao li hai wo ji cuo le you hao fang yuan tong zhi yi sheng da jia yi kuai zhu hang zhou (Wow you are so great my memory made a mistake please notify me of good real estates there let's live in Hangzhou together)
8:11 PM	Lili	ni da suan lai hang zhou fa zhan ma? huan ying a! yi ding yao dai ni de zhun lao gong guo lai a! (Do you want to move to Hangzhou for career development? Welcome! Please come to visit with your fiancé!)
8:18 PM	Wei	mei you zhi shi zhao ge luo jiao de di fang shun bian ji dian gu ding zi chan (No I only want to find a place to settle down and gain some fixed assets on the way)
8:35 PM	Lili	he he! ni de jing ji tou nao hai shi zhe me fa da! (Ha ha! You are still so money-wise!)

In this case, Lili was accompanying a company recruiter to a career event at school that evening. Feeling bored and because she had heard news of an engagement about her college friend and roommate Wei, who was currently in Cixi, she texted her. They exchanged updates about recent life situations. As Lili did not like to use instant messaging programs and seldom used email at that time, here text messaging served as a combined function of instant messaging and email.

Compared to her text conversations with friends, her work-related conversations were much shorter:

		TEXT SNIPPET 6.2	
Time	Sender	Message Text	Place
3:38 PM	colleague	zhu tou hui kai de ru he? (How is the stupid meeting?)	at the meeting
3:40 PM	Lili	hai zai jin xing dang zhong, ting shun li de! Chen chu zhang you wen qi ni a! (Still in the middle of the meeting, and making progress smoothly! Director Chen asked about you again!)	at the meeting
3:41 PM	colleague	ni zen me shuo (What did you say about me)	at the meeting

Influenced by this use situation, two-thirds of her text messages fell into the personal sphere and one-third into the work sphere. It is important to note that Lili had the highest percentage of work-related messages among all participants. Text messaging was one of her most-used daily communication technologies, and it was highly embedded into her life. However, like Text Snippet 6.2, most of these work-related messages occurred in the context of friendly chats with old friends or colleagues. The purpose of such discussions was to keep up to date about recent situations or report at-the-moment experiences rather than accomplish work-related tasks in a work context.

Since Lili tended to chat with her friends about recent life situations, she employed a large percentage (47.8%) of text messages with informing purposes (see Figure 6.1). That percentage was much higher than the average at the Chinese site (31.6%), which was higher than that at the American site (26.2%). Her percentage was actually at the high end of the category for informing purpose among all 41 participants. In some way, hers was a parallel case to Sophie's at the American site. One of the major differences between the rhetorical purposes of American text messages and Chinese text messages was that American participants texted more for expressing purposes and Chinese participants texted more for informing purposes. Sophie and Lili are two representative cases with high percentages in these two distinctive categories. The distribution patterns of Lili's other purposes are similar to the overall pattern at the Chinese site: 23.9% of messages had the purpose of expressing (vs. 25.6% at the Chinese site), 13.4% for the purpose of co-experiencing (vs. 16.8%), 11.9% for the purpose of instructing

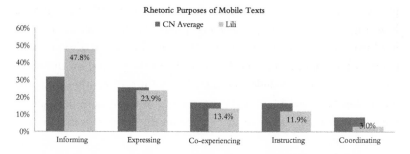

FIGURE 6.1   Lili Sent More Texts for Informing than the Chinese Average

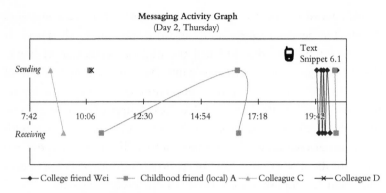

FIGURE 6.2   Temporal Pattern

(vs. 16.5%), and she had a smaller percentage of messages for the purpose of coordinating (3% vs. 8.4%).

Figure 6.2 illustrates a typical temporal pattern of Lili's text messaging activity found in her message log with Text Snippet 6.1 mapped on it. Most of the text messages she exchanged were between her and her friends. She also texted two colleagues, as it was a workday.

Persistent Texting

A half-day shadowing study conducted one year later showed a similar pattern from the diary study and confirmed the important status of text messaging in Lili's personal communication. That morning she exchanged five text messages with her childhood friend, Dong, during the work break.

It was a Monday morning at the end of the spring semester. Lili's office was located near the woods on a small hill, and thus the cell phone reception was not very good. Lili arrived at the office at 7:30 a.m. Entering the office, she put her cell phone on her desk along with her Little Smart wireless phone, side by side. There was also an office phone a few inches away on the desk. Then she turned on the office computer behind her desk and logged into QQ. Recently she would stay in her "on" status as long as possible in order to raise her rank in the QQ user community so that she could do more customization of the program.

Her primary task that morning was to fill out some forms for the Housing Office. After working for an hour on the forms, her supervisor came in and announced that staff vacations would start on July 18. Lili was so excited about the upcoming break that she sent a QQ message to her friends, "We are going to start summer break on July 18!" She got a QQ response five minutes later but did not notice because she was busy with the forms.

At 9:15 a.m., Lili was about to complete the forms and decided to take a break. She sat in front of the computer and laughed at some funny cartoon pictures she received on QQ. Then she turned back to the desk, picked up the cell phone, and started browsing a few old text messages sent over the weekend by her friend Dong. He just told her he was going to the U.S. the following month to pursue an advanced degree. Lili had been considering studying abroad for a while, but she had not yet taken the TOEFL and GRE examinations. Dong's success motivated her to begin her preparation. Seeing a well-known resource site for studying abroad that Dong had recommended in his text message, Lili went to the website and with one hand started to text Dong, who was vacationing at his parent's place:

"wo hai nan bu qu le, xue xiao yao 18 hao fang jia, wo kuai yun fan le! wo lao ma ta men da gai zhe ge zhou mu hui qu, ni zao dian guo lai chi fan o! zui zhu yao de shi yao mian shou jing yan a, ha ha! (I'm not going to Hainan, our school will start the break on the 18th, and my schedule is so crazy! My parents are probably going home this weekend, please come to have dinner together as soon as possible! The most important thing is to share your insights of American graduate school application, haha!)"

Unfortunately the signal was not good, and she got an alert of "Delivery Fails." She stood up and walked toward the office window to send it again, with no luck. She walked around in the office and tried again, but it still failed, so she left the office. Walking outside, she kept trying but got the same alert. She crossed the hallway, stepped down the staircase, circled around in the small courtyard in front of the building, and finally stopped at the end of the yard facing the big lawn downhill, where she got a better signal. It took her three minutes to get the message sent.

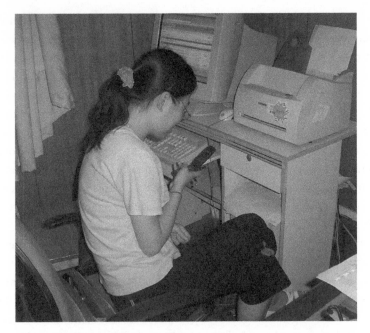

FIGURE 6.3   Texting at an Internet-Connected Computer

FIGURE 6.4   Sending a Text in the Courtyard for Better Signal

The reply arrived smoothly one minute later, fortunately:

"hao de. wo guo lai le jiu lian xi ni (Sure. I'll contact you when I'm in town)."

Because Lili was given a small project by her boss, she did not reply to the message right away. Once she had time, she exchanged another three messages with Dong, which included two messages sent and one received. In both cases of sending messages, Lili had to walk around outside to get the message sent. It usually took two or three minutes. For once, Lili was so desperate about sending it that she stared at the screen praying, "Go go go!"

It should be noted that, while Lili struggled with sending text messages, there was one landline phone and one Little Smart wireless phone sitting quietly on her desk, as well as the QQ instant messenger and an email client available on her computer.

Texting and Lifestyle

Text messaging played a significant role in Lili's everyday life because it implemented and enhanced a socially meaningful activity that was important to her, maintaining long-term and sometimes long-distance relationships with friends and relatives in a considerate-yet-unobtrusive way.

Indispensable Means of Communication in a Social Network

As shown from fieldwork, text messaging was an important means of communication in Lili's daily social network. She used text messaging to stay in contact with childhood friends, college friends, colleagues, and relatives. In fact, Lili defined text messaging as "an indispensable means of communication" in her life, and she believed that most of her friendships and family relationships were maintained and enhanced by text messaging.

Lili usually communicated to important people in her social network in the following manner: She called her parents in her hometown at a fixed time once a week and had longer conversations. With her husband, she usually had quick exchanges on the phone because they lived together and saw each other every day. For cousins, childhood friends, and college friends, she preferred to text them to keep in touch or to talk to them on the QQ messenger, but QQ was neither as available nor accessible as text messaging.

Unlike the informal status of text messaging in American social life, text messaging is acknowledged as a formal genre for Chinese daily social activities. When I first interviewed Lili, she was busy preparing for her upcoming wedding ceremony, and she had just sent out the first round of invitations for their wedding banquet to her friends via text message. She liked the affordance of getting quick feedback from text messages. Friends typically texted her with congratulations, told her whether they would be able to come, and reported the number of people likely to attend. Especially for friends at a distance, it was more convenient to send text messages than to mail invitations. Lili also prepared a few paper-based invitations. These were primarily reserved out of respect for her work colleagues, with whom she enjoyed good but not necessarily close relationships.

The implicit communication style and format of text messaging sometimes helped her to iron out the wrinkles of her relationships due to years of no contact. There was an interesting episode involving Lili texting to her old college friends about her wedding. She forgot to notify Lan, who was one year ahead of her at university and whom she had not seen since Lan graduated, though they were once very close at school. Another friend reminded her, and Lili felt so sorry that she texted Lan immediately with a short note about how she missed her and included the invitation. Lan was very moved by Lili's text message. She felt so happy that Lili still missed her even after years of not being in touch and had invited her to the wedding. Lili was happy to be reunited with an old friend. She commented on how text messaging helped her to solve a communication problem and fix a social blunder where other technologies might not have been as effective. It was abrupt to call people to say that you miss them and invite them to a wedding party after years without contact. Text messaging bypassed this awkward feeling with the affordance of its written form and implicit style. She concluded: "It is a very beautiful thing to convey feelings this way."

Indifferent but Pure Like Water

In the broad sociocultural context, text messaging was indispensable for Lili, as it suited her personality and enhanced her role in the sociocultural norms in which she was situated.

As a very social type of person, Lili liked to make new friends and cherished long-time relationships with old friends. However, she did not like to make phone calls with friends all the time, nor did she like to go online to chat via instant messaging with many friends at the same time, which she thought did not agree with her personality. To her, it was abrupt to call people and check in after a long time without contact. She did not know what to say at those moments, though she cared for her friends. Moreover, she said it was not genuine to chat with different friends at the same time through instant messaging.[6] She valued simple friendships and one-to-one communication. Text messaging, which affords one-to-one communication in an implicit way, satisfied her needs and fit with her personality, allowing her to use it comfortably and happily. On reflection, she said that she would not have been able to stay in touch with old friends if they were not texting. A few years later, they might just turn into strangers.

By using text messaging for maintaining and enhancing her social network, Lili actually identified herself strongly with the sociocultural norms surrounding her. In a collectivist culture, relationships are relatively long lasting, and individuals feel a deep personal involvement with each other. This long-term relationship orientation is mediated nicely with the instrumental and social affordances of mobile messaging that allow people to stay in touch in an unobtrusive way. She confessed in the interview: "Sending text messages helps me understand [the saying] 'the friendship between gentlemen appears indifferent but is pure like water (*Jun zi zhi jiao dan ru shui*)' in a deeper way. It makes me feel good by texting and greeting friends occasionally." The phrase "the friendship between gentlemen appears indifferent but is pure like water (*Jun zi zhi jiao dan ru shui*)" is a Confucian motto regarding how to socialize with friends. It has been followed for thousands of years in China and is deeply rooted in Chinese people's daily social practices. People are taught that they should treat their friends genuinely with reserved warmth and reasonable distance. The best friendship is like pure water, not tainted with personal interests and excessive contact.

In Lili's opinion, many of her friends were old friends. Their friendship was not maintained by constant contact but by years of care and trust. Texting was a good way to show care and consideration. She liked to text to a friend occasionally to ask how her or his life was and whether s/he was busy with work.

Lili savored her mellow taste of friendship mediated by text messaging as she went through different phases of the post-college life: landing her first job, settling down in a new city, changing jobs, and getting married. In the second interview, she told me that she did not chat as much as she did one year ago via text messaging, but she made sure to check in with friends regularly. For example, when her friends broke up with girlfriends or boyfriends, she would send messages of support to them. And usually she was notified of life updates of friends by text messaging. Recently, after receiving Lili's monthly greeting message, one of her childhood friends revealed via text message that he was divorced after a few months of marriage. This friend was an introvert who did not like to talk about his personal life, and thus what Lili could do was send him warm text messages occasionally to cheer him up.

Texting with Goodwill

It is noteworthy that text messaging gradually entered the public discourse as a formal genre in China: The Beijing mayor sent all Beijingese a text message of Happy New Year on the eve of the Spring Festival in 2006 (SINA, 2006); more and more journalists conduct interviews via text messaging (Xinhua Net, 2006); and listeners text in to join the live discussions of radio programs instead of calling in (personal observation). In Lili's case, she found herself using more text messaging for her work. In her second interview, she revealed that a large percentage of her text messages came from her students asking permission for sick leave, for example, and inquiring about course work. Senior colleagues would also send her text message reminders about work. In one case, the college dean, who was in her 50s, texted Lili about the status of business documents. However, it would be inaccurate to consider text messaging as a business genre in China. The business-related use uncovered from the fieldwork showed that text messages were usually used as a polite reminder, a cautious inquiry, or a subtle check-in. As documented in the diary study, most of these work-related messages still remained as meta-communication. And messages were often sent with the goodwill that the sender did not want to interrupt the receiver's work flow.

Text messaging had blended into Lili's life so naturally that some-times sending a text message was just an instinct. When she heard that a student from her class was sick, her first reaction was to text him to forward best regards. She explained that it was just more convenient for someone who was sick in bed to get a text message than answer the phone. She also remembered how she was touched when reading warm messages like this from students the last time she was sick: "It feels very bureaucratic and impersonal when you call a sick student, but text messages can convey more subtle feelings." Similarly, though a poor signal made texting Dong very inconvenient, Lili chose to do so regardless of other options available (e.g., an office phone, Little Smart wireless phone, instant messenger, and email application).

While Lili enjoyed the social affordance of the text messaging technology, she was also bothered by its instrumental limitations. As Lili tended to use text messaging to chat with friends by employing messages for informing purposes, she found that her care and consid-eration were confined to the size limit of a text message. She usually liked to describe things in a clear way with cause and effect, and thus her messages were a bit complex. This was particularly true for the first few turns with her friends when she told them about what had hap-pened recently in her life. About 70% of the time she was composing text messages, she would receive a prompt telling her that she reached the size limit. Then she had to go back and delete some of the words without ruining the meaning of her message. It was annoying to go through this process daily, but she had no other way.

Reflection Notes on Cross-Cultural Design

Similar to Sophie's case, Lili's use experience of mobile messaging technology is situated at the interaction of her immediate context and the surrounding conditions, while manifested in different ways. Lili first adopted text messaging because of its convenience and its wide acceptance in China. She stayed with it when she found that text messaging helped her to avoid abrupt phone calls to old friends and stay in contact with them as she adjusted to post-college career and life. Lili enjoyed using this technology not only because text messaging fit with her lifestyle but also because text messaging helped her to maintain her daily social network. It also helped her to be better situated within her sociocultural context and connected her to thousands of years of social tradition. Here both action and meaning are mediated nicely by the technological genre of text messaging.

In this case, social affordance became so important to the user that she ignored the poor usability of the technology. Lili had a high tolerance for the inconveniences of the technology for the sake of its social affordances. She stuck to mobile text messaging technology even though she had to delete extra characters to fit her long messages into the size limit. The power of social affordance became so strong that Lili persevered in her efforts to send text messages and ignored other technologies available during the shadowing study.

Local uses of mobile text messaging were the outcome of the interactions of various cultural factors on different levels. Lili's personal use of the technology was influenced both by her gendered identity on the local level and by ethnic cultural factors on the global level. The feminine phone, "Dancing Queen," that Lili used manifested how the technologies of wireless phones and mobile text messaging were localized for female social practices. These social practices were Lili's way of negotiating a form of "pure water" relationships between friends in her sociocultural contexts. If Sophie's experience highlights the subjectivity of technology use, Lili's experience underlines the importance of "integration" with the surrounding contexts.

As we uncover how various cultural factors are articulated into user localization, it becomes clear how culture is situated in the localization process: Culture is situated in concrete use activities within concrete contexts, which should be approached in a dynamic fashion and in a broad way. The analysis of Lili's use of messaging technology shows that her local uses were shaped by dimensional cultural factors such as a high-context communication style and collectivist culture, but these dimensions were not abstract and isolated ones; they also interacted with the local conditions in the immediate context and with Lili's own personality. This suggests that we should move toward designing local technology with rich understandings of use activities in context instead of simply applying cultural conventions to localization work.

Notes

1. A famous Chinese motto about friendship.
2. It is a local wireless loop service that was popular in China between 2001 and 2007. This service allowed users to make wireless phone calls at the rate of landline phones. As the cost of mobile phone services dropped, Little Smart® lost its market and was scheduled to end its service by the end of 2011.
3. QQ is a popular instant messaging application in China like AIM in the U.S.
4. Wei's text messages do not have punctuation marks.
5. This number is Wei's QQ number, a popular instant messaging system in China. She was suggesting switching from text messaging to instant messaging.
6. See Chapter 7 for the comparison between text messaging and instant messaging in Brian's case.

7

Brian's Story: Conversations Carried through My Fingers

> *"My instant messaging use, you know, definitely shaped my desire to text messaging, or my predispositions, maybe, towards using text messaging a lot, because I find it, at this time, after I have been using AIM for eight years, a very natural form of communication.... I think instant messaging has taught me how to carry on conversations through my fingers instead of my mouth."*

Profile

"Brian," 22, grew up in a middle-class family in Rochester, NY, with two younger sisters. He majored in chemistry in college but switched to finance for his graduate study at the same university and was planning to pursue a PhD right after completing his master's degree. Brian paid his own bills and worked during the summer to support his education. At the time of the study, he worked as a lab assistant and volunteered in a friend's Taekwondo gym in exchange for free membership. One month after the survey and diary study, Brian was shadowed in two different settings within one week. He had one follow-up interview two months later, and another five months after the first one.

Brian liked sports and enjoyed practicing Taekwondo and playing video games. He had a pilot's license and would fly once a month. Living with three boys in a campus apartment, he socialized with a large group of male and female college students who were either seniors or first-year graduate students. He had been dating Mindy, who attended the same college, for a while.

Like most college students, Brian's daily communication technologies included a wireless phone, landline phone, instant messaging (AIM), text messaging, and email. His top three communication choices were instant messaging, text messaging, and wireless phone. Most of his communication occurred with his friends; he would occasionally call his mom and instant-message his sisters.

He got his first cell phone after a fight with his mom at the age of 16 as a marker of his independence: He wanted to talk on the phone to his friend who needed comfort and support after a terrible breakup, but his mom allowed him to use the landline phone in the house for only five minutes. Brian was so mad that he bought a cell phone for himself the next day with his own money. At the start of the study Brian used an Ericsson R278d, which was his fourth phone over eight years. It was an old model without T9 or vibrating function—all of his text messages logged in the study were sent by the multi-tap method, which Brian was pretty good at. He replaced it with the LG 4010 at the later stage of the study and liked its T9 function.

Brian discovered text messaging one year before the study, in the fall of 2002. He and his good friend and roommate, Tom, met an old female friend on campus who told them that she hardly talked on her phone anymore but instead used text messaging all the time. Fascinated, Brian and Tom tried text messaging each other. Brian still remembered that "wow" moment: "We were both sitting here (their apartment), like, 'Oh, this is so cool!' That's really a hit to me." It so happened that his wireless carrier, Cingular, offered a promotion of free text messaging at that time, and he immediately added this feature to his plan. As more of his friends heard about texting and began texting, it became more fun to text. He sent three or four text messages a week for the first month. In the second month, the volume jumped to a couple of messages daily, averaging 100–200 a month. He quickly became addicted to this innovative way of messaging friends other than his favorite instant messenger before he realized he would need to pay $10 a month for the messaging plan when the promotion ended after two months. Since he found text messaging "very convenient" and was excited about its "tremendous novelty," Brian decided to keep this feature, although he had to be very careful about his spending budget. He did not want to walk away from the texting community that he had already formed with so many friends.

The purposes of using text messaging for Brian were to make plans with friends, update them on interesting details of his life, and share random thoughts in places where other communication was not appropriate, for example, in class or at work. His messaging speed spiked when he had to travel often for his summer job; he learned to text without looking at the keypad and mastered fast-typing with multi-tap. Consequently, his usage rate reached 600 pieces a month. After the 16th month of text messaging use, Brian felt the novelty wear off and became concerned about his grim prospect for a summer job. He thus downgraded his $10 unlimited text messaging plan to the $5 package first and then the $2 package of 100 messages. After the change in his messaging package, he exchanged text messages mostly to make plans and maintained a range of 80–100 messages a month. He noticed that most of his friends did not need to watch their messaging use as closely as he did because their parents paid their phone bills.

Texting in Action

The diary study and two follow-up shadowings observed how Brian used text messaging to coordinate with his friends and co-experience and share mundane life details in his busy graduate school life.

Patterns of Daily Use

Brian was an interesting texter in the participant pool. In a research pool that was widely dominated by female participants because of the criteria that a participant must text a certain number of messages daily (see Chapter 10 for further discussion), he had the highest volume of daily text messages at the American site. In a period of four days and two following observation sessions, he exchanged a total of 109 messages with seven correspondents in nine places, with a daily average above 20 messages.[1] He primarily texted to friends and his girlfriend from places such as home, work, class, and the gym (ranked in the order from most to least). He sent 49 messages and received 60, some of which came from the instant messaging application AIM, as he linked his cell phone to his AIM account at that time.

Figure 7.1 shows the messaging activity on a weekday when he logged 46 messages in his diary, which was not common in 2003, when

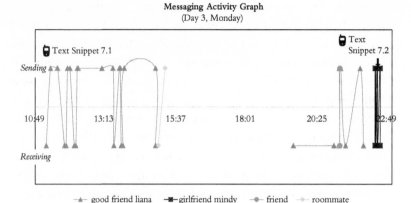

FIGURE 7.1   Brian: When Did He Text?

text messaging started to take off in the U.S. He exchanged text messages with his good friend Liana, girlfriend Mindy, another female friend, and his roommate. There were conversations going on between him and Liana and between him and Mindy. Compared to other American participants, his conversations tended to be longer ones that were similar to those found at the Chinese site.

For Text Snippet 7.1, Brian and his good friend Liana were making plans to have lunch together while Brian was working in the lab and Liana was in class. Liana proposed a plan one hour before lunchtime,

TEXT SNIPPET 7.1			
Time	Sender	Message Text	Place
11:12 a.m.	Liana	Yo (you), mp (acronym for a restaurant) after class? Around 12 15?	work
11:21 a.m.	Brian	M and w i work gy //Monday and Wednesday I work, Guy.	work
11:35 a.m.	Brian	RSVP ASAP	work
11:36 a.m.	Brian	Out if u wanna pick me up in the car @ my building and txt me when u (you) r (are) there they will let me sneak out long enough 2 (to) go eat w (with) u (you) if u (you) r (are) quick	work
			(Continued)

		TEXT SNIPPET 7.1 (Continued)		
Time	Sender	Message Text		Place
11:50 a.m.	Liana	Yeah, i guess thats (that's) fine, i can be there around 12 25		work
11:53 a.m.	Liana	K (ok), my teacher just said not so much.		work
11:56 a.m.	Brian	Ok cool txt me when u get in the car on bk (acronym for a school building)		work
12:01 p.m.	Brian	Lol i cant wait til ur a fesor guy almost time 2 reg 4 ur gre better tell ur dad u need 300 //Laugh out loud. I can't wait till you are a professor. Guy, (it's) almost time to register for your GRE. (You'd) better tell your Dad you need 300 bucks.		work
12:10 p.m.	Liana	Oo you want to go to the tk (acronym for a school building) instead?		work
12:13 p.m.	Liana	Then lets (let's) do that, want me to meet you at your offices?		work
12:16 p.m.	Brian	Whatev is bst 4 u //Whatever is best for you		work
12:18 p.m.	Brian	DT256 BK side of the building		work
1:07 p.m.	Brian	Bye guy		work

and then they discussed where to meet with a few messages exchanged back and forth. Meanwhile, Brian considerately reminded Liana of the GRE test she needed to register for shortly. It took a few exchanges for them to reach the agreement about lunch. Around 12:30 p.m. they had lunch together and then said goodbye at 1:07 p.m.

In Text Snippet 7.2, while walking home from the restaurant after dinner, Brian texted his girlfriend Mindy for the night. He greeted Mindy first, updated her about his status, made plans for tomorrow's dinner, and invited her to go out. The invitation mediated by text messaging sounded sweet and romantic here.

These two text snippets represented the major trend of Brian's text messages: 82% of his text messages fell into his personal life sphere; he

		Text Snippet 7.2	

Time	Sender	Message Text	Place
10:27 p.m.	Brian	Sup //What's up?	Walking home
10:27 p.m.	Mindy	Not a thing u (you)	Walking home
10:29 p.m.	Brian	Walkin (walking) bak (back) from freedom (building name), Keggers (restaurant) cooked dinner. Alas another nite (night) i should have done work wasted.	Walking home
10:29 p.m.	Mindy	Ha ha, at least u ate well	Walking home
10:32 p.m.	Brian	True. Xcept 4 thed burned squash. R u goin 2 cheap din 2mor //True. Except for the burned squash. Are you going to Cheap Dinner tomorrow	Walking home
10:32 p.m.	Mindy	O (oh) U (you) Know it:)	Walking home
10:32 p.m.	Brian	Hmm, I was gona skip but if u r gona b there i gota go //Hmm, I was going to skip but if you are going to be there I got to go.	Walking home
10:32 p.m.	Mindy	only if u want to	Walking home
10:33 p.m.	Mindy	Sure where r u	Walking home
10:37 p.m.	Brian	wana come outside 4 a few its really nice // want to come outside for a few minutes? It's really nice	Walking home
10:38 p.m.	Brian	Right outside	Walking home
10:38 p.m.	Mindy	OK	Walking home

often texted to share feelings, co-experience, and coordinate. Examining his messaging pattern in the American participants' group, many of his rhetorical patterns did not deviate from other American participants. As shown in Figure 7.2, 27% of his messages were exchanged for the purpose of expressing (33.1% at the American site), 23.4% were for the purpose of informing (26.2% at the American site), 20.4% were

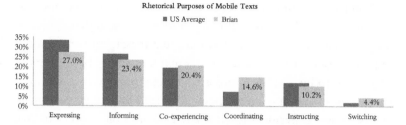

Rhetorical Purposes of Mobile Texts

■ US Average   ■ Brian

FIGURE 7.2   Brian Sent More Texts for Coordinating than the American Average

for the purpose of co-experiencing (19.3% at the American site), and 10.2% were for the purpose of instructing (11.9% at the American site). However, he exchanged 14.6% of messages for the purpose of coordinating, which doubled the American average of 7.2%. This pattern synced with his interpretation of the messaging technology discussed later.

The text snippet[2] below (7.3) is an example of the rhetorical purpose of co-experiencing. This messaging conversation occurred on Halloween when two friends reported to each other what they were doing and what they saw that night.

TEXT SNIPPET 7.3			
Time	Sender	Message Text	Place
10:51 p.m.	Liana	There is a guy here dressed like Reno 911, the guy w the short shorts.	at Halloween party
10:59 p.m.	Brian	Lol	at party
11:06 p.m.	Liana	How is your halloween going	at party
11:16 p.m.	Brian	Home alone just remembered I have a flight sort. I shoulda gone out where u @?	at party
12:05 a.m.	Brian	Where u @	at bar (CJ's)
12:09 a.m.	Liana	CJ's	at bar (CJ's)
12:10 a.m.	Brian	On my way	at bar (CJ's)
12:10 a.m.	Liana	K	at bar (CJ's)
12:12 a.m.	Liana	I think we are going to Town Tavern soon.	at bar (CJ's)
2:09 a.m.	Liana	Yo. There is a Mineva here.	at Town Tavern

Compared to instant messaging conversations, the text messaging conversations have the following features: First, unlike "one-to-many" instant messaging conversations, text messaging conversations are mostly "one-to-one." When using text messaging, Brian found it much easier to hit "reply" in order to directly respond to a text message instead of creating a new message to send to another person. In contrast, it was convenient to click any person's icon in order to chat on a computer's instant messaging application. Because of this particular instrumental limitation (a.k.a., affordance), Brian usually would not initiate a new text messaging conversation with another person until he had finished the current conversation. Second, text messaging conversations tended to go much slower than instant messaging. In the case of Text Snippet 7.1, 12 messages were exchanged over one hour. The exchange between Brian and his girlfriend Mindy (see Text Snippet 7.2) was much quicker, but this frequency was not common in Brian's diary.

Texting to Coordinate

Two shadowing conversations were conducted to see how Brian texted in two settings in which he stayed the most: in class and at work. For the former, he was shadowed in one of his 90-minute classes; for the latter, he was followed on a Sunday afternoon for six hours at the gym where he volunteered.

In Class

The class met from 2:30 p.m. to 4:00 p.m. and was an upper-level undergraduate finance class with around 60 students present. Though familiar with the course subject, Brian was required to take this course because his undergraduate major was not in business.

The class began with a 15-minute quiz. After students turned in their answers, the female professor reviewed the quiz. Brian was about to take notes by opening his notepad when he noticed that he had received a text message from Liana at 2:44 p.m.:

Huh?

This was a follow-up of the previous exchange. Half an hour before the class, Liana had texted to Brian asking about Mindy's recent situation when Brian was walking to a meeting with two professors. He replied as he walked at 1:59 p.m.:

> No big deal I have meet w 2 profs now ill txt u when I get to class. // No big deal (about Mindy). I have to meet with two professors now. I'll text you when I get to class.

Apparently Liana was confused by his message and questioned him. Unable to reply to this message at that moment, as he needed to take notes, Brian whispered "Shoot…" and placed the phone under his left buttock.

The quiz review took three minutes and the professor then asked students to turn in a milestone for the group project. Students rose to assemble group work and handed projects to the professor, who then began that day's lecture with PowerPoint slides at 2:52 p.m. Listening to the lecture, which lasted the rest of class, Brian reached for his phone and started to compose a reply message to Liana. He usually would use two thumbs to text for faster speed, but he could use only his left thumb to type in this stealthy situation as a left-hander. Because he

FIGURE 7.3   Texting in Class with One Hand

did not want the professor to notice what he was doing, it took him a few minutes to work on the message, and he did not send it out until 2:56 p.m.:

> No change w mindy in class ttyl // No change (about the meeting plan) with Mindy's current situation. (I'm) in class. Talk to you later.

After sending the message, Brian put his phone back into his right pants pocket and focused on the class. He raised a question to the professor, which she acknowledged as a good one with a nod. At 3:08 p.m., he reached into his right pocket and checked his phone, and this time he saw Liana's response sent at 2:57 p.m.:

> O ok. TTYL (Talk to you later).

For the rest of the class, Brian listened to the lecture, took notes, and read the textbook as instructed. He checked his phone at 3:18 p.m., 3:22 p.m., 3:34 p.m., and 3:44 p.m. and checked his watch at 3:13 p.m. and 3:31 p.m.—his phone did not have the vibrating function. A few students in the class also checked their phones occasionally.

Toward the end of the class, at 3:47 p.m., he grabbed the phone out of his pocket and quickly typed to Mindy with his left hand. As the classroom atmosphere was more relaxed than the beginning of the class, he sent this message in one minute:

> U have class 2nite (tonight) what time?

Mindy responded right away:

> 545 (5:45)

Seeing the response, Brian put the phone back in his pants pocket at 3:48 p.m. The last 10 minutes of the class were for group work. Brian locked the keypad of the phone, concluding this use session as he walked to his group to join the project discussion.

At the Gym

On the afternoon of a Sunday, which happened to be the first day in the fall when the clocks were adjusted back from the daylight saving time schedule, Brian arrived at the Taekwondo gym at 12:18 p.m. There were already three staff members and instructors and a few students in the training hall. For almost one year Brian had volunteered at the gym between noon and 7:00 p.m. on Sundays. The reward was a free membership and a free guest pass for each visit, which was attractive to such an enthusiastic Taekwondo learner as Brian. The workload was not heavy and included showing new customers the basics of the sport, providing class information, and helping instructors. Most of the time he read gym magazines; occasionally he would bring homework.

Around 12:30 p.m., Brian greeted his first guests of that day with a coupon for a free trial class. He went through the first-visit protocol with them, such as filling out forms, showing them around, and introducing them to the instructor. The whole routine went on for approximately 30 minutes. While Brian was watching customers practice, he checked his phone and found a message that Mindy had sent twenty minutes earlier. Obviously he did not hear the text alert sound—he would not turn off the phone's volume in the gym because it was noisy there anyway. Brian typed back with two thumbs while in a standing

FIGURE 7.4   Texting in the Gym

position in order to keep an eye on customers. Mindy did not reply at that time.

After the new guests began their class, Brian sat on a picnic table to have a better view of customers. At 1:13 p.m. he began to compose a text message to an ex-girlfriend who lived in Rochester. He was following up with their recent phone conversation, but this was a difficult message to draft: First, the situation was a bit complicated; second, he knew that her phone bill was paid by her mom, who complained that her daughter got too many messages, so he wanted to keep his message to her short and concise—a long message exceeding word limit could be divided and sent as multiple pieces by the wireless carrier. Brian made a few changes as he typed on the keypad. Once he was interrupted by a customer who needed some help getting a drink that had gotten stuck in the vending machine. Brian sent the message at 1:17 p.m.

> Thanx (thanks) 4 (for) calling. Sorry if I seemd (seemed) curt. It was a shock 2 (to) hear u (you) after a month. Have a good week @ work. Cal (call) me soon when u have mor (more) time 2 (to) talk. Miss u (you).

Without much to do in the gym, Brian wandered around, picked some magazines to read, and chatted with another staff member about a recent movie. When Mindy's reply came 50 minutes after the initial

		TEXT SNIPPET 7.4
Time	Sender	Message Text
12:35 p.m.	Mindy	Just woke up surprisingly my contacts (contact lens) don't hurt[3]
12:59 p.m.	Brian	Cool good thng (thing) we set theclock (the clock) bak (back) it would b (be) 2pm again. What 8p (up) 2 (to) 4 (for) the day // Cool, good thing. We set the clock back; it would be 2 pm again. What are you up to for the day?
1:47 p.m.	Mindy	Going tanning gym and babysit
1:47 p.m.	Brian	Til (till) when?
1:49 PM	Mindy	9

message, he exchanged another three messages with her. They were updating each other about that day's plan (see Text Snippet 7.4).

The rest of the afternoon passed as Brian oriented new customers, helped set up two birthday parties, and watched customers practice. Liana and her sister came to the gym around 2:35 p.m. and stayed for two hours. There were around 30 people in the gym by 3:00 p.m., but there was not much for staff members to do. For Brian, one advantage of this job was that he could text freely. Thinking about the video game he wanted to play after work, he exchanged three messages with his roommate (see Text Snippet 7.5).

TEXT SNIPPET 7.5		
Time	Sender	Message Text
3:52 p.m.	Brian	4 player bond when I get bak (back)
3:53 p.m.	Roommate	That's right guy
4:04 p.m.	Brian	Sweet

The last chat of that afternoon was between Brian and Liana (see Text Snippet 7.6). As the first day to be back from the daylight saving time schedule, the night seemed suddenly to fall around 5:00 p.m. on this rainy day.

TEXT SNIPPET 7.6		
Time	Sender	Message Text
5:00 p.m.	Brian	The dark is killing me
5:03 p.m.	Liana	Yes. Im (I'm) sorry guy. We will move to an island as soon as we finish grad school.

Texting and Lifestyle

As a veteran user of instant messaging for eight years, Brian found text messaging "a very natural form of communication" that corresponded with his lifestyle: He had many good friends across campus with whom he liked to socialize on a daily basis, but he was busy with his graduate course work and part-time jobs. Text messaging was a good way to

keep him up to date on his friends' schedules. He localized text messaging technology as a coordination tool with friends. This user localization matched his perception and interpretation of this technology.

Convenient Tool

Brian was first attracted to the messaging technology for its "tremen-
dous novelty" and soon realized that this technology was a convenient
tool to coordinate with his friends and co-experience and share everyday details of his busy life.

As a first-year graduate student, many of his classes were three
hours long, and it was not appropriate to talk about personal business
on the cell phone when at work either. Text messaging afforded him
the ability to communicate with people in places where he would not
have been able to before, e.g., in the middle of a three-hour class, or
at work—"you can almost text anywhere except a few situations." He
remembered that he had once texted to Liana from the helicopter he
was flying, and the reception was quite good at 3,000 feet high.

> Text messaging allows you to communicate with somebody you
> are not with, you might be making plans later on, you might just
> have something funny to tell, too. You know, if you have a funny
> story during the day; you are always going to save it in your head
> till the end of the day to tell your best friend, your girlfriend or
> whoever. You don't have to do that, you can send the funny story
> right away, rather than waiting to tell them later.

On the aspect of social affordance, text messaging also met "a
human desire to tell people what happens to you during the day." In his
community of friends, more and more people started using text messaging to text each other. Texting was a communication mode for friends.

In addition to sharing experiences, Brian delegated certain communication practices to text messaging, for example, "If you just have,
like 'What time are we having dinner?' there is no reason to call for
that." He used text messaging to sync schedules with friends about
dining and play, as evidenced by many messages logged in the diary
study and shadowing observations. For him, these types of communication practices were not worth making a phone call and costing

expensive phone minutes to discuss. Just type on the phone, send, wait for the confirmation or negotiation, and then you're done. And oftentimes, plans for dining and play were usually made either in class or at work, which made text messaging a more convenient tool to use to quickly get in touch with someone without disrupting local communication protocols:

> "I find it (text messaging) very useful, especially in class."
> "If I have a class from 9 in the morning before a lot of my friends get up, they get out at noon, three hours later, when I could meet somebody for lunch, (texting allows me) to be able to make up lunch plans while I'm in the class."

Brian was conscious of his messaging practices in class. He admitted that "one of the major reasons that I have text messaging is because I'm taking classes, and I can't talk on the phone in the class, but a good number of my classes are three hours long." He knew texting could be considered very rude, so he did not want to offend his professors by letting them see him texting. He would always try to keep the phone stealthily located or covered when he texted in class. This is why he would wait for a better time to work on the text message and patiently spent five minutes sending it during the observation. Because his phone did not have a vibrating function, he tended to check his phone "a minimum of two or three times in a class" unless he was busy or particularly engrossed in the class.

One episode that occurred in the study proved that Brian was very good at sending text messages in a stealthy situation. I was anxiously waiting to meet Brian to shadow his texting practices in class, but he did not show up at the scheduled time. Ten minutes later I got a text message from him: "Wil cal u in 2 (Will call you in two minutes)." He called me shortly, apologizing that he was late because the meeting with his two professors ran late. He also revealed that he had sent me the text message right in the meeting with the two professors, who apparently did not notice he was texting.

Later, when Brian had to reduce living costs and downgraded his monthly messaging plan from $10 to $2, he dedicated the role of text messaging in his life to making plans. For this reason, he made it particularly clear to his friends that they should send him messages only when they had something to say or if they wanted to meet, and he did not welcome text messages "to just say 'Hi' or 'How is your day going?'" The act of reducing messaging use itself shows that Brian found the niche of text messaging in his lifestyle and localized the technology for the maximum benefit according to his understanding of the technology and his identification with it. No other technology could replace this one in his current lifestyle with the same affordances as text messaging. On the other hand, it shows that low cost is an incentive for new users, but might not be the main reason for users staying with the technology.

Messaging as Conversation

Brian's use experience with messaging technology came from the outcome of its congruent situatedness in his lifeworld and developed as a result of the cultural meanings he built surrounding this technology as well.

For Brian, his enthusiasm with text messaging did not come from the technology itself but from its predecessor, instant messaging, which he believed greatly shaped his appreciation of text messaging technology.

> If text messaging had come out (at a time) that has never been a
> chat room, never been such things as instant messaging, two-way
> typing communication on the Internet, I don't think it would have,
> for me, and probably for the society, I don't think it would've caught
> on so fast, because people wouldn't been thinking of in terms of
> typing their words as a way of communicating in two ways.

Brian still remembered his fascination with instant messaging when he was first introduced to it. Between the ages of 14 and 15, when he was a sophomore in high school, he would sit at the computer all night. He signed on and waited for people he knew to pop up in the full-blown AOL desktop before the separate instant messaging application AIM was released. In a nostalgic reflection, it looked similar to a date: One was waiting for someone one knew to be online and anticipating text-based conversation at a time when not many people had Internet access. Brian and his friends thought it was "so cool," and no other technology seemed to be able to recreate that enchantment—Brian joked that he would not sit by the cell phone to wait for a text message like he had waited for an instant message eight years before.

For Brian, instant messaging had played a huge role in his life. He considered instant messaging to be his first-degree means of communication, while either wireless phone calls or text messaging would be the second degree, depending on the time periods when asked. Text messaging was ranked as his second communication mode before he reduced his cost, and down to third after that.

In fact, Brian's text messaging practices were interlinked to his instant messaging practices. When someone sent him a text and he happened to be near his computer, he would send the person an instant message reply first. If he got the instant message answer, he would talk to the person on AIM. If not, he would assume the correspondent was not around his/her computer and would reply to the text directly. In addition, when Brian had the $10 messaging plan, he linked his AIM account to his cell phone. The diary book logged some messages that were routed through AIM.

With eight years of prior experiences with instant messaging, Brian had been very accustomed to reading and replying on the screen, typing to others to communicate rapidly, and sending texts back and forth. He felt "very comfortable" about this two-way typing communication and defined this as "conversations." He differentiated messaging-based communication from written letters and emails, and would call the latter "correspondences" because of the exchange rate and the words transmitted. He believed that this form of two-way written communication would be more common in the future.

> My instant messaging use, you know, definitely shaped my
> desire to text messaging, or my predispositions, maybe, towards
> using text messaging a lot, because I find it, at this time, after
> I have been using AIM for eight years, a very natural form of
> communication....I think instant messaging has taught me how to
> carry on conversations through my fingers instead of my mouth.

Text-based communication is currently my primary means of communication with friends.

Brian realized this was a literacy skill that was not available in a non-technical society where people would not type to each other. Though he had been comfortable with and good at this typing communication, he was still amazed to watch how fluidly and how fluently his 12-year-old sister "talked" back and forth on the computer using an instant messaging application. It took him a while to get used to this communication mode, but apparently it became a "natural ability" of a younger generation.

Texting in a Male Perspective

Gendered identity plays an important role in the constructed meanings around mobile messaging technology. As in the cases of other participants presented in this book, Brian's messaging use was also shaped by the gendered discourse.

As a young man, Brian understood the power of implicitness from text messaging for establishing and maintaining a romantic relationship, and he skillfully used it to achieve its rhetorical beauty. Text messaging provided a good comfort level for both parties at the beginning of the relationship. He was once interested in a girl who gave him her phone number. Two days later, Brian deliberately chose to text but not call her as most men would have done before the emergence of text messaging. He sent something similar to "Hey, I don't know if you got text messaging or not, but if you do, this is Brian, you now have my phone number. Give me a call sometime." She quickly responded, "Yeah, I do got text messaging." They texted back and forth, and indeed they texted a lot before they started hanging out. In addition, texting is also a fun and intimate rhetoric to use after one has been seeing a girl for a while; for example, Brian invited Mindy out for a romantic night with a text (see Text Snippet 7.2). Other flirtatious messages were also found in his messaging log. Here texting helped to explore intimate relationships and set up romantic agendas (for similar uses in a Filipino context, see Elwood-Clayton, 2005; Pertierra, 2005).

Brian served as a good case to examine female messaging practices from a male perspective, as the only male participant profiled in this book. For example, most of his text messages were exchanged between him and his girlfriend or between him and other female friends; he adopted text messaging practice because of the introduction from a female user. The act of purchasing his first cell phone after the fight with his mom could be read in a wide context of gendered communication practices too.

In Brian's opinion, his text messaging contacts split evenly between both genders, but the number of text messages to female contacts was indeed much higher because the conversations with female friends tended to go longer. He contributed the high volume of text messages from girls to a female style of communication. For the same purpose of making plans, he usually needed to exchange six or seven messages with Liana to get things settled (see Text Snippet 7.1), but it would take him only two or three messages with a male friend (see Text Snippet 7.5).

Reflection Notes on Cross-Cultural Design

Brian's use experience with messaging technology suggests that the complexities of designing for culturally localized user experiences cannot be accomplished by studying only cultural dimensions.

Users adopt, use, and stay with mobile text messaging based on both the instrumental affordances and social affordances of the technology. Here instrumental affordances come from built-in design features, and social affordances arise out of instrumental affordances through users' interactions in local contexts. So the same instrumental affordance (for example, quick, quiet, discreet) might lead to different social affordances and support different social uses when affordances are realized in different contexts. Both Brian and Sophie utilized the quick, quiet, discreet instrumental affordance of the technology at work, but they ended up developing different social affordances, either making plans discreetly or providing emotional support.

It should be noted that Brian and Sophie came from the same American culture, but their uses went to different paths due to their gender, age, and economic differences, and due to their different perceptions and meaning-construction of the technology. If only cultural dimensions were applied here, such great use difference between Brian and Sophie would have been missed.

A major weakness of the models of cultural dimensions is that they escape the history of a technology, ignore the dialogical nature of a technology in its contexts, and thus fail to understand the complex and dynamic interaction between a technology and its surrounding social, cultural, technological, and economic conditions. Many more factors than cultural dimensions come into play in the use of a technology. Brian chose text messaging because it was situated well in his way of life as a convenient communication tool for his school and work schedule and because of the constructed meaning he brought to his use experience as a veteran user of instant messaging. Genre theory suggests that a new genre usually evolves from an old genre, or its predecessor. At the American site, the predecessor for mobile text messaging was instant messaging. In Brian's case, instant messaging shaped his use of text messaging and his perception of the writing practices engendered, i.e., text messages as casual conversation. At the Chinese site, instant messaging was not the predecessor of mobile text messaging, as many participants adopted these two technologies almost simultaneously. With a strong written tradition in China, Chinese participants interpreted text messaging as a written genre that could have a formal status, as shown in the case of Lili.

Because the interaction between use and local contexts is so complex, simply applying cultural conventions in cross-cultural design would be unable to capture local contexts' messy complexities. As Weisinger and Trauth (2002) observe from their studies of the workplace culture in multinational IT firms of Ireland, broad cultural dimensions might not be useful for analysis "at the level of interaction where a variety of contextual factors can affect behavior" (p. 315). A focus on use activities is needed to develop a deeper understanding of technology design for culturally diverse users. In the next chapter, we will look at the case of Chinese user Mei, who interpreted text messaging differently from Brian due to her cultural background, and further examine how this interpretation difference played out in the text messaging use patterns between the two cultures.

Notes

1. An average American participant in the study texted to 5.5 people from 5.8 places with a daily average volume of 10.5.
2. This snippet was logged in the diary book of Liana, who also participated in the first stage of this study a few weeks later than when Brian did the diary study. The place here refers to where Liana was.
3. Mindy forgot to remove her contact lenses before going to bed the night before.

8

Mei's Story: "Idioms Solitaire" between Sports Fans

> *"Maybe I just wanted to make a random comment (about the game I'm watching), but the text extended as responded by my friends, on and on, endlessly. Like playing idioms solitaire, one would not stop until other players want to withdraw.... Sometimes we would be so engrossed in this texting game that we did not care what was going on in the real game..."*

Profile

Like Brian, 23-year-old "Mei" was in her first year of graduate study at the time of her participation in the survey and the diary study. She had a phone interview six months later and was then interviewed again in one year with a follow-up contextual visit.

Coming from a lower middle-class household in Hangzhou, Mei went to the same university in her hometown for both college and graduate school and majored in sociology. Her on-campus dorm accommodations were upgraded when she moved to graduate school; she now shared a dorm room with three girls instead of five girls like before, which was a standard accommodation in Chinese universities. Other than that, her graduate school life was not much different from her undergraduate years. The course load was light, as most humanities curricula offered in Chinese universities were, and her internship at a local newspaper office would not start for a year, so she spent most of her time in the following places, from most to least: in her dorm surfing the Internet and listening to music from the desktop computer she brought from home, at school attending class, and at home watching TV.

As an avid sports fan, her favorite sports were tennis and soccer, though she was not good at either of them—in fact, she was not athletic at all. Like many young women, she was fascinated with energetic and charming sports stars like Roger Federer and David Beckham. She followed international sports events regularly with a group of college girlfriends who were also passionate about sports, and she particularly liked to watch televised live games. These international games were usually broadcast late at night or early in the morning due to the time difference, to which Mei was accustomed from her childhood: At the age of nine, she watched her first nightly TV soccer game for the FIFA World Cup in Italy with her father, a soccer junkie, and she has been enchanted ever since. Because there was no TV set in her dorm room, she either went to other people's dorms or returned home to watch games on TV, and occasionally she would invite friends home to watch together.

Mei bought her first computer in the summer of her sophomore year. She was so excited about owning a computer that the computer occupied all of her summer time. She exchanged a lot of emails with friends at the time when most people did yet not have wireless phones. One year later, in May 2002, when the wave of owning a cell phone hit her school and her hometown, she purchased her first cell phone, following the trend. It was a Nokia 3330 that cost 1000 yuan, amounting to two months' worth of expenses for a college student at that time. She replaced it two years later with a Samsung Anycall SGH-X108, a sleek bar-style phone, in the middle of the study. Like Lili, she began to use text messaging on the first day she had her cell phone. It was a natural process for "a late adopter," described by Mei herself, to simultaneously take on wireless phone calling and texting since everyone around her seemed to have a cell phone with a texting function. It also seemed a natural move for her to text about her hobbies. She soon found that she could not part with her phone anymore; she kept her phone with her everywhere for the peace of mind.

Texting in Action

Mei's messaging diary shows how an enthusiastic sports fan utilized the text messaging technology to pursue her passions: Mei liked texting to her sports friends to share her excitement and to exchange reviews while following late-night games on TV at home.

Patterns of Daily Use

At the first stage of the four-day diary study, Mei sent 30 messages and received 33 messages, for a total of 63 pieces. Texting largely occurred at her home, in her dorm, in the classroom, in the school dining hall, in the library, or on the streets, and half of her texts occurred at home. She communicated with eight college friends and her father. The top three correspondents were her sports fan friends. Indeed, sports were the main theme of those text messages: 30 out of 63 messages were about sports games.

Figure 8.1 illustrates how this themed texting practice was situated in Mei's overall messaging activity. There were some tennis matches and soccer games going on that week, which Mei and her friends had been following for two consecutive nights (Day 2 and Day 3 for the diary study). The first night she stayed in a friend's dorm room to watch the game (see Text Snippet 8.1), and the second night she went home to watch the game (see Text Snippet 8.2).

In China, overseas games such as tennis and soccer, even recorded, are often scheduled late at night because only a small group of avid sports fans would watch them. Often one would not know whether a particular game would be televised or not. In Text Snippet 8.1, Mei asked Bo (her sports fan friend 1) not to forget to notify her of the upcoming

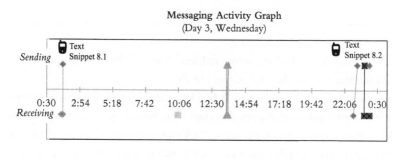

FIGURE 8.1   Mei: When Did She Text?

		TEXT SNIPPET 8.1	
Time	Sender	Message Text	Place
10:46 p.m.	Mei	you bi sai lu bo gao su wo o. (Please let me know if there is a pre-recorded telecast of the game tonight.)	dorm
10:47 p.m.	Bo (fan friend 1)	hao de (Sure)	dorm
11:50 p.m.	Bo	tong zhi men, da jia yao chi de kuai chi bao, yao shui de jiu kuai xing lai! da jia kan zhu tou bei da a! ha ha. (Comrades, please feed yourself if you are hungry and wake up if you are sleepy! Let's see how the Clumsy Fool will be beaten in the game! Haha.)	dorm
1:33 a.m.	Bo	na cai pan shi na li ren ya, dang xin hui jia de shi hou bei ren bian a (Where did the umpire come from? He needs to be careful when going home. People might hit him)	dorm
1:40 a.m.	Bo	gang gang ta men la di xian shi, you ge qiu zhu tou chu jie le cai pan mei pan, hai hao hai shi ying le (When they were rallying a moment ago, the umpire didn't call out a shot from the Clumsy Fool that was out; fortunately we still won)	dorm
1:40 a.m.	Mei	en, shi de, jin tian hao xiang mei yu qi de jing cai a (En, yes. Well, the game today didn't seem as exciting as expected)	dorm

tennis match. Bo indeed informed her shortly. They exchanged some comments toward the end of the match.

Text Snippet 8.2 occurred at Mei's home. Mei had text conversations with two friends in that period as they were watching a game. Similar to Lili's text messages (see Chapter 6), Mei's messages often consist of two or three sentences, much longer than what was found at the American site.

The two text snippets above showed how Mei and her friends, although in different places, co-experienced exciting sporting events

		TEXT SNIPPET 8.2	
Time	Sender → Receiver	Message Text	Place
10:44 p.m.	Bo→Mei	kan lai jin tian shi bie shui le. xian shi fei de bi sai, zai shi huang ma de guan jun bei. (I'd better not sleep tonight. There will be Federer's tennis game first, and then Real Madrid's game for the UEFA Champions League.)	home
11:01 p.m.	Mei→Bo	xiao fei jin tian da de tai gao xiao le, ma sa gen ben wu neng wei li (Federer is so powerful today that Massu has no way to fight back)	home
11:31 p.m.	fan friend 2→Mei	xiao fei zui jin hen qiang a (Federer has played very well recently)	home
11:33 p.m.	Mei→fan friend 2	he he, ni de luo di ke zai nian zhong ye hen you you shi a (hehe, your Roddick is also at an advantageous position toward the end of year)	home
11:55 p.m.	Mei→Bo	jin tian lai le hao duo ren na (It came a big crowd today)	home
11:55 p.m.	fan friend 2→Mei	hai you fei de le bu rong xiao qu (But there is a Federer who can't be ignored)	home
11:57 p.m.	Bo→Mei	gu di ye lai le, jiu zai ma su hou mian (Guti also came, who is sitting behind Massu)	home

together with the help of text messaging. Of Mei's messages, 14.1% had the rhetorical purpose of co-experiencing.

A large number of the text messages in Mei's diary log present a rhetorical pattern of informing. Compared to the average of 31.6% of messages that were informing at the Chinese site, 40.6% of Mei's has this pattern. Text Snippet 8.3 is such an example when Mei and her friends were informing each other about game scores.

Figure 8.2 paints an overall picture of how Mei's text messages were communicated during the study. It is clear that more than 50% of the

		TEXT SNIPPET 8.3	
Time	Sender → Receiver	Message Text	Place
3:30 a.m.	Mei→fan friend 3	kun le, qiu sai bu kan le. shang ban chang 1:0 (I'm sleepy and not going to watch the game anymore. The score for the first half is 1:0)	home
10:19 a.m.	fan friend 3→Mei	bi sai jie guo ru he? (What's the score?)	home
10:20 a.m.	Mei→fan friend 3	bu xiao de. zhi dao le gao su ni (I don't know. I will let you know after I find it out.)	home
10:30 a.m.	Mei→fan friend 1	bi sai jie guo zhi dao le ma? (Do you know the score?)	home
11:00 a.m.	fan friend 1→Mei	hai shi 1:0. jiu jing le yi ge. (Just 1:0. Only one goal was scored.)	home
11:02 a.m.	Mei→fan friend 3	1:0	home
11:03 a.m.	Mei→fan friend 3	xi huan pi pi zai ren he chang ci jin qiu, dan bu yuan shi zhe chang, yin wei zhe chang qiu dui a bei tai te shu le. (I like Piero's goals on any game, but not this one, because this game is extremely special for Beckham.)	home

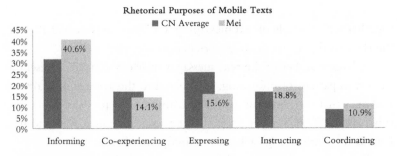

FIGURE 8.2   More than 50% of Mei's Texts Sent for Informing and Co-experiencing

messages were exchanged for co-experiencing and informing. Other than the topic of sports, Mei's messages also covered getting a takeout dinner for a roommate and bringing a textbook for a classmate, etc., which corresponded with the high frequency of the instructing purpose.

Ruling Passions and Texting Practices

Mei's texting practices remained the same between the time period of her diary study and the first phone interview, and then her texting frequency increased, largely due to the changes in her life: She was dating a boy who was at his first job out of college, and she had begun her internship in a newspaper office. As either an entry-level worker or an intern, they were cautious of not making personal phone calls at work, so texting was a good choice to stay in touch. She reported that she would send 20–30 messages a day and receive an equivalent amount of messages. Most of the time, her text amount exceeded the limit of 500 free text messages provided by her phone plan. With all the changes, however, sports still remained the major topic of her text messages. For example, she exchanged 20 messages with Bo and her boyfriend about the Wimbledon tennis matches televised the night before the second interview.

The contextual visit to Mei's home right after the second interview showed me the pervasive power of sports in Mei's daily life. I chose a contextual visit over a shadowing observation because it would have been invasive to follow a female sports fan into her bedroom to watch how she texted late at night when lying in bed watching a TV game.

We went to her apartment on a Tuesday evening in mid-summer after having dinner together. She received two text messages during the dinner on her Samsung phone, which she had owned for one year by then, but she did not notice them because the alert beep of the Samsung was much quieter compared to her previous Nokia phone. The first one was a message generated by her wireless carrier about a new service available. The second was a message from her classmate asking about school work, but she did not reply right away because she felt it was not urgent.

Mei lived with her father and grandmother in an old apartment downtown. She moved back home from school half a year ago to save on transportation time as her internship became busier. Her room was both her bedroom and a study. In addition to other furniture, there

Pennant of
Real Matrid

Landline Phone

Cell Phone

FIGURE 8.3   Going Online in the Evening

were an old TV set and a computer brought back from school. A landline phone was on her desk, next to the desktop computer. In a room
filled with furniture, sports-related decoration caught my attention:
A big poster of Michael Jordan was hung above the computer; next
to it was a pennant of Real Madrid, a famous European soccer team
(see Figure 8.3); and a poster of Roger Federer was posted on the door
of the wardrobe.

Her daily routine consisted of going to the newspaper office in
the morning, working at her internship, and coming back around 6:00
p.m. After a simple dinner, she would turn on the computer to surf
the Internet and listen to music. Her first stop was usually the sports
section of SINA—SINA is a popular web portal in China, like a combination of Yahoo! and CNN. Sometimes she would visit the entertainment section. She went to sleep around 1:00 a.m. or 2:00 a.m. if
there were no late-night games to watch that day.

Mei showed me her treasures on her computer: an extensive file
collection of her favorite sports stars. For example, she had collected
many photos of Roger Federer in her undergraduate years. At that time
she would crazily save any photo of Federer that she could find on the
Internet. She even went out of her way to make notes of each photo,
such as where the photo was taken, for what game, etc. In smaller
sizes, she also had collections of her favorite movie posters and songs.
She felt sad that she no longer had time to engage in these hobbies as
she got busy with her current work. In those frantic days with sports,

she once almost missed a course exam scheduled in the morning because she had stayed up to watch a game the night before.

In their study of socially situated literacy practices in Lancaster, UK, Barton and Hamilton (1998) introduced a concept of "ruling passions" to illustrate how ordinary people's everyday literacy practices are guided and influenced by their interests and hobbies. In Mei's case, her texting practices were shaped by her ruling passions for sports. Mei explained about her messaging content in her interview: "My hobbies are sports, and accordingly my messages would focus more on this aspect. Just like other people who might like shopping, they would text more about their shopping plans and activities."

Texting and Lifestyle

So far, other participants profiled in this book adopted and localized text messaging technology because they found the niche (i.e., situatedness) for the technology in their busy schedules first, e.g., the need to communicate to a close girlfriend at work (i.e., Sophie), the goodwill to stay in contact with old friends with little overhead (i.e., Lili), and the desire to make plans with friends in class (i.e., Brian). As they became glued to the technology, they found that texting actually made sense of their lives. Mei's case is a bit different. Her texting use started from and centered on her passion for sports, and thus she localized this technology according to her identity as a sports fan from the beginning. The constructiveness of the technology is vital in Mei's culturally localized user experience. Her ruling passions illuminate what she used messaging for and why messaging mattered to her.

Co-experience as Sports Fans

For Mei, it came naturally to use text messaging to express the fun and feelings of watching games and to exchange thoughts about games. She and her friends talked about sports a lot before they had cell phones, so when everyone had a cell phone, one more method of communicating about their sporting experiences was available. The instrumental affordance is appreciated here: A phone ringing at midnight might first disturb the sleep of family members, and the speaker's voice might tend to grow louder and louder as she gets excited about the development of a game. But texting provides "a personal space" (Mei) where one could freely voice her opinions and share her pleasures, anxiety, and disappointment in her fan community.

The social affordance is more valuable for the identity of an avid sports fan: First, sports fans always enjoy the sense of community and would increase shared interests through this bonding process. Texting adds more fun while watching a game with someone who shares the same interest, even though this person is not physically near. Second, one does not have to wait until the next day to utter her excitement or frustration about a game. Mei thought it was important to relay her excitement to her friends right at the moment because her feelings might have changed a day later. It did not matter when her friends would receive the message (because a phone might be shut off at night); she just wanted to vent it in her "personal space," a space created by the cell phone where her sports fan friends were welcome to join and interact with her. This was the space layered on her physical place. It is the "genius loci" where Mei stitched the "physical situatedness" of mobile messaging technology with the "constructive subjectiveness" of the technology as she localized this technology into her life (Sun, 2009b).

Mei referred to the streams of text messages traveling late at night between her and her sports fan friends as "idioms solitaire":

> Maybe I just wanted to make a random comment (about the game I'm watching), but the text extended as responded by my friends, on and on, endlessly. Like playing idioms solitaire, one would not stop until other players want to withdraw.

> For example, one of my favorite soccer stars who didn't score a goal well. Sighing with emotion, I sent a text message out to a friend, with no clue of what she was doing at that time and no clue of whether she would like to engage in a conversation— I was just sending an abrupt message over. To my surprise, she was also watching the same game, and her response resonated with the mood of my message. Then we would follow each other's message back and forth. Sometimes we would be so engrossed in

this texting game that we did not care what was going on in the real game. Because your attention shifts away from the game to the words you work on when you text.

In her messaging diary, she noted that most of the text messages sent as "idioms solitaire" would not have been sent if there had not been a text messaging technology at all. Mobile text messaging encouraged and created new communication practices that afforded sports fans the opportunity to participate in a collective fan culture in a novel way. Similar to other types of fan creations, such as contributing to fanzines and writing fan novels, composing "idioms solitaire" through text messaging escalated and consummated the experience of being a sports fan.

Messaging as Letter

The characteristic of "idioms solitaire" struck Mei as the literacy nature of text messaging. Here literacy refers to a writing culture in contrast to an oral culture (Ong, 1982). She told me about a remarkable moment she had with text messaging in one interview. Her best college friend was departing to Beijing for graduate school. Feeling lonely and realizing she would not be able to see Mei and other friends for four months until school was over, she sent Mei a text message after they saw her off at the train station: *"It is a pity that all of you are four months away."* The poetic and nostalgic presentation suddenly hit on Mei's emotional chord, and she recognized that the same meaning would not have been able to be conveyed face to face or over the phone, as that text message hovered in her mind for quite a while. She commented on the power of literacy as this: "The presentation is totally different when you express the same thing in the written form. You could use more effective words to describe what you experienced, and the receiver would be impressed by what you wrote. The verbal conversation is much blander."

There are two translation variations for Short Message Service in Chinese: *duan xin* and *duan xiao xi*. The literal translation of *duan xin* into English is "short letter," and that of *duan xiao xi* is "short message." The former is much more widely used in Chinese daily discourses due to its conciseness and its link to the traditional style of communication, letter and mail. Indeed, I argue that *duan xin* should be officially acknowledged and fully explored to understand the contribution of Chinese text messaging practices to the global discourse of texting, as the Japanese term *Keitai* has done to our understanding of the role of cell phones in Japanese mobile communication (Ito, 2006).

As depicted in Lili's and Mei's technology use histories, text messaging technology entered the Chinese people's daily lives shortly after the computer did, at the turn of this century, due to the developmental pace of local technology infrastructure. Therefore, text messaging technology was adopted by the public in Chinese cities almost at the same time as email and instant messaging were. Mei reflected on the interactions of her use of email, instant messaging, and text messaging: She had her own computer one year before she owned a cell phone. During the first summer she had a computer, she exchanged a lot of emails with her friends and used instant messaging often. She was attracted to email because she found the email exchanges often had a florid prose style, different from the daily conversations she and her friends had. When the New Year was approaching, they started to replace paper greeting cards with email greeting cards, which seemed extremely cool at that time. Before email was solidified in her literacy life, along came text messaging. She and her friends realized that text messaging was much easier and more convenient to use than either email or instant messaging. They could text almost everywhere and did not have to be bound by a computer. These mobile texts could be casual, formal, artistic, humorous, or personal, whatever style the texter wanted. Her use of email started dropping since she started using a cell phone, and continued dropping as she reported in two follow-up interviews. She defined email as a tool to transport files, used only to send documents to another party. All other communication needs could be taken care of by text messaging.

Mei's experience was echoed many times by other Chinese participants during the interview stage of the study. While it is common to hear Americans say this in daily conversation: "I'll send you an email to ask about it/to remind you of this/to explain this/to give you further details of this...," one should expect to hear from Chinese people say this: "I'll send you a *duan xin* to ask about it/to remind you of this/ to explain this/to give you further details of this..."

Mei explicated her use change of email and instant messaging with her own "pie theory." In her eyes, all daily communication needs form one big pie. If some communication channel covers more needs by taking a bigger slice of pie, other communication channels would get much smaller pieces than before. While email is opted out of the personal communication horizon, text messaging in China has the advantage of covering both personal needs and public needs for a young generation like Mei's.

Unlike Brian, who had been "trained" and coded into the conversation mode of instant messaging and formed a mental model of text messaging based on that, Mei's mental model of text messaging came from her previous experiences of writing letters and emails. When I asked, she was at a loss about the connection and resemblance between instant messaging and text messaging; apparently the link between these two never occurred to her, though she could articulate lucidly the influence of email use on her text messaging use.

Reflection Notes on Cross-Cultural Design

Mei's culturally localized user experience with mobile messaging technology fully exemplifies the dialogical nature of technology in cross-cultural technology design. Many factors, other than cultural dimensions, contributed to this particular local use.

Following the previous chapter, this chapter looks further at issues of orality and literacy between two cultural contexts and discusses how different cultural preferences led to different use and genre patterns of text messaging: While Brian related text messaging to instant messaging and interpreted text messaging as conversation, Mei saw more resemblance between text messaging and email and was fascinated by the literacy power of text messaging. Through Mei's case, we are able to see the history of a technology and its dialogical nature on a broader horizon.

The interpretation and adoption of text messaging technology comes not only from its predecessor, but from its literacy tradition and its technology infrastructure as well. Mei's interpretation of text messaging as letter was situated in a broader sociocultural context where literacy culture is highly valued, and people are attracted to and fascinated by the literacy capability remediated through an emerging technology such as mobile text messaging. Certain literary formats surrounding text messaging technology appeared in China (Yan, 2003), and the career of the SMS writer emerged. These writers, hired by big web portals and telecommunication companies, compose text messages for various occasions. At the peak of SMS (before mobile Internet and 3G service were widely adopted by Chinese users), there were websites devoted to the literature generated through SMS (e.g., cell phone novels), national SMS writing competitions, and books collecting fun and smart text messages.

Some people might argue that the models of cultural dimensions do cover the difference of orality and literacy; however, these differences should be investigated in local conditions with a dialogic approach. In Mei's case, local literacy traditions interact with the developmental phase of local IT infrastructure, which shaped Mei's messaging use. Because computers and cell phones were introduced to the public at almost the same time to Chinese local users, cell phones have won a more favorable status due to their mobility, convenience, and pervasiveness.

Mei's case also epitomizes the importance of "constructive subjectiveness" in technology design. She adopted, appropriated, and localized the texting practice, a new literacy practice, to exchange game reviews and increase bonds with other sports fans because of her ruling passion for watching sports. Her identity as a sports fan was a driving force in her creative way of using and localizing a technology. This orientation to "constructive subjectiveness" will be further explored with Emma's case in the next chapter.

Unfortunately, the dynamic factors discussed above tend to be ignored in the models of cultural dimensions. All of this stresses the importance of approaching cross-cultural technology design with a dynamic vision of local culture informed by a dialogical approach.

9

Emma's Story: More than a Nice Gesture in a Technology-Mediated Life

"For me, text messaging is a quick and easy way to contact people. It is fun, and it's a nice gesture to let people know that you care" (at the beginning of the study).

"I use the phone, a lot more, the actual phone now. Instead of actually calling to say a lot of things, I just text it" (three years later).

Profile

"Emma," a 20-year-old American college junior majoring in business at the beginning of the study, enjoyed her dorm life and was busy with schoolwork and a part-time job at a local golf club on the weekends. She completed the survey and messaging diary and was then shadowed and interviewed six months later. Shortly thereafter she took a year off from college and worked in a local doctor's office as a secretary. When we met again for a follow-up interview one year later,[1] Emma was 24, back in college, living off-campus, planning to graduate at the end of that year, taking classes for getting a realtor license, and bartending on the side. Reflecting on the past three years, she commented that her biggest change was that she had become more mature, which was indeed attested to by her use trajectory of text messaging technology.

Getting her first cell phone in her sophomore year of high school, Emma started using text messaging as a college sophomore in January of 2003. At that time, text messaging was becoming popular. She sent her first text message from the Nextel website and found it to be fun. As text messaging became more popular, she also texted to people in other networks and increased her use. She changed phones twice and switched from Nextel to Sprint PCS during the period of study.

Emma had an ensemble of daily communication technologies. At the beginning of the study, when she still lived in dorms, this ensemble included a wireless phone, landline phone, AIM, text messaging, walkie-talkie,[2] email, and letter writing (listed from used most to least), among which, wireless phone calls, AIM, and email were the technologies she "always" used, and text messaging was ranked as the fourth. She had a clear rationale for choosing a particular technology for communication: "Basically I use the technologies people have and that are convenient to them." Therefore she used wireless phone calls for conversations she thought were important for family members, friends, and special people. The walkie-talkie was used for "quick and stupid" (her words) conversations when the other party was also a Nextel subscriber, saving money during peak hours. She chose AIM to "shoot the breeze" with friends online and switched to text messaging for "quick, easy, and fun" conversations when she or the other person was not at a computer. She chose email for school communication or to transfer files. The landline phone was used only for calls from the school or from home during peak hours. Occasionally, she wrote letters to her then-boyfriend, Dirk, a professional baseball player in Alabama.

Three years later, Emma found herself more mature, ready to transition into a post-college life. She was no longer interested in starting random communication via instant messaging but rather in having conversations with people for whom she really cared. Text messaging became the most important communication means in her life while other technologies phased out from her ensemble. She used only text messaging, wireless phone, email, and AIM (ranked in the order from most used to least used).

Texting in Action

Text messaging was a big part of Emma's college life. We will look at two patterns of messaging use in Emma's life at different stages: how text messaging was situated in her daily life and in her ensemble of communication technologies at the beginning of study—the dorm life period; and how text messaging was used and perceived in her technology ensemble at the end—the off-campus life period.

Patterns of Daily Use

In the four-day period of diary study conducted at the beginning, Emma sent 16 messages and received 42 pieces, for a total of 58. The total number of different places from which she sent messages was 10. Most text messages were sent from the dorm or from the workplace. One fifth of her messaging practice occurred in vehicles. A small amount of messages were sent from restaurants, at sporting events, and in class.

Similar to the overall distribution pattern of rhetorical purposes at the American site, as shown in Figure 9.1, 32.8% of Emma's messages were exchanged for the purpose of expressing (33.1% at the American site), 19.4% were for the purpose of co-experiencing (19.3% at the American site), and 25.4% were for the purpose of informing (26.2% at the American site). However, she sent more text messages for the purpose of instructing (17.9% vs.11.9% American average) and that of switching (4.5% vs. 1.8% American average), and she did not send any text messages for the purpose of coordinating during the diary study.

Two-thirds of Emma's text messages fall into her personal life sphere. Another third of the messages are about her school sphere and work sphere. During the four-day period, the people to whom Emma texted were her roommate (a good friend), a boyfriend she was dating before she moved into the relationship with Dirk months later, and her coworkers. Half of the text conversations occurred between Emma and her roommate, Paula. Those conversations were about daily life activities, such as getting up in the morning, taking work-out classes together in the afternoon, downloading music, or chatting

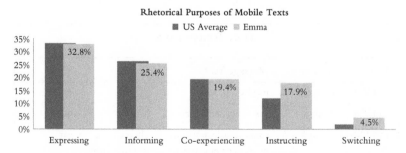

FIGURE 9.1   Emma's Top 3 Texting Purposes Were Consistent with the American Average

<table>
<tr><td colspan="4" align="center">TEXT SNIPPET 9.1</td></tr>
</table>

Time	Sender	Message Text	Place
9:24 AM	roommate	Wake up!	in bed
9:51 AM	Emma	I'm uppp	in bed
10:15 AM	roommate	Did you leave?	dorm
10:19 AM	roommate	Bfast (breakfast)?	dorm
10:19 AM	Emma	no, where are you?	dorm
10:19 AM	roommate	Gym	dorm

about a guy they met in a bar. Text Snippet 9.1 is a typical conversation between Emma and her roommate, in which there are messages with a co-experiencing purpose and an instructing purpose: That morning, Paula got up early and went to the gym. She texted Emma to get up and not to miss that day's work.

Her old boyfriend sent 16% of her incoming messages. He did not have a cell phone, but sent Emma one-way text messages from the Nextel website with the expressing purpose of showing his love and care:

"xoxoxoxoxoxoxoxoxoxoxoxoxoxoxoxoxoxoxoxo (love and kiss) luv ya (love you)."
"Just wanted to say hi! I'll TTYL (talk to you later)."

The text messages Emma exchanged with her coworkers included personal messages and work-related ones. In Text Snippet 9.2, coworker A was comforting her about her recent life situation. In Text Snippet 9.3, the same coworker texted to find out when he needed to come into work.

<table>
<tr><td colspan="4" align="center">TEXT SNIPPET 9.2</td></tr>
</table>

Time	Sender	Message Text	Place
4:54 PM	coworker A	maybe a smile?	work
4:59 PM	Emma	I just feel inadequate	work
5:08 PM	coworker A	so do I, but we still have a choice if we want to or not so just fing (f**king) smile	car
5:18 PM	coworker A	Smile no one can take that away from you	car

TEXT SNIPPET 9.3			
Time	Sender	Message Text	Place
12:39 PM	coworker A	What time am I in?	work
12:42 PM	Emma	2:00 PM	work

Figure 9.2 illustrates a typical one-day messaging activity chart from Emma's diary log. Text snippets 9.1 and 9.2 are mapped on the chart. As seen in the chart, Emma seldom initiated conversations, though she often responded to incoming messages. During the interview, she explained that she did not like typing on the phone keypad during the first two years in which she used text messaging. She felt it was annoying to do so even though she could type very fast on a small keypad with T9 while driving. Sometimes she would simply call back to respond to the sender. But she would reply via text messaging to her roommate, as they had a more special bond than Emma had with others. Thus they texted each other frequently.

Messaging in a Technology-Mediated Life

Emma commented about text messaging this way: "It's a little surprise when you get a text on your phone, just like the movie *You've Got Mail.*" As the fourth most-used technology in her daily life, text messaging had its own niche in Emma's ensemble of technologies with its instrumental and social affordances.

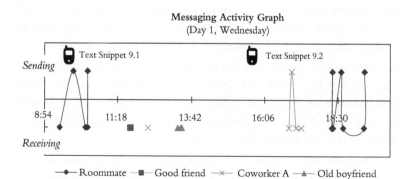

FIGURE 9.2   Emma: When Did She Text?

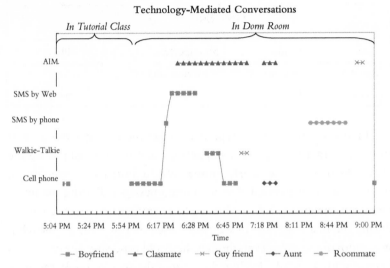

FIGURE 9.3   Technology-Mediated Conversations (Sun, 2009b, p. 256. Used with permission from ©2009 Baywood Publishing Co., Inc.)

Figure 9.3 provides a snapshot of how technologies were deeply embedded in Emma's life during a four-hour period on a typical Tuesday evening that occurred six months after the diary study. It also shows how mobile text messaging practices were situated in Emma's technology-mediated life. Emma had a language tutorial class from 5:00 p.m. to 6:00 p.m. After class, she stayed in her dorm room for the rest of the evening, working on homework, watching TV, and chatting with friends online. Except for the hour she was in class, her communication technologies were always on. Emma was engaged in different modes of communication the entire time, either in wireless phone conversations, walkie-talkie chats, text messaging chats, or AIM conversations. She was communicating to different people about different aspects of her life: with her boyfriend Dirk about a recent relationship crisis, with a classmate about schoolwork, with a friend about leisure activities, with her aunt about her family relationships, and with her roommate Paula about day-to-day relationship and friendship situations.

I selected her dorm as the main observation site because, according to her log, Emma tended to text a lot from the dorm. Also, the dorm was the place at which she stayed the most, as noted in her diary workbook. It was a typical dorm room for two college girls, with two beds on one side of the room. Beside each bed was a desk with a computer on it. Three TV sets were scattered in different corners. Assorted sizes of posters of celebrities and models covered every inch of the four walls in the room, among which stood out Greek flags of various sizes: A big curtain-sized Greek flag was hung in front of her window, a small Greek flag was pinned to the wall near her bed, and a mini-sized flag was pasted to the mirror. Clearly, as the second generation of Greek immigrants, Emma was very proud of her ethnic heritage—even her Nextel i730 had a Greek flag as its wallpaper, and she was very close to many members of the large extended family of her parents in the U.S.

Emma received a phone call from her boyfriend Dirk before the class, which she returned right after the class (about 5:54 p.m.) while walking back to the dorm. Emma had met Dirk, a baseball player in Alabama, two years before, but they did not move into the relationship until recently. Since then Emma had visited him four times. That day they were in the middle of a relationship crisis about a recent event. Emma had gone out with a male coworker the previous Friday night and told Dirk about it right away. Because Dirk had some bad experiences with his previous girlfriends, he was very upset about this and wondered if Emma was cheating on him. Emma told him she was not one of his previous girlfriends and wanted him to get over it. So they were arguing about this on the phone.

Emma communicated to Dirk primarily via wireless phone calls and walkie-talkie. Dirk's phone was not able to send text messages, but he could receive them. He also had a computer at home, but it did not have Internet access.

When we arrived in her room, Emma was still arguing with Dirk on the phone. The TV beside her bed had the volume on high. The electric fan was on to cool down the room from the sunshine. Her computer was on, with the AIM window layered on top of all other programs on the desktop. The 22-minute phone conversation did not seem to go anywhere. Frustrated and disappointed, Emma started to compose a breakup text message to Dirk at 6:18 p.m. She completed two key presses on her phone keypad and then stopped. She sat at the computer and went to the Nextel website because it would be quicker to type on the keyboard for a long and difficult message:

As much as it kills me to do this, I am deleting your number from
my phone. I care about you too much for you to be treating me
this way. I hope you find whatever it is that makes you happy in
life. I will always be 823[3].

A silent and immediate text message seemed to be the best way
to convey her emotions and avoid confrontation, since Emma did not
want to talk to Dirk.

While Emma was composing the message and then hesitating to
send it, a classmate greeted her on AIM (6:22 p.m.). She exchanged
some quick messages with him while reading the breakup text again
and again. Then Dirk beeped her using the walkie-talkie at 6:24 p.m.,
which was a free feature on both of their plans. When Emma was
pressing the walkie-talkie button, she accidentally clicked the SEND
button on the Nextel website, sending the breakup message! "No,
I don't want to send this one!" she exclaimed. "I wouldn't have made
this mistake if I didn't talk to him... He is receiving this message
now..." She hid her face in her hands, and the beeping walkie-talkie
suddenly became silent.

Two minutes later, Emma decided to walk away from this awkward situation, since finals week was just two weeks away and she had

FIGURE 9.4   Working with a Classmate on an Online Quiz via AIM

a few projects due soon. She logged on to the Blackboard website to work on an online quiz. It was nice that her classmate on AIM was also working on the same quiz. So they started to chat on AIM about quiz questions.

Dirk's response finally came with a beep from the walkie-talkie at 6:36 p.m. Emma did not have the courage to face him and decided to ignore the call. The beeping continued until it got so annoying that she turned it off. At 6:43 p.m., the ringtone of her cell phone invited her to take a phone call—it was Dirk calling. Emma answered the phone call and spoke with him over the phone, calmly this time. She ended the phone conversation five minutes later and started to work on her timed online quiz.

She was distracted once more two minutes later when a guy friend Kerry, also a baseball player, beeped her via the walkie-talkie about baseball games this weekend. Emma loved to watch baseball games, and she asked Kerry to keep her posted on game schedules.

Emma returned to her online quiz, reading the textbook carefully to find the answers. Around 7:18 p.m., she got a cell phone call from her aunt. As she had not talked to her aunt for a while, she was excited about receiving this phone call. She told her aunt about what was happening recently, being very open about her family situations: "I hate my family right now, and I don't want to talk to them." She complained about her mother's gossiping habit: "I called her the other day about Dirk and wanted her to give me some support. She didn't give me any support, but commented on me, and told my dad about this…" Emma walked around in the room, unpacking stuff from her backpack as she talked. Realizing that the online quiz was timed, she returned to the desk to work on the quiz while continuing to talk to her aunt.

The phone call ended 16 minutes later; Emma did not have much time left to work on the quiz, while her classmate had already completed his quiz and gone offline. Seeing a bad score on the last screen of the quiz, she was so disappointed that she comforted herself by saying that "I'm not going to care about this." Feeling bored, she played with her cell phone a bit and changed the ringtone. Then she leaned on her bed and started watching TV—first a baseball game and then her favorite show, *American Idol*.

		TEXT SNIPPET 9.4
Time	**Sender**	**Message Text**
8:39 P.M.	Emma	Are you on your way back yet?
8:40 P.M.	roommate	Yeah 2 Hours to go
8:41 P.M.	Emma	How'd the games go?
8:43 P.M.	roommate	Split lost one in the 7 Typical huh
8:44 P.M.	Emma	yeahhh
8:51 P.M.	roommate	Are you gonna be in the room or do you have work to do?
8:51 P.M.	Emma	No, I'll be here.

In the middle of watching TV, Emma thought of her roommate Paula, who was playing a softball game in Vermont, and texted to her (see Text Snippet 9.4).

Paula was also Emma's best friend at that time. They had a close social bond and shared many daily activities. Because Paula was not

FIGURE 9.5   Texting to Roommate

on the Nextel network and did not have walkie-talkie service, the women tended to update each other via texting. Text messaging is good for these daily life exchanges because such details are not very important in the sense of their meanings but important in maintaining close friendships. The informal format of text messaging helps to express caring in a discreet way, and the mobile form affords frequent contact almost everywhere.

At 8:54 p.m., Emma heard an IM sound from the computer and jumped from the bed: Kerry had IMed her about the baseball schedule. Emma brought out her schedule book and wrote down the schedule. Emma preferred to do scheduling via AIM or text messaging because she could keep the schedule on the computer or in the phone for later reference.

I left Emma's room at 9 p.m. as scheduled. While showing me the way out of her dorm building, she began to dial Dirk's phone number in Alabama. She told me that she was going to fight with Dirk for the rest of the night, since now it was off-peak hours for unlimited minutes.[4]

Growing Mature with Texting

The wallpaper on Emma's cell phone was a close-up of her made-up right eye when we met again in her off-campus apartment after she returned to college. This visual statement subtly echoed what Emma revealed in the interview: "The biggest change in my life is that I matured a lot. I became more interested in my education, my life, my future, not sitting around…" Because of that, her way of using text messaging changed "absolutely." She confessed that she texted 20 times more than at the beginning of study: She would send 200 messages a day and receive another 100 or 200—"Sending around 10 messages an hour is easy." Similar to Brian's observation[5] (see Chapter 7), Emma's phone bill was paid by her father, and thus she did not worry about the cost. There were 154 messages received that day in her inbox and 137 in the sent box the same day by 6 p.m., and usually she went to bed around 2 a.m. The majority of text messages were sent to her current boyfriend Josh and roommate Anna. She would text all day to these two people. "Texting them is what is counted for these 137 messages (sent today)." [6] And Josh was the one she texted the most. She explained it in this way: "All I want to do is talk to Josh and Anna, people in my life that matter, and my family. I don't care about stupid conversation that means nothing."

Consequently, Emma's ensemble of communication technologies changed. She disconnected her landline phone and dropped the walkie-talkie feature from her wireless phone after she moved out of the dorm. She seldom used instant messaging, which she thought was "part of the dorm life" when students would instant-message everyone they knew on campus. She was not interested in being everyone's friend anymore. A proof to this statement was that her computer was shut off during the entire interview, unlike the time of our last meeting in her dorm room when her computer was on with AIM on all the time. The wireless phone was her most important communication technology these days: "I use the phone, a lot more, the actual phone now. Instead of actually calling to say a lot of things, I just text it." In addition to texting to the two people who mattered, she also called her parents or work, and this was her major use of her wireless phone.

Emma used text messaging everywhere. She described what she would text in her own cynical manner:

> Anything if usually stupid, just pointless, just so you can have
> communication, while you are doing something boring, you can
> have it. Or during bartending, somebody is coming in who I hate,
> you know. I'll send out a text like this...You know...Anything.
> Stuff like this. Anything that goes through my mind.

This description was consistent with the messaging patterns revealed in her messaging diary at the beginning of the study, when she texted mostly for the purposes of expressing and co-experiencing. Because of her desire to express her feelings in words, she was not fond of picture messaging.

Typing on the keypad was no longer annoying or inconvenient. In fact, Emma taught 31-year-old Josh how to text after they began dating. It took Josh a couple of weeks to become a fast typist on the phone. Now Josh thought texting was interesting and had sent about 1500 messages to Emma and his guy friends the month before.

Texting and Lifestyle

Emma's messaging use experiences over three years serve as a good example of a temporal pattern of culturally localized user experience. A dynamic and complex process of user localization occurred while Emma looked for and refined a communication technology to fit her changing lifestyle. Though the messaging use experience was situated in her technology-mediated life from the beginning, the meaning of "constructive subjectiveness" evolved as Emma matured. Compared to Mei, whose messaging experience was driven by her unchanged ruling passion for sports, Emma's use experience was constructed around her developing identities in a process of becoming.

Technology Affordances and Rhetorical Persuasion

The four-hour observation at an early stage of the study illustrates how Emma unconsciously designed rhetoric to accomplish her daily communication goals with various technology affordances (including both instrumental and social aspects). Within the immediate context of the dorm room, different technology affordances are organized to accomplish the art of persuasion in Emma's daily communication practices. As shown in Figure 9.3, in every communication situation, Emma skillfully chose the best technology that was available, easy, and convenient for both parties to better communicate her points based on the instrumental and social affordances of the technology. In two out of the five situations, she employed more than one technology to communicate and mediate practices, and switching between technologies enhanced her communication. Classic rhetoric divides the art of persuasion into five "canons": (1) invention, (2) arrangement, (3) style, (4) memory, and (5) delivery. Technology affordances are related to arrangement and style. For the former, technology affordances provide the proper means of persuasion to structure an argument and fuse form, function, and content into a coherent presentation (Hart-Davidson, Cushman, Grabill, DeVoss, & Porter, 2005); for the latter, they help to create voices and thus identities of the communication.

To handle a relationship crisis with her long-distance boyfriend, Emma used four forms of technology: cell phone conversation, walkie-talkie voice chat, text messaging by phone, and text messaging by web. Affordances of each technology are used here to arrange a stronger rhetoric. Cell phone conversation allowed her to argue with her boyfriend at a distance, with the richest information exchange and the highest level of flexibility: They were connected no matter where she was—in the classroom, on the way back to the dorm room, and in the dorm room. However, it cost money during peak hours, and the constant verbal flow might not be effective in a dramatic situation. Walkie-talkie conversations occurred to counteract the disadvantages of cell phone conversations: Discrete conversation flows with sentence pauses helped them to focus on the content they wanted to convey without being extraordinarily emotional. It also saved money. However, it does not have the clear quality that a phone conversation does, and it is less formal and genuine because of its cheap cost, as shown at the moment when Emma refused to answer Dirk's walkie-talkie call. Text messaging allows the user to avoid confrontation while contacting the other party right away, but this technology demands more effort to type on the phone keypad, especially for a long and important message. Thus Emma switched from the phone to the computer. Unfortunately, a flawed design for sending text messages on the Nextel website (it did not incorporate the function of asking for a confirmation to send the message like other websites such as Verizon Wireless and Sprint PCS did) caused a communicative breakdown, complicating the situation.

The conversation about baseball games and its switching from walkie-talkie to AIM was simpler. According to Emma, schedules, date times, and work-related issues were not important enough to be discussed on a cell phone. The walkie-talkie is a good way to handle these kinds of "quick and stupid" conversations. However, walkie-talkie conversations cannot be saved for later reference. In addition, Kerry did not have the schedule available when he was using the walkie-talkie. When he had the schedule available, he instant-messaged Emma. An AIM conversation here helped to mediate the scheduling practice by providing a reminder note at the top of the computer display.

In other communication situations, Emma communicated with her aunt using a cell phone because a) that was an important and longer conversation for her, b) her aunt didn't use walkie-talkie or text messaging as Emma's generation did, and c) she was responding to a phone call that actually did not involve a rhetorical arrangement from her perspective. She chatted with a classmate about the online quiz via AIM, since AIM allows for cutting and pasting questions and exchanging answers right away. In the last case, she texted to Paula because of its low cost and little overhead for exchanging mundane life experiences and maintaining friendships.

By examining text messaging practices in their immediate context, we see text messaging situated in Emma's life within its own niche. With its instrumental affordances (e.g., quick, direct, silent, and convenient) and social affordances (e.g., avoiding confrontation, staying in contact, and showing care), text messaging might not have been the most important technology for Emma at the beginning of the study, but it already played a particular role in her technology-mediated life that other technologies could not replace.

As Emma matured, text messaging ascended to be the most important communication means in her life. This use change stressed how the affordances of text messaging suited her rhetorical priorities—she was not interested in being everyone's friend but only in communicating with a few people for whom she cared, no matter where she was or when it was. No other technology except text messaging could provide such instrumental affordances (i.e., silent, quick, and direct communication, convenient use, discreet action, inexpensive communication, and multitasking) and social affordances (i.e., staying in contact, expressing feelings and sharing support, having fun, and protecting privacy) for her needs, or could be dedicated to such intimate emotional exchanges, and thus could fit into her lifestyle.

Identities Mediated by Phone

The affordances of technologies not only helped Emma to create a stronger rhetoric for daily communication needs, but also presented different identities for various life spheres in a broader sociocultural context.

Emma was sophisticated in mapping different groups of people for different technologies during her daily communication practices from the beginning, though she seemed to achieve this unconsciously.

For parents and relatives, she called them; for friends, she called, emailed, instant-messaged, texted, and used the walkie-talkie; for her boyfriend, she called, texted, and used the walkie-talkie; for work contacts, she called and emailed them. This sophistication was also shown when she had a smaller technology ensemble later: She would call her parents or workplace but reserved text messaging to close correspondents for the most important and meaningful communication.

In Emma's ensemble of technologies, each technology had its own role and worked well with the other ones. Each helped her to mediate different identities and important relationships. In a four-hour period indicative of her daily life experiences in her dorm-life period, we see Emma busily shifting her identities between a lover, a classmate, a niece, a casual friend, and a close friend using a range of technologies. Technologies made the emergence and co-presence of these various identities in one place possible, and they also interconnected the identities to form Emma's subjectivity within the messy complexities of everyday life. Here, each instance of technology use was "carefully and strategically knitted and stitched into a web of her relationship, which shows both the 'situatedness' of the technology and its 'constructive subjectiveness' as well" (Sun, 2009b, p. 257).

While Emma was smart in orchestrating different technologies for her communication purposes at that time, she was only passively consuming technologies. As she described why she would adopt new technologies in an early interview, "the world keeps coming with new technologies. They're out there, and you might have to have them." Because of this she was also frustrated with the pervasive power of communication technologies: "Oh my God! There are so many ways to communicate with somebody! Unbelievable! You can always get hold of somebody, either by computer, by cell phone, or by work phone..." She disclosed that during the four hours with me, it was actually her least amount of time on the phone: "Everyone knows that I'm always on my phone." The impulse to communicate—and the various identities coming with that impulse—makes her sometimes feel exhausted and consider "throwing my phone out of the window."

As she transitioned to an off-campus, post-college life, Emma became more selective about her communication technologies. She realized that the people with whom she really wanted to communicate were her boyfriend, her roommate, and her family. Therefore, she got rid of her landline phone and walkie-talkie, and phased out from instant messaging. She was not fond of emerging communication channels, such as blogging or social networking websites, either. Clearly, not all of these were important to her communication priorities. As a proficient "cultural expert," Emma chose communication technologies based on her communication needs and persuasion goals, and thus her identities were constructed through her careful arrangement of technologies in her daily life.

In Emma's case, the mobile messaging technology was integrated into her local context as well as articulated into a process of constructing her subjective experience according to her lifestyle and identities. This user localization process links the instrumental aspect of the mere use process to the subjective use experience situated in a particular cultural context and demonstrates how Emma actively localized the technology to fit into the fabrics of her everyday life to establish and maintain her multiple identities. When she started to use the messaging technology, she often texted to her roommate, friends, and coworkers, for it was "a nice gesture to let people know that you care" and "a fun surprise" for the people she cared about. In an early interview, she said she occasionally texted to her parents to say "love you." They did not respond because they did not know how to, but they liked that surprise. It was also a persuasive rhetoric when she did not want to talk. Later, when she moved out of the dorm, text messaging helped her stay up to date on "the most important stuff." By choosing the mobile messaging technology to communicate, she was positioning herself in a specific life sphere with a certain identity. Here the messaging technology was chosen as the favorite technology because it provided opportunities to construct multiple identities in her relationship networks. As Geser (2005) observes, "the mobile phone endows individuals with the capacity to accumulate diverse roles simultaneously as well as to maintain 'pervasive roles'" (p. 213).

Reflection Notes on Cross-Cultural Design

Emma's case points out the importance of meaning construction and identity work in cross-cultural design in this postmodern era. It directs our attention to the role of subjectivity in design and urges the design community to consider the needs of individual users.

Postmodernists believe that multiple identities are constructed in numerous layers of cultural contexts through a process of becoming. Our identities are never fixed but keep changing through our cultural consumption experience when we localize technologies within meaningful social practices. Emma's case shows the ongoing development of multiple identities in the process of becoming. Since these identities are not fixed, it is hard to describe them with static values like cultural dimensions, and it is also pointless to capture those changing multiple identities into values at all. This raises the question of how to design for a changing entity in an era when the only constant is change, and shows the necessity of allowing for multiple interpretations in design. A design that can be interpreted in different ways will leave plenty of room for user localization and let individual users define their own meanings and grow with the technology, as Emma did.

Emma's case sketches the dynamic and complex journey of user localization where a user kept looking for a technology to find herself and fit her lifestyle. When Emma began to use the technology, she was attracted only to its novelty and used it as a nice gesture to friends among an ensemble of communication technologies in which she engaged for fun. She did not like typing on the keypad, and she had a serious breakdown, as observed, when she tried to send a breakup message to her then-boyfriend Dirk. However, text messaging does provide good social affordances to maintain intimate communication between close friends, which became a high rhetorical priority in Emma's daily communication as she got older. She overcame her discomfort of typing on the phone and loved text messaging. When text messaging acquired a central role in her everyday communication practices as a hub for important relationships as well as a site for her identities, just like the Greek flag on her phone screen displayed her ethnic heritage or her self-reflecting eye implied her maturity, this technology was thus localized by Emma and became *her* technology. And as an advocate for her own technology, Emma enthusiastically taught her people—in this case her boyfriend Josh—to localize the same technology to fit their lifestyle. In addition, the change in Emma's use over the years could be read against a larger context where the SMS traffic of the U.S. was catching up with the rest of the world.

It is interesting to look at the gender factor through the angle of Emma's case. It was not just coincidence that four of the five case studies in this book profiled female users. Though originally designed as a general study to compare use patterns across cultures, two-thirds of the participants turned out to be female because the criterion-based sampling procedures emphasized a high volume of daily messaging exchanges; data from the fieldwork also present distinctive patterns of use between participants of different genders and show that the gender factor played an important role in the use of text messaging. Female participants used text messaging more than males and enjoyed text messaging more. The study also observes that the enthusiastic uses of text messaging were constant for these young female users as they went through life-changing events: Emma increased the use volume of text messaging when she was about to graduate from college, and Sophie embraced new messaging technology (e.g., picture messaging) when she moved into motherhood. In both cases, changing identities played an important role in determining their use practices of mobile messaging.

Notes

1. I was not able to contact Emma for a while at the time when she was out of college, since she had changed her phone number and email address.
2. Here, walkie-talkie refers to a feature that the wireless carrier (Nextel) provides. The full name of this service is Walkie-Talkie (Direct Connect ®).
3. 823 means "thinking of you." Each digit corresponds to the number of letters of the words.
4. It is possible that Emma waited till 9 p.m. to call Dirk because she didn't want to argue with him in front of me.
5. Brian and Emma did not know each other.
6. See Endnote 3 of Chapter 5.

PART III

IMPLICATIONS

10

Culturally Localized User Experience as Situated and Constructed

The five individual use cases in Part II have painted a vivid picture of assorted culturally localized user experiences that are both situated and constructed in their local contexts. Based on the empirical study, in this chapter I extend the discussion of culturally localized user experience by drawing a general trend of local uses, situating individual cases in broader contexts, and further developing the CLUE framework as outlined in Chapter 3.

My primary goal in this chapter is to contextualize key concepts of the CLUE framework—situated action, constructed meaning, a dual mediation process, and affordances—in a panoramic view of mobile text messaging use across two sites, and thus build the concrete mold of the CLUE framework. Through exploring both the "situatedness" and the "constructiveness" of technology use in local contexts in the first two sections, I demonstrate how action and meaning are integrated in culturally localized user experience. Here, *situatedness* refers to both action and meaning and seeks to weave both, while *constructiveness* focuses on meaning. Built on this holistic view of user experience, in the third section I connect technology affordances to a dual mediation process of technology use and survey where affordances emerge from and how they arise as dialogic relations from a situated and constructed experience of mobile messaging use. I end this chapter with a discussion of the value of the CLUE framework for the cross-cultural design community.

I would like to emphasize that the case study approach is used to develop a deep understanding of situated phenomenon, and I do not intend that the five selected cases should be able to represent *all* the rich cultural scenarios in every local context. If so, I am doing the same thing as those cultural essentialists whom I criticize in this book. What I suggest is that these individual cases will provide insights to the cross-cultural design community in helping us to connect local cultural ethos and individual subjectivity in technology design, and eventually in assisting users to achieve "genius loci."

Situated Use Activity as Articulation of Local Influences

I explore the "situatedness" of mobile messaging technology use in this section; while I do not aim to provide a complete picture of the use scenarios (it is not possible to have a complete picture in terms of postmodernism), I want to demonstrate how various contextual and cultural factors from local contexts are incorporated and reflected into local uses. It will serve as a backdrop for understanding diverse use activities from their local contexts presented in a panoramic view.

Mobile messaging technology mediates different social practices in different contexts. The five use histories illustrate how individual users articulated myriad contextual and cultural factors into use as they localized a hard-to-use technology into their personal lives. Local uses of mobile text messaging were the outcome of the dynamic interactions of various contextual and cultural influences on different levels. These factors and effects come from immediate and material contexts, from varied communities, and from broader sociocultural contexts. They have played an important role in determining how the technology was adopted, used, and consumed in a particular locale as participants used the technology to embrace their lifestyles and improve their forms of life.

Immediate contextual factors largely come from a particular participant's life situation; for example, Sophie was not able to check email at work due to her busy schedule, Brian could not make phone calls to friends for lunch plans in class, and Mei found it inappropriate to call sports fan friends about games at midnight. But there are some contextual factors common to participants from the same site, such as the socio-technical system determined by local IT infrastructure and economic conditions, which affect the use of mobile messaging.

Table 10.1 sketches each participant's information on mobile phone use between the two sites based on data collected in the fall of 2003 via a questionnaire survey (see Appendix A). By no means do I want to

TABLE 10.1   Comparison of Mobile Phone Use between the Two Sites

Categories	US Participants	CN Participants
Average Use History of Phone (Months)	30.89	19.50
Average Use History of SMS (Months)	14.42	18.09
Average Monthly Phone Cost	$66.94	56.14 yuan[1]
Average Monthly Text Cost	$6.63	32.05 yuan

suggest that a brief cross-site comparison could represent the local use patterns of two cultures; that would never be the goal of a qualitative study like this, not to mention the fact that the sampling procedure and sample size would not be able to generate this inference at all. My goal here is to offer a situated view to help us understand the five local use scenarios profiled earlier.

The survey results show that American participants had a longer adoption history of cell phones than their Chinese counterparts (11 months longer), but a shorter adoption history of text messaging (3.5 months shorter). It is noted that most Chinese participants started using text messaging almost at the same time they adopted their cell phones, while American participants adopted text messaging 16 months after they purchased their cell phones. This explains the "wow" moment Brian had with his friend Tom when they first tried text messaging as well as Lili's practice of texting people to notify them of her phone number after she got her first phone.

Table 10.2 describes the daily communication tools available to participants at the two sites.[2] For this pool of participants, Americans had more communication tools available to them than Chinese—89.5% of American participants reported using wireless phone calls, mobile messaging, instant messaging, and emails "usually." For Chinese participants, 95.5% reported using mobile messaging "usually," but only 68.2% used cell phones "usually." The percentages of those "usually" using instant messaging and email were much lower, 59.1% and 54.5%, respectively. This scenario was consistent with the development of the IT infrastructure in these two countries at that time (see Table 4.2). It also explains the high volume of text messages found at the Chinese site.

Apparently, the access to different communication technologies shaped local uses. Most American participants have had a wide

TABLE 10.2   Comparison of Daily IT Use

Percentage Using IT	US Participants	CN Participants
90.0%–100%	Wireless phone calls (100%)	
	Mobile messaging (94.7%)	Mobile messaging (95.5%)
80.0%–89.9%	Instant messaging	. . .
	(89.5% also *always* using)	
	Emails (89.5%)	
70.0%–79.9%	Landline phones (73.7%)	. . .
60.0%–69.9%	. . .	Wireless phone calls (68.2%)
50.0%–59.9%	. . .	Instant messaging (59.1%)
		Landline phones (57.1%)
		Emails (54.5%)
<50.0%	Letters (26.3%)	Letters (9.5%)
	Faxes (5.3%)	Faxes (4.8%)

range of communication technologies available to them and have had more access to computers, the Internet, email, and instant messaging. For quick communication, they had a selection of technologies from which to choose, accomplishing the same purpose without having to bang away on a phone keypad. In contrast, the technologies that were available to most Chinese participants were mobile messaging and wireless phones. Since text messaging had a higher penetration rate at the Chinese site, it was more convenient for participants to use text messaging to contact people for various work and personal activities. In the cases we have seen, Brian's use of text messaging was influenced by his earlier use of instant messaging. In contrast, at the Chinese site, Lili did not use instant messaging until later in the study; as an earlier adopter of email compared to Lili, Mei reflected on how texting took over the charm of emailing.

The text conversation below describes how a Chinese user employed a variety of communication technologies to connect with friends for a task-related purpose. Friend A wanted to borrow a large amount of money from Ling, whom she was not able to get in contact with. She knew the participant in the study maintained contact with Ling and asked for help via text messaging.

		TEXT SNIPPET 10.1	
Time	Sender	Message Text	Place
9:43 AM	friend A	bang wo lian xi Ling, wo you ji shi zhao ta (Please help me contact Ling, I have something urgent.)	office
9:44 AM	participant	wo ye zhi you ta de MSN, ni hen ji ma? Gei ta fa Email hao le (I only have her MSN (messenger) contact, is it urgent? Just send her an email.)	office
9:45 AM	friend A	wo gei ta fa you jian ta dou bu hui. wo you ji shi zhao ta, ni zai MSN shang kan dao ta, jiao ta gen wo lian xi (She never replies to my emails. I have something urgent, if you see her on MSN (messenger), please ask her to contact me.)	office
9:49 AM	participant	hao de. ta gang shang xian, wo ba ni de shou ji gei ta le (Sure. She just came online, and I gave her your cell phone number.)	office
10:02 AM	friend A	wo que qian, fang zi yi shi mai bu diao, ni bang wo zhuan gao kan kan ta na li neng fou jie wo 5 wan, 4 wan ye xing, ming nian kai chun huan ta. (I need money. My condo can't be sold right away. Please ask her whether she could lend me 50K, 40K is also ok, I will return it to her the coming spring.)	office
10:02 AM	participant	wo gen ta shuo le, ta jiao ni bie ji, ta wan xie shi hou chu qu mai dian hua ka gei ni dian hua. (I just forwarded this to her. She doesn't want you to be anxious, and she will go buy the phone card later and call you.)	office
10:04 AM	friend A	ni jiao ta ba you xiang qing kong, wo jia dian hua ******, wo zai jia li deng ta. (Please ask her to empty her email box (so that new messages can be received). My home phone number is ******, and I'll be waiting for her call at home.)	office
			(Continued)

		Text Snippet 10.1 (Continued)		
Time	Sender	Message Text	Place
10:05 AM	participant	hao le, ni qu shen qing le MSN ba. ta zai shang mian, wo zuo shi le, 88. (Well, you should apply for an MSN messenger account. She is there online, and I need to go back to my work, bye-bye.)	office
10:06 AM	friend A	en, hao de, ma fan ni le. (Ok, well, thank you.)	office

Other than the issue of trial and error of various communication channels between friends, this conversation indicates that texting technology is deeply embedded in ordinary Chinese people's everyday lives. Chinese participants texted about a variety of topics, such as borrowing money, buying a house, sending gifts to the boss, exchanging job information, and so on—in short, every aspect of daily life.

In comparison, a high percentage of chats found at the American site were exchanged for conveying users' care and feelings, where there was a salient messaging pattern for the purposes of expressing and co-experiencing (Sun, 2004). In the following two examples, participant A was male, and participants B and C were female, and they shared the similar messaging use pattern of having quick exchanges about what was going on. This pattern was described by some of the American participants as "small talk." Researcher danah boyd (Knies, 2009) defines this as "social grooming"—even though the messages look pointless to outsiders, it is "a particularly critical process for young people" to "figure out how the social world works."

		Text Snippet 10.2		
Time	Sender	Message Text	Place
9:05 PM	participant A	What you doing tonight	car
9:14 PM	friend	movie then bar	car
9:16 PM	friend	want to come?	car
9:21 PM	participant A	Sure, im (I'm) callin (calling) you now	car

\multicolumn{4}{c}{TEXT SNIPPET 10.3}
Time	Sender	Message Text	Place
12:29 PM	participant B	I love you	in class
12:30 PM	participant C	Where the hell are you?	meeting
12:31 PM	participant B	In my student government meeting	meeting
12:32 PM	participant C	Ah i see i thought we were eating at 1230	meeting
12:34 PM	participant B	nope my meeting is at 1230	meeting
12:34 PM	participant C	K (ok)	meeting
12:46 PM	participant C	Me and jenna love you Uuuuuu (you)	meeting
12:48 PM	participant B	Aww amanda and me say we love too	meeting

As discussed in Brian's case, participants' experiences with instant messaging influenced their experiences with mobile messaging. Most American participants had used instant messaging for a few years before they adopted text messaging. During the interviews, I found that the conceptual model of instant messaging was so deeply rooted in some participants that they often compared mobile messaging to instant messaging. This frequent comparison often leads to one conclusion: Mobile messaging is just instant messaging without computers but not as easy to use. During daily use, participants tended to reserve longer conversations for instant messaging. In contrast, most Chinese participants started using mobile messaging and instant messaging at the same time (some of them had never used IM before the study); they did not have a conceptual model of instant messaging when they started using text messaging. Furthermore, for most of them, the Internet was not as easy to access as a cell phone was. Participants tended to regard them as two parallel technologies and seldom combined them during these interviews, as shown in Mei's case.

Additionally, the structure of cell phone plans affected the use of text messaging. This is instrumental affordance that comes from the service network. As described in Chapter 4 (see Table 4.3), phone minutes and text rates were calculated differently at the two sites. At the American site, participants usually had phone plans with free night and weekend minutes along with monthly minute allowances, sometimes making it cheaper to call than to text. At the Chinese site, participants' phone plans usually did not include free phone minutes but had discounted text packages. Therefore, some people thought texting saved money. Whereas it is hard to compare the monthly costs of mobile telephony between the two sites, the average ratio of call cost vs. text cost for American participants was 10:1 (see Table 10.1), and the average ratio for Chinese participants was 1.75:1. This shows that texting was a big part of mobile use for Chinese participants.

Generally, the cost factor seems to play a more important role in enticing new users to adopt text messaging than persuading frequent users to stay with the technology. Sophie once downgraded her texting plan in the middle of the study, but returned back to an unlimited plan after she found the fun of using picture messaging as a young mother's brag book. Cost was the concern for a budget-conscious consumer who supported himself for graduate study such as Brian: He adopted text messaging because a free plan was available at that time. However, after his plan's free promotion ended, the cost concern adjusted his messaging practice, but he did not cancel the texting plan because all of his friends were texting. For Chinese participants, the cost factor was not as apparent as that of the American site since texting was already part of a cell phone bill. The question about the cost was translated into whether one wanted to have a cell phone or not, but not whether one wanted to have a texting plan.

The issue of community might be more important for frequent users than cost concern. According to Rogers (1995), technology adoption usually goes through five stages: innovators, early adopters, early majority, late majority, and laggards. The American site was still at the early adoption stage for text messaging when the study began (see Figure 4.1), so it had not reached a critical mass, and a texting discourse community had not yet come into shape. However, the Chinese site was at the stage of early majority, and it had already reached the critical mass. Participants at the American site usually went through an adoption moment triggered by a series of events, as shown in the cases of Sophie and Brian. Particularly in Brian's case, one reason he was able to catch on to text messaging quickly is because a texting community made up of his friends began forming at that time. Chinese participants usually took the adoption of this technology for granted, and it was natural for them to join in such a large community of texters.

TABLE 10.3   Overview of Logged Messages

Sites	Average daily messages per person	Logged places per person	Logged correspondents per person
US	10.48	5.79	5.47
CN	18.79	6.59	10.05

Table 10.3 provides an overview of messages logged in the diary study conducted in the fall of 2003. Over a period of four days (chosen by participants themselves), the Chinese participants sent more text messages and texted to more people than American participants did, but the number of different texting contexts was similar across sites. Participants texted to friends, lovers, classmates, colleagues, coworkers, and relatives—most messages were sent to friends and lovers. As the penetration rate of text messaging was higher in China, it was not surprising to see that the number of people that Chinese participants texted was double the number for the American site.

On the one hand, we see communities forming based on the messaging technology. On the other hand, messaging practices strengthened established communities (Ling, 2008), such as the social circles found in Brian's case, the cohort of college classmates from Lili's case, and the sports fan community revealed in Mei's case.

More than the effect of community, other *broad sociocultural influences* from national/ethnic culture (e.g., power distance, collectivism vs. individualism) and from subgroup culture (e.g., age group, gender, and organizational affiliation) defined technology use in their own ways.

According to the questionnaire survey, Chinese participants named staying in contact with friends or loved ones their top reason for messaging,[3] which was ranked as the seventh most important purpose by American participants. This helps to explain why more text correspondents were recorded in the diary workbooks of Chinese participants. In comparison, Americans reported that the top two purposes for sending messages were for fun conversations with friends and passing the time. The former was ranked a fourth at the Chinese site, and the latter was ninth.

The survey results are consistent with the collected messages. Social motives provided by the mobile messaging technology, taking the form of local purposes, are represented in different messaging patterns logged in their diaries. Many of the Chinese chats from the message logs were exchanged between participants and their local, distant, and online friends. Those conversations often consisted of informing-oriented communication for staying in contact, which was part of the collectivist culture at the Chinese site (see Text Snippet 10.4). In a collectivist

TEXT SNIPPET 10.4

Time	Sender	Message Text	Place
1:17 PM	friend	Yuanyuan ni hao a. Wo shi Zhang Xia. Hai ji de ma? You mei you ba wo wang ji a? (Hey Yuanyuan. I'm Zhang Xia. Do you still remember me? Or have you forgotten me?)	Dorm
1:23 PM	participant	Hao jiu mei ni xiao xi le ai. Xian zai hao ma? (I haven't heard from you for a while. How are you doing?)	Dorm
5:27 PM	friend	Yuanyuan, wo shi Zhang Xia ji de ma? Ni gao zhong tong zhuo tong xue, wo zhong wu gei ni fa le xin xi. Ni shou dao mei you ne (Yuanyuan, I'm Zhang Xia. Remember me? I'm your high school classmate who shared a desk with you. I sent you a message at noon. Did you get it)	Dorm
5:46 PM	participant	Wo zhong wu yi jing hui ni le ya. Gang cai zai da dian hua (I replied to you at noon. I was talking on the phone a moment ago)	Dorm
5:51 PM	friend	Shi wo mei you shou dao a ni xian zai zen yang a zai na li shang xue a. Wo men hao jiu mei you lian xi la ni de dian hua wo hai shi xiang Ling Gang wen de ne (I didn't get it How are you doing Where are you going to school We haven't contacted each other for quite a long time and I got your phone number from Ling Gang)	Dorm
5:54 PM	participant	Wo zai hang zhou. ri zi ma hai hao. wo QQ shi 2*******8, ni zai nan jing o. (I'm in Hangzhou. I'm doing well. My QQ is 2*******8, you are in Nanjing, right?)	Dorm

(*Continued*)

	TEXT SNIPPET 10.4 (Continued)		
Time	Sender	Message Text	Place
6:02 PM	friend	Ni zen me zhi dao de, wo shi zai Nanjing. qu nian wo zai Tianjin du le yi nian xian zai you hui dao Nanjing du le. wo de qq shi 2*******. (How did you know that? I'm in Nanjing. I went to Tianjin for school for a year, and now I'm back in Nanjing. My qq is 2*******.)	Class
6:12 PM	participant	Deng Lan gao su wo de. Wo xian zai zai shang ke, xia ci liao o. (Deng Lan told me about that. I'm in class, talk to you later.)	Class
6:30 PM	friend	Ni you mei you Wu Dong de dian hua a ni you he ta lian xi ma. (Do you have Wu Dong's phone number Do you stay in touch with him)	Class
6:32 PM	participant	Mei you. wo dou mei he ta men lian xi guo. (No. I didn't stay in contact with them.)	Class

culture, long-lasting relationships are valued and individuals feel a deep personal involvement with each other. This long-term relationship orientation is mediated nicely by mobile messaging because it allows people to stay in touch in an unobtrusive way.

In contrast, as an individualist culture, American culture does not have a strong orientation toward long-term relationships. The cultural characteristic of individualism shapes the use in another direction: Mobile messaging was primarily regarded as a means for quick exchanges between peers and close friends where fun and amusement for individuals were emphasized (see Text Snippet 10.5).

	TEXT SNIPPET 10.5		
Time	Sender	Message Text	Place
11:57 AM	friend	Hey! Hows (How's) Albany?	Class
12:00 PM	participant	Urgh–2 (too) much to type. I'll call U (you)	Class

Text Snippet 10.4 is a typical chat between friends at the Chinese site. In this example, a participant named Yuanyuan was reconnecting with her old school friend, and they exchanged several messages with an informing purpose. The implicit affordance of text messaging makes this contact less abrupt. The whole conversation took 10 turns.

Text Snippet 10.5 is of an American participant who was also reconnecting with her former school friend. After a quick exchange, they decided to switch to a phone conversation.

In addition, as illustrated in Brian's and Mei's cases, local cultural preferences for literacy or orality furthered the use of mobile text messaging in different directions. With a script-based language and 4,000 years of written history, literacy culture is highly valued in China. Text messaging is interpreted as writing rather than as conversation. During their interviews, Chinese participants spoke about how they were attracted to the power and beauty of the written communication of text messaging. As text messaging is recognized as a popular genre, the career of the SMS writer emerged. Some SMS writers have their own columns on the bigger web portals. People enjoy circulating well-written text messages among friends, and dozens of these messages were logged at the Chinese site. Similar interpretations of texting as literacy practices also happen in Indonesia and the Philippines (Barendregt, 2008; Elwood-Clayton, 2005).

In contrast, at the American site, text messaging was regarded as orality instead of literacy, similar to what Ling (2004) reports in his study of Norwegian teenagers' text messaging use. All logged text messages had conversational styles, and many colloquial and slang words can be found. There were no circulated messages. But this does not necessarily mean that the message-composing process was treated lightheartedly at the American site, as we can see from Sophie's texts, which used popular languages in a humorous way in order to be cool.

Other than notable use patterns across two types of ethnic cultures, data from the fieldwork also presented distinctive patterns of use between participants of different genders, as discussed in the cases of Brian and Emma. Two-thirds of the participants turned out to be female because the criterion-based sampling procedures emphasized a high volume of daily messaging exchanges, and female users generally tend to send more text messages than males.[4] Indeed, gender has played an important role in the use of phones both historically and globally. Female users adopted landline phones for "rapport talk" after the phones were first introduced in the early 20th century (Rakow, 1992; Tannen, 1990). Cell phones were adopted by working mothers for domestic purposes such as remote mothering and parallel shifts in the early 1990s (Rakow & Navarro, 1993). The emergence of short text messaging service provides more possibilities for female users. Various research conducted in the U.S., Europe, and the Asia-Pacific found that female users were apparently more enthusiastic about using text messaging as a means of communication than male users (e.g., Hjorth, 2009; Igarashi, Takai, & Yoshida, 2005; Lin, 2005; Lin & Tong, 2008; Ling, 2004; Peters, Almekinders, van Buren, Snippers, & Wessels, 2003; Shade, 2008; Uy-Tioco, 2008). Some female participants of this study claimed that "text messaging is my form of communication."

The gendered practices of mobile text messaging technology also serve as interesting examples of local/global dynamics. In Lili's case, her personal use of the technology was influenced by both her gendered identity on the local level and ethnic cultural factors on the global level. The feminine "Dancing Queen" phone she used exhibited how the technologies of wireless phones and mobile text messaging were localized for female social practices. These social practices were also her way of negotiating a form of "pure water," a social relationship between friends in her sociocultural contexts. Similarly, in a comparison of four qualitative studies of female mobile phone users in Tokyo, Seoul, Hong Kong, and Melbourne, Hjorth (2009) maintains that the diverse "gendered performativity" surrounding mobile phones in different cultures is "part of broader processes of globalisation and postmodernity in the region" (p. 74).

As a matter of fact, different representations of mobile messaging technology within local cultures played a significant role in its local uses. Mobile text messaging has been regarded as a driving force of Internet economy in China. A few of the major Chinese web portals that suffered from financial deficits began to turn a profit after they provided text messaging services around 2001. This huge market success makes text messaging an eye-catching cultural phenomenon celebrated by the mass media, wireless carriers, phone manufacturers, and even the government. Some Chinese participants mentioned during their interviews that at the time they adopted text messaging, it was being promoted as a new technology, a new means of communication, and even a new cultural practice that no one should miss. It represents the direction of an advanced culture within the Chinese discourse context of the "Three Representations".[5] Another study of Chinese mobile phone users conducted in 2000 found that "the adoption of...mobile phones in China has symbolic significance: not only are they communication devices, but instruments of social status" (Wei, 2006, p. 992). A young Chinese generation was eager to integrate mobile phones into "their conspicuous, westernized and socially active lifestyle" (p. 991).

In comparison, besides TV commercials, the biggest marketing campaign for text messaging at the American site was the text-to-vote for *American Idol*, a popular talent show on the Fox TV network. Text messaging is primarily seen as a fun and entertaining means of communication.

So far I have traced a big picture of situated uses in two local contexts and noted contextual influences, including the following: factors that come from a material context such as technology access, mobile phone service design, and cost; and factors that come from a broad sociocultural context such as community, cultural dimensions including collectivism vs. individualism and orality vs. literacy, gender, and technology representations in local culture. Of course, this is not a complete list, and we could add other factors to enrich and complicate this sketch, such as individual factors (e.g., personal background, values, and interests), ways of life, past use experiences, daily activities, and interpretations of all these life experiences.

To be sure, an activity of local use mediated by a technology is never a random phenomenon, but always situated in the nexus of myriad contextual influences. At the same time, the local use forms as an articulation of these complex interactions. This articulation, as a way of context mapping in a technological culture—as we discuss in Chapters 1 and 3—integrates practices and meanings. All of the contextual elements reviewed above that make up the articulation not only shape user action but also build user interpretation of the studied technology, particularly those elements that come from the sociocultural context like community, gender, and representation. Even elements derived from a material context—for example, the service design of a cell phone—can be read as a regulation process on a cultural circuit (du Gay et al., 1997), which impacts user's perception of the messaging technology.

Thereby we see localized social motives being realized in concrete use practices through the genre of mobile messaging technology and being articulated as numerous modes of local uses. Situated in the middle of the dynamic interactions, the local use of text messaging presents the duality of the technology on various contextual levels. Drawing from Giddens' structuration theory (1984), Orlikowski (1992) argues that technology use in an organizational context is not only socially constructed in human interpretive actions "through the different meanings they attach to it and the various features they emphasize and use" but also a "part of the objective, structural properties of the organization" (p. 406). The local use of text messaging shares this similar duality. In the individual context, Emma was observed to be actively attaching meanings to the new technology (such as text messaging) in her life sphere and weaving them into her ensemble of communication technologies with agency. However, by doing this, she also confined herself to a structure and a system of technologies in which she would get lost and overwhelmed. In the sociocultural context, Lili was observed to employ the implicit style of text messaging for her communication with friends as it fit her personality and identity. But at the same time, her use was indeed reinforcing the structuring factors and the social norms surrounding her.

To conclude, a local use of mobile messaging technology is situated at the intersection of various contexts, including the immediate context, the community context, and the sociocultural context. Each use has a local purpose and a social motive. On the one hand, participants used this technology to accomplish tasks in their immediate contexts. For example, Mei chose text messaging for exchanging thoughts with sports fan friends when watching late-night TV games because she did not want to disturb other family members. On the other hand, these users texted in order to achieve social motives recognized in the sociocultural context. In the same case, Mei wanted to share her game-watching experience and excitement with her friends and in so doing increased bonds within their fan community. Here, both activities and meanings are mediated by the technological artifact in the use process. They are integrated and make up for a holistic user experience. In the next section, we will look closely at the meaning-construction aspect of text messaging use.

Meaning Constructed out of User Localization

Meaning construction is important to achieve culturally localized user experience. Without constructed meanings involved, situated use interactions cannot be regarded as use experience, but only use activities. When a user is able to make sense of his or her particular technology use activity, we say that the user experience has come into being. What makes a culturally localized user experience different from a *common* user experience is that CLUE emphasizes the agency of users, through which users creatively customize and localize a technology to fit into their ways of life, contributing to their identity-building processes.

Culturally localized user experience acknowledges and is founded on user localization. The forming of culturally localized user experience depends on whether a user has successfully localized a technology into his or her local context. In the case of mobile text messaging, frequent users developed various localization strategies to integrate the technology into their life styles. Messaging technology was Sophie's sweet chocolate to share with girlfriends in a stressful work environment, Lili's pure water to savor for long-lasting friendships, Brian's convenient tool to coordinate with friends, Mei's idioms solitaire to engage with other sports fan friends late at night, and Emma's nice gesture to her people as she grew and matured in her nomadic way of life. Each of them used the technology differently and interpreted it differently, and their interpretations played a significant role in shaping their use experiences.

To extend the discussion of Chapters 2 and 3 about meaning-making in technology design, I next connect these concrete use cases with the influence of consumer culture on technology design and with the mediation of meaning on a cultural circuit. I argue that user localization efforts of mobile text messaging contribute to the dynamic meaning-making process of technology *design* as cultural consumption.

Active Meaning-Making during Cultural Consumption

As one element of a cultural circuit, cultural consumption is indeed an important issue for British cultural studies. Historically, schools of cultural theories (e.g., the Frankfurt School and structuralism) have treated consumption as a coercive practice determined by social structure. Accordingly, this negative image of consumers who passively consume what is in their hands without making a creative contribution has been carried over to technology design. However, the Latin root of consumption, *consumare,* actually means "to consummate" and to "bring to completion." Thereby consumption is "simultaneously destroying (using up) and creating (bringing to fulfillment)" (Paterson, 2006, p. 8). To be sure, consumption is never "a mere shadow of production," as Storey (1999) indicates (p. 168). Using Gramscian hegemony theory, he describes today's popular culture as a "compromise equilibrium" consisting of both "resistance" and "incorporation," "structure" and "agency." This characterization shares a great resemblance to the same "enabling and constraining" theme we have seen from the use cases of mobile text messaging. It also explains why cultural studies is always interested in "the way these cultural commodities are appropriated and *made* meaningful in acts of cultural consumption; often in ways not intended or even envisaged by their producers" (p. 150, emphasis as it is), because these acts of cultural consumption, or user localization, are the crucial matter of our everyday lives.

This form of cultural consumption is production "governed by agency" (p. 159). For example, subcultural studies of punk culture and queer culture have been examined and celebrated by scholars for their rebellious acts against mainstream culture through their peculiar consumption patterns. In this way, creative appropriation—using an object in an unintended way—is a form of cultural production, such as repurposing text messaging technology from a voicemail alert service to a communication channel between peers. Michel de Certeau (1984), a proponent of the "pleasures of consumption," maintains that consumption is production in its own right. Engaging in consumption as a productive activity, consumers apply creative strategies to attach meanings to the objects they consume and make sense of their everyday practices. This kind of creative power clearly surfaced in Mei's efforts to localize mobile text exchanges into idioms solitaire in her fan community, or from the tactics Sophie employed to provide emotional support within her work environment. When consumers are actively making the technological objects in hand meaningful through the process of consumption, consumption is no longer the end of a process—production—but a continuation of the production, or the "secondary production," where meanings are actively constructed. It should be referred to as "the 'work' of consumption" (Mackay, 1997, p. 7).

The consumption itself is "the articulation of a sense of identity" (ibid, p. 4). Storey (1999) further posits that identity became an issue in British cultural studies starting in the 1970s, and the relationship between identity and consumption is a key feature of postmodernism. Compared to a traditional identity interpreted as fixed and coherent, a postmodern view of identity is taken as a plural form, and as multiple and mobile identities "constructed and always in a process of becoming, but never complete, as much about the future as the past" (p. 135), constituted in multiple layers of cultural contexts. Emma's use story of text messaging over the years illustrates this becoming process of identity formation. In this sense, consumption is a means of performing for establishing and changing identities. We define ourselves with the way we use and consume everyday objects; for example, the tendency to use the iconic iPod rather than another MP3 music listening device in college, or to use OpenOffice rather than MS Office in a community of knowledge workers. *I use/consume, therefore I am.* No wonder some participants claimed that "text messaging is my form of communication."

A dialogic view of meaning creation is "an active process rather than a static entity" (Wertsch, 1991, p. 52). The notion of *double articulation* illuminates how meanings of interactive technologies are circulated and generated on a cultural circuit as a dynamic process, as Silverstone and Haddon (1996) maintain. The first articulation occurs as "the meanings of all objects and technologies are articulated through the practices and discourses of their production, marketing, and use" (p. 62). The meaning of mobile messaging technology was prescribed and embedded in the process of production, for example, a voicemail alert service, or a technology seemingly "useless" to wireless carriers for which the telecommunication network could charge a low cost or offer for free. Then the prescribed meaning was recognized, acknowledged, and altered as the text messaging technology entered the social circulation. In the processes of consumption, identity, and representation, original meanings were challenged, and new meanings were added as some Western European teenagers took over the technology as their communication channel. Meanwhile, the vigorous meaning-making process went through a process of regulation as the technology use adjusted and responded to the development of local technological infrastructures, the design of messaging service, and other changes of cultural, economic, and political conditions, e.g., when SMS was used to organize smart mobs in the Philippines (Rheingold, 2002) or when messages of political jokes were circulated among Chinese cell phone users during the SARS outbreak (Yu, 2004).

The second articulation comes from the communicative nature of the technology. As an interactive technology, mobile messaging "carr[ies] a second level of meaning" in culture with "their programmes, narratives, rhetorics, genres, and the software" (Silverstone & Haddon, 1996, p. 62). Therefore, the second articulation and the meanings produced are results of the first articulation. It should be pointed out that, while individual users contributed to the collective meaning-making that occurred on the cultural circuit, a personal discursive practice from the process of localizing technology can be different from the collective one.

Overall, the first articulation occurs as users adopt, use, and localize the technology to fit within their lifestyles. In this articulation, strategies for the use of text messaging technology are developed, and the role of this technology is confirmed in the ensemble of communication technologies, including wireless phone calls, instant messaging, email, and landline phone calls. The second articulation appears out of the first articulation, wherein the meanings of identities and social relationships emerge from the rhetorical and generic rules of the mobile text messaging technology. In Lili's case, she used the messaging technology not only to represent and enhance her identity but also to identify with a social tradition.

Genius Loci: Situatedness and Constructive Subjectiveness

Cultural consumption based on a process of double articulation is "reflexive" in its nature. Through double articulation, "we learn how to consume and what to consume. And through our involvement in consumption, we learn to display who and what we are" (ibid, p. 65). In the process of constructing their identities, consumers are developing their expertise as "cultural experts" to localize technologies according to their lifestyles, as shown in Chapters 5–9. In this sense, a local use is an articulation work of self and locale,[6] which involves concrete use activities surrounding the user's identity and self in his or her local context. *Genius loci* epitomizes "constructive subjectiveness" arising from a locale. Originally from architecture and Greek mythology, it has been used to refer to the "spirit of the place." In the HCI context, Eriksén (2002) extends "genius loci" to characterize "a place where the subjective and objective meet and define each other in and through action" (p. 442). Therefore the notion of *genius loci* moves forward from the "situatedness" and the embodiment of the interactions and encounters in a local context to the "constructive subjectiveness" at the intersection of self and locale. Users chose text messaging to help them create, present, and maintain their identities to navigate through daily activities in different life spheres for genius loci. And the technology acquires meanings through social practices.

In Mei's case, her bedroom, decorated with sports memorabilia, was a site for situated use and identity construction. When she engaged in messaging conversations with her sports fan friends late at night, "genius loci" thus emerged from the idioms solitaire she and her friends played, which strengthened the sense of unity within her fan community. It exemplifies both the "situatedness" of the technology and the "constructive subjectiveness" as well. In terms of constructive subjectiveness, the meaning of a technology was able to be constructed and completed with Mei's participation and use. This technology was thus localized by Mei and became *her* technology. This process of "artful integration" (Suchman, 2002) is what user localization aims to achieve for a culturally localized user experience.

In another case from the fieldwork, 23-year-old Chinese male journalist Ding compared wireless phone calls to text messaging to a metaphor from Maslow's hierarchy of needs. He defined phone calls as something located on the bottom level of physiological needs, such as food and shelter, while text messaging was on an upper level, which deals with spiritual needs. One primary function of messaging for him was a writing contest among his close colleagues to show who was wittiest. The person who outsmarted everyone else in one's message composition won. He and his colleagues exchanged text messages in settings where it was perfectly appropriate to have a direct face-to-face conversation, e.g., sitting together in the backseat of a taxi, but they still preferred texting because meaning differed in the written form from the verbal one. In this instance of genius loci, the subjectivity overshadowed the objectivity of the technology.

The meaning construction of genius loci is deeply rooted in an energetic process of user localization: Genius loci emerges and originates from a user's efforts to localize a technology into his or her life sphere. User localization links the instrumental aspect of the mere use process with the subjective use experience situated in a particular cultural context and demonstrates that frequent users actively localize technologies to fit into the fabrics of their daily lives in order to establish and maintain their identities.

Clearly, meaning construction is not separated from situated action in this process, but closely intertwined. Indeed, both aspects are two sides of one coin. For example, the gendering practice of text messaging use, discussed in the previous section, can be read from both the lens of situatedness and that of constructiveness, and serves as a good example of genius loci in a postmodern globalization age (see Hjorth, 2009). In one case, Uy-Tioco (2008) studied Filipina overseas workers in the U.S. who maintained transnational motherhood via frequent text messaging in order to stay involved with family routines half a world away, such as checking in with children about their school day, reminding them to do their homework, assisting in planning for dinner, and bidding good-night. In another case not related to gender, Barendregt (2008) discusses the identity formation of Indonesian mobile young Muslims through their peculiar text messaging pattern—using a form of street language for chat and wordplay to "allude to contemporary events or current politics and developments in mass culture"—in the post-1998 period after the fall of the Suharto dictatorship (p. 166). Such examples of genius loci—the weaving of situatedness and constructed subjectiveness—are abundant in the research of mobile phone culture (e.g., Bell, 2005; Campbell, 2008; Horst & Miller, 2006; Shade, 2008). In all the cases above, users are self-conscious cultural experts who construct, maintain, and perform their identities with active user localization according to their lifestyles.

The social circulation process of text messaging is both enabling and constraining. On the one hand, Mei and Ding were such proficient cultural experts that they chose an interactive technology based on their communication needs and persuasion goals, and they constructed their identities by utilizing the genre convention of this technology in their own ways. On the other hand, multiple layers of contexts are articulated into use, and various cultural influences are integrated into this "stabilized-for-now" (a.k.a., genre) through the identity work, including power and ideology. For instance, the same texting technology that empowers migrant mothers "further entraps them in the web of transnational migrant labour, perpetuating the divide between the global North and South" (Uy-Tioco, 2008, p. 121).

To sum up, culturally localized user experience represents a stance toward respecting use practices of individual local users, as described in Chapter 3. This design approach starts with an in-depth study of situated user activities for insights and continues in a cycle of rigorous user-centered design emphasis as users localize a technology to fit their lifestyles and make sense of it. An ongoing dialogic interaction[7] occurs between developer localization and user localization in which developers closely watch users' reactions and timely upgrade technologies in order to support emerging users' activities in context and improve future localization performance. The dialogic nature of user localization offers opportunities to incorporate the complex subjectiveness of technology use into an objective design process, and therefore constitutes an energetic and co-constructive relationship between designers and users. Accordingly, designers will be able to design better resources to support various local uses that resonate with users' lifestyles.

More important, the fruitful contributions users have made to the meaning-making process through technology use promote them to crucial co-designers in the design process, someone who is involved in or assists in "determin[ing] the detailed interfaces in all their forms that implement technology in everyday life" (Heskett, 2005, p. 136), for they bring precious user knowledge and need expertise to the table, as illustrated in the discussion of mobile messaging use. With regards to meaning making as an active process in constituting user experience, much of the meaning circulated on the cultural circuit comes from users, rather than prescribed by designers or embedded in the structure. This finding elevates the status of users as co-designers in the design process and signifies the necessity of extending design to use and converting use outcome into design resources in a cyclical view of design, which I will further explore in the next chapter.

Technology Affordance as Mediation Property

After developing a lucid understanding of the essential features of culturally localized user experience through local uses of mobile messaging technology, situatedness and constructiveness, a natural question to ask is "What could the cross-cultural design community do to invoke, encourage, and assist local users to create their culturally localized user experiences?" To answer the question, I will discuss how the community could help local users achieve structured affordances by examining the dialogic relationship between affordances and a dual mediation process through technology use. I will also demonstrate and review how structured affordances play out in various culturally localized user experiences and discuss the role and functions of affordances in a cross-cultural design approach that integrates action and meaning.

Designers have been accustomed to equating affordances to technology features. Quite often the references to technology affordances in conference papers and magazine articles actually denote program functionalities. As discussed in Chapter 3, this static vision of affordance contributes to the mindset of focusing on lower-level interaction modalities in technology design, and this mindset complicates the problem of poor use experience in cross-cultural design. Contrary to this, an activity approach like CLUE suggests regarding affordances as the action possibilities posed by an artifact in use. It represents a three-way dialogic relationship between a technology, a user, and a user's concrete activity, situated in a concrete context. This approach is closely related to a dual mediation process, which consists of mediation of action and mediation of meaning.

In Chapter 3 I describe technology use as a dual mediation process. Technology affordances unfold in this praxis of use and develop as a result of the interplay of habituated uses and sociocultural influences. As action possibilities, affordances emerge when action and meaning

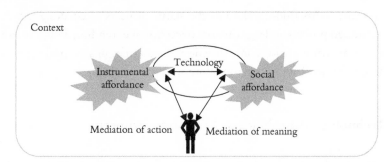

FIGURE 10.1   Structured Affordances Arising from a Dual Mediation Process

are mediated through technology use, so affordances, as properties of interactions, are indeed properties of mediation. Observed with the lens of rhetorical genre theory, technology affordances, functioning like the forms of a genre (with its history and addressivity), are designed to invoke use action, meaning construction, and thus a conversation between a user and a technology.

Structured affordance emerges out of a dual mediation process (see Fig. 10.1). Operational affordance and instrumental affordance of a technology invoke and compel particular user action, which forms the mediation of action. Meanwhile, social affordance of the technology arises as meaning is constructed from the mediation of meaning. Put another way, when a meaning of a technology is invoked and created by a user, then comes the social affordance. Though social affordance comes from meaning construction, this does not necessarily suggest that the meaning constructed is meaningful to a user in his or her local context. When a social affordance does not make sense to a user, one will not recognize its value, and he or she might just walk away from that technology. For instance, when text messaging technology was first introduced to the public as a voicemail alert service, though people were able to use and interpret it, few people could relate to its social affordance and make sense of it. Accordingly, the technology did not grab people's attention until a few years later when new meaning was introduced by some teenagers with their innovative use and when new social affordance came into shape. Clearly, structured affordances emerge as the material and the discursive are fused together through technology use.

Findings across the American and Chinese sites suggest that frequent users adopted and developed a variety of local uses of mobile text messaging as a result of the combined affordances of the perceived technology. During the *instrumental mediation*, when users interacted with the technology, instrumental affordances (e.g., silent, quick, and direct communication; discreet action; delayed responses) built into the mobile messaging technology through design emerged to support users' daily communication activities situated in context. At the same time, social affordances (e.g., unobtrusively staying in contact, expressing feelings, and sharing support constantly and almost everywhere) came out in the *communicative mediation* and afforded particular sociocultural practices when users were making sense of their practices. From these patterns of use, the instrumental affordances of mobile messaging technology supported personal communication tasks in particular situations so well that they filled personal communication gaps other technologies were unable to complete. As users were able to acquire meanings through those practices, they began to value the social affordances of mobile text messaging and see its role in their lives. Thus, various uses of this technology in the personal life sphere were found in fieldwork. Participants used the technology to stay in touch with old friends at a distance, to connect with family members, to socialize with new acquaintances introduced to them by friends, to coordinate schedules, to exchange sports reviews late at night, to look for people in a quiet place like the library, to amuse and cheer up friends, and so on. For more detailed discussion of the interaction between the two types of affordances, please read the individual case studies presented in Chapters 5–9.

The fieldwork also sheds light on the complex relationships between instrumental affordances and social affordances in use. As discussed in Chapters 3 and 7, social affordances arise out of instrumental affordances through users' interactions in local contexts, and thus the same instrumental affordances (quick, quiet, discreet) might lead to different social affordances and support different social uses (for fun or for staying in contact) when affordances are realized in different contexts.

Participants adopted text messaging as it fit within their lifestyles and their local IT ecology. They constantly made media choices from a range of communication technologies, selecting the one they felt fit best for a particular communication situation and their audience. Text messaging was not the only communication technology participants used to augment their life and work. The patterns of mobile messaging use should be understood and interpreted in a web or an ensemble of different technologies situated in local contexts. The fieldwork found that participants had developed sophisticated strategies to use different technologies for different audiences, as shown in Lili's and Emma's cases. Some participants mapped different people into an imaginary "communication matrix." For others, they unconsciously did this. Text messaging was a particular way for participants to communicate with a particular group of people in their lives.

Just as social affordances are closely related to users' lifestyles, they were so important to some users that they would ignore the poor usability of the technology. In Lili's case, she had a high tolerance for the inconvenience of the technology for the sake of its social affordances. She stuck to mobile text messaging technology even though she frequently had to delete extra characters in order to fit her long messages into the size limit.

Participants acknowledged and valued the social affordances of mobile text messaging technology. In the survey, they ranked social-related purposes as their top reasons to participate in text messaging and mentioned how they loved the social affordance of the technology:

> "It's like you get a little greeting card in the mail every day. It's nice to know you thought of someone that made you laugh."

> "It's fun to get a message. Like the movie *You've got mail*. It is always a surprise."

> "You xie qing gan de biao da neng tong guo duan xian lai wan chen, shi yi jian te bie mei li de shi qing (It's a very beautiful thing to convey certain feelings with text messaging)."

> "Tong hua shi yi shi zhu xing, duan xiao xi shi jing shen ceng mian shang de (Calling is like food and shelter, which fulfills my basic needs, but texting fulfills my spiritual desires)."

As a dialogic three-way relationship between a technology, a user, and a user's concrete activity in a concrete context, there are interactions between instrumental affordances and social affordances, as described above, and interactions between a technology and the surrounding context. For example, affordances of a technology not only afford uses but also constrain uses. First, in the cases of Chinese participants Mei and Ding, the instrumental affordance of mobile messaging resulted in a reduced use of email. Second, while text messages could be sent almost everywhere and anytime with more creativity and humor, the message size limit also shaped the nature of communication—for instance, only brief exchanges were privileged, even though 70 Chinese characters are able to convey more meanings than 160 English letters. While being a general characteristic of affordance, this "enabling" and "constraining" characteristic becomes more remarkable in cross-cultural technology design. Cross-cultural design is never neutral or instrumental, as seen in the water hyacinth effect from the case of mobile messaging use between hateful tribes in Kenya and Nigeria, as discussed in Chapter 1.

The various personal uses of mobile messaging actually depart from the intended use of the original design. Chapter 4 describes how mobile text messaging was designed, introduced, and marketed as a business technology. Due to the combined affordances of the technology perceived by participants, text messaging was used for personal communication rather than business communication across sites, contrary to the designer's original intention. There is a large gap between the intended use and the actual uses, since most of the actual uses fell within the private life sphere. This might be beyond the designer's thoughts, but it is a logical development, considering the affordances of the technology. We might want to ask: What kinds of business tasks do the affordances of mobile text messaging best support in context? How do these affordances work for situated activities in context? Do people have to rely on affordances such as quick and direct communication of mobile messaging to accomplish business tasks when they can use other available communication technologies? We do not want to forget that affordance is a three-way dialogic relationship between a technology, a user, and a user's concrete activity. Just focusing on a technology itself without considering a user and his or her concrete activity in a surrounding context will not help designers go very far toward accomplishing user goals.

For the cross-cultural design community, the discussion of a dual mediation process of technology use and the structured affordances that originate demonstrates the importance of fostering a holistic view of user experience. This holistic view will help to link action and meaning in the design process with a dialogic feature and cultivate affordances for culturally diverse users. In this mass-production-focused consumption era, when new technological products are pushed onto the market every day, a usable but not meaningful product will not be able to stay long on the market. By the same token, a product that has been proved successful in one local market because of its usefulness and meaningfulness for users in that locale could turn out to be usable but incomprehensible in another cultural context.

A structured view of affordances informed by a dual mediation process can help us locate user needs and prioritize design goals in the design process. In the case of mobile text messaging, the fieldwork findings clearly state that users valued social affordance, an affordance on the activity level. Users want a technology that they find both usable and meaningful. It is time for the cross-cultural design community to think about designing for higher-level activity and aim beyond instrumental affordances.

Conclusion

The goal of this chapter is to further develop the CLUE framework as outlined in Chapter 3, to illustrate the interaction and integration of action and meaning with examples of local uses of mobile messaging technology, and to elevate the role of users to co-designers in the design process. I situate five individual cases on a broader horizon, the American and Chinese contexts, and even the global context, and then review the trends of user localization across the sites. Thereby I illuminate how a holistic view of user experience is both situated and constructed in local contexts: To explore the "situatedness," I look at how a local use of mobile messaging technology is situated in the surrounding contexts as the outcome of the interactions of various cultural influences on different levels. To investigate the "constructiveness,"

I demonstrate how user localization functions as cultural consumption and how "genius loci" is achieved by integrating situatedness and subjective constructiveness. Based on this holistic view of user experience, I examine affordances as dialogic relation through a dual mediation process of messaging use and suggest designing beyond operational affordances and cultivating social affordances for local use.

Because my goal here is to fully develop and highlight the CLUE framework, I chose to place the three major intellectual traditions reviewed in Chapter 3—activity theory, British cultural studies, and genre theory—as the backdrop and deliberately mark out their influences on the CLUE framework, to a lesser extent, when I went over the key features of CLUE via a consolidated case discussion or presented lively user experiences earlier in those use case chapters. I believe good theories "illuminate" what we are watching in research as a spotlight (Maxwell, 1996), and it is most important to be able to watch things clearly. Think of a metaphor of pebbles in a creek at dusk, which I'd like to use to compare to the research subject of this book. The creek can be regarded as our everyday life experience, which flows in its own path, and various sizes of pebbles are various use actions surrounding the mobile messaging technology, which are hard to see in dusky light. As researchers, we use certain spotlights in order to see the distinctive and interesting patterns of the pebbles and appreciate their existence (and their meanings) in the creek. While we see these patterns, such as action, meaning, genre, affordances, and so on, we do not have to be constantly reminded of what spotlights are held in our hands as we marvel at the wonder of the nature, in this sense, theories like activity theory, British cultural studies, or genre theory. To me, the key features of the CLUE framework are more important than their intellectual roots when cases are reviewed.

On the other hand, we should be aware that we have been able to see those interesting patterns because of the particular spotlights used in this study—the integrated perspective developed from activity theory, British cultural studies, and genre theory allows us to see the dynamic interactions between practices and meanings, and between various contextual and cultural factors on different levels. For example, if activity theory had not been used in analysis, we would not have been able to see how a local use of a technology is situated and shaped by the concrete use activity other than by cultural dimensions, and we would not have been able to see the relationship of instrumental affordances and social affordances in local uses. If British cultural studies had been missing, we would have lacked a perspective to interpret the mediation of meanings in everyday life practices, and we would have missed the complex process of "constructive subjectiveness" emerging from user localization. Last, if genre theory had been neglected, we would not have been able to see technology affordances as mediation property, and we would not have been able to observe how affordances "enable and constrain" technology uses in cross-cultural design.

Furthermore, the key concepts informed by the three theoretical constructs interact with each other in an integrative approach. Here, "meaningful action" comes from activity theory but is also influenced by the discursive angle of British cultural studies; "situated meaning" is shaped by British cultural studies, but this "situatedness" clearly derives from activity theory; and genre theory welds these two sides of a coin into the concrete uses of mobile messaging technology via activity-based affordances. As the three approaches are combined into one spotlight, there might not be such a need to point out what beam of light comes from which bulb.

The CLUE framework presents much potential to enrich current cross-cultural technology design practice and research, and will address the weakness resulting from the cultural dimensions approach. Inspected with a dual mediation process view, clearly models of cultural dimensions are lacking in the following areas:

First, because this approach of cultural dimensions primarily relies on solidified cultural values to account for cultural differences, meaning is not treated in a dynamic mediation process but rather is mostly regarded as a static virtue. In this manner, meanings are not constructed but are attached or added at a later stage of design, replaceable for different audiences and for different contexts. Discounting the complexity of meaning construction and the multitudes of interpretations, this design mechanism functions like a psychology test for young children. When a sketch of an apple is presented to a toddler, a tester will feel happy if the toddler, with his limited life experience, is able to recognize it as food. However, we cannot expect that our local users in a concrete context will behave like a toddler—they may interpret the sketch of an apple as a product brand, the knowledge taken by Adam and Eve from the Tree, or some other meaning. Many interpretation possibilities could arise, but unfortunately they will probably be ignored with a narrow and static vision of meaning.

Second, as discussed in early chapters, the mediation of action is missing in this design approach because models of cultural dimensions attend only to the discursive aspect of a design, though in a narrow way, as described above. Third, because the mediation of action is a blind spot in this approach, the mediation of meaning is not coordinated, synced, or integrated with the mediation of action. In the perspective of Vygostky (Wertsch, 1991), who was an early founder of activity theory, meaning is "part of and *mediate* human action" (p. 29, emphasis as it is). This indicates that meaning cannot independently exist outside of action. This stance inquires into the logical foundation of and the methodological legitimacy of the current practice of adding meaning at a later stage of the design process.

As an integrated approach, the CLUE framework regards action and meaning as two sides of the same coin, which is incorporated into a coherent dual mediation process. In this mediation process, both action and meaning are linked, synced, and coordinated in a dynamic way. For many years, designers have been asking one question: "How can we make a technology more usable?" The CLUE approach suggests that we go further: "How can we make a technology both usable and meaningful?" This goal is achieved through a deep understanding of the user experience of local users, a mediation process that includes tool-mediated production and sign-mediated communication. Only with this dual mediation process in mind can we design technologies that work in local contexts successfully.

In Chapter 3, I outline seven defining features of the CLUE framework:

1. The CLUE approach highlights the praxis of use.
2. Local culture constitutes the dynamic nexus of contextual interactions and manifests numerous articulations of practices and meanings.
3. User experience is both situated and constructed.
4. Technology use is a dual mediation process.
5. Structured affordance comes from dialogic interactions.

6. Culturally localized user experience respects use practices of individual local users and values their efforts at user localization.

7. Design is both problem solving and engaged conversation.

The first six features are further developed and presented in this chapter through a review of the essence of the CLUE framework—situated use activities and constructed meanings of use—and a discussion of the exigency to design for culturally localized user experience. It should be noted that the review is done with a focus on how various users actively designed and consummated their culturally localized user experiences of text messaging from their local contexts. Here, users are designers who make and craft their own use experiences with creative agency and cultural expertise, and these user localization efforts are illuminating to the design community on how to achieve cross-cultural design for individual users in this participatory culture.

In the next chapter, I will explore the last distinctive feature of this framework, dialogicality, and point out future directions the cross-cultural design community could take with the stance of dialogicality, in order to invoke and sustain culturally localized user experience. Realistically, culturally localized user experience is accomplished and consummated at the user's site, and it is the individual user who will decide whether she or he enjoys this experience. What the design community could do is design *for* culturally localized user experience and invoke, support, and sustain that experience.

Notes

1. See note 7 of Chapter 4.
2. See Q23 of Appendix A.
3. See Q21 of Appendix A.
4. The gender divide in the group of American heavy texters in 2009 is reported like this: "Older teen girls ages 14–17 lead the charge on text messaging, averaging 100 messages a day for the entire cohort. The youngest teen boys are the most resistant to texting—averaging 20 messages per day" (Lenhart et al., 2010).
5. The "Three Representations" was developed by the former president of the Communist Party of China, Jiang Zenmin. This policy claims that the

Party must always represent the requirements of the development of China's advanced productive forces, the orientation of the development of China's advanced culture, and the fundamental interests of the overwhelming majority of the people in China.

6. Locale is a concept informed by "a practice-oriented vision and a focus on subjective experience" (Sun, 2009b, p. 248). Extending the meaning of physical features of a place, it centers on an activity and its engendered relationship and interactions.

7. Please see Chapter 11 for further discussion about dialogic interaction.

II

Future Directions

After the CLUE framework is fully presented, I'd like to look at the broader implications it brings to cross-cultural technology design. Therefore, in this concluding chapter, I map out my suggestions for future directions the design community should take to craft a usable and meaningful technology.

Following the previous chapter, which extended the empirical study of text messaging use to show how culturally localized user experience is formed at the user's site, this chapter explores how the cross-cultural design community could learn from those user localization efforts to design for, invoke, nurture, encourage, support, and sustain culturally localized user experience—the consummate experience—for emerging technologies. I study the characteristics and value as well as the role and functions of user localization in a technology's whole design, production, and use cycle and discuss how to route those user efforts into the design process to better address user needs and expectations in this *glocalization* age. When needed, I supplement with real-world examples to further the discussion beyond the case study.

The subject matter of this chapter is dialogicality. In order to channel user innovations into cross-cultural technology design, we need to have a deep appreciation for the dialogical nature of culture and that of design. The dialogicality of culture is examined in Chapter 1, and the CLUE framework is built on this very dialogical understanding of culture. As a result, a CLUE perspective asks the design community to extend our view of design from problem solving to engaged conversation in the era of participatory culture.

Dialogicality

A dialogic methodology originating from Bakhtin's notion of dialogicality (Bakhtin, 1981, 1986) shapes the view of design in the CLUE framework. Building on his studies in speech genres and social language, Bakhtin notes that nothing is isolated in the world, and any unity is accomplished dialogically. As the cornerstone of Bakhtinian philosophy, dialogicality can be traced throughout Bakhtin's writing (Wertsch, 1991). With such profound influence on the 20th-century humanities and social sciences, Bakhtin's dialogism is characterized as "an ontology and epistemology of the disciplines requiring mutual acknowledgement of two or more consciousnesses" (Marková, 2003, p. 14).

Dialogicality is indeed a critical and fundamental concept for IT fields, such as human–computer interaction, interaction design, and professional and technical communication, because the terms "interaction" and "communication" connote a dialogue between at least two entities (a person, a subject, an object, an actor/actant, a meaning, a perspective, a voice, and/or consciousness, etc.) aiming for negotiating, constructing, and creating something new. Tracking Bakhtin's interest in Socrates' dialogue form and situating the development of Bakhtinian dialogicality in the rhetorical tradition, Zappen (2004) argues that Bakhtin's dialogism transforms the relationship between speakers and listeners, or designers and users in our context, in which multiple voices are introduced into the discourse to "test and contest and create or re-create ideas tacitly and unreflectively held to be true," thereby "render[ing] ourselves accountable to others in an ongoing exchange of voices" (p. 15).

Wright, McCarthy, and Meekison (2003) declare that Bakhtin's dialogicality is his "central contribution" to experience design (p. 45). According to McCarthy and Wright (2004), a dialogic worldview believes that "any unity is composed of many voices in unfinalized conversations that cannot be reified monologically" (p. 72). They state that this dialogic worldview connects action and meaning through "intoning," i.e., "how individuals make acts their own, how they make them unique, personal experiences through the particularities of interpreting, feeling, and making value judgments and distinctions that are ethically worthwhile" (p. 56). Based on this dialogic methodology, they argue for a holistic approach to experience consisting of "the creativity of action and the dialogicality of meaning making" (p. 184), which is also adopted in the CLUE framework.

Of course an interactive, dialogic, and dynamic characteristic marks many contemporary humanistic and social science approaches (e.g., hermeneutics, pragmatism, and phenomenology), among which Bakhtinian dialogism might be one of the most influential; however, this is not the major reason that I chose it to underline the CLUE framework. Bakhtinian dialogism is fundamental to the CLUE framework for the following reasons: It treats different voices independently and respectfully, and thus users' voices will not be ignored or discounted; it stresses the role of the self, the subjectivity, in a dialogue and thus emphasizes users' agency; and it promotes an energetic, multivoiced view of communication rather than a static transmission model and thus values users' contributions. All of these will help to address problems of integrating action and meaning in context that have been undermining cross-cultural design practices for a long time, as shown in the following two cases.

First, Bakhtin's dialogicality is instrumental in integrating meaning and cognition. Cultural psychologist Wertsch (1991) asserts, "human communicative and psychological processes are characterized by a dialogicality of voices" (p. 13). In his studies of language use in the schooling practices, he appropriates Bakhtin's social language and speech genres to investigate how influences from the sociocultural setting shape the development of individual psychological process with his mediated action approach. Though Wertsch does not examine technology as meditational means in his studies, his findings are insightful for the HCI field. On the one hand, user modeling based on cognition has been a driving force in HCI design, but it is not well connected with the interpretative aspect of actions, as shown in Hutchins' work (1995). Usually the two aspects have been treated as two separate factors that overdetermined a design. On the other hand, as universalistic approaches of cognitive models overshadowed other cognitive approaches in HCI designs for a long time, particularly during the 1990s, the sociocultural situatedness of cognition was ignored. Accordingly, user models based on a universal and individualist design philosophy have caused many problems in cross-cultural technology design, e.g., a Maori user's frustration with a digital library as shown in Chapter 2. So when Wertsch illustrates the sociocultural situatedness of mediated action (i.e., user tasks accomplished with a technology) in a convincing argument with the Bakhtinian notion of dialogicality, it manifests the necessity to start cognition modeling from a local context and shows us possible ways to connect user modeling to interpretation on an upper level.

Second, a multivoiced, dialogic approach makes it possible to have multiple, potentially competing interpretations that coexist in design, as I have argued in other places (Sun, 2009a). In HCI design and cross-cultural technology design, the dominant communication axiom follows a transmission model that assumes a single, univocal message is transmitted from sender to receiver. For example, design approaches based on cultural dimensions models aim to transmit one univocal meaning from designers to users through narrowly localized interface features. Here, the design goal is just to convey meanings, and these meanings are regarded as fixed entities, neatly packaged to be transported from one context to another. In contrast, a dialogic model of communication takes meaning as produced through "an ongoing process of articulation constituted in (and constituting) the relations of meaning and power operating in the entire context within which messages move" (Slack et al., 1993, p. 25), as shown in the discussion of meaning making from the previous chapter. The entire context includes the contexts of designers and users, and the technology itself, in the case of cross-cultural design practice. This mode expects that new meanings will be added and created through users' involvement. To this end, the communication process is "an articulation of voices, much like what Bakhtin has characterized as the orchestration of 'heteroglot, multi-voiced, multi-styled, and often multi-languaged elements'" (p. 31), where multiple interpretations come into fruition.

The notion of dialogicality has the flexibility to be explored in various ways to conceptualize the CLUE framework: as the *interaction* between technology and users, between technology and its surrounding local conditions, and between the local and the global; as *conversations* between designers and users; and as a *defining feature* of the design process. For example, as the defining feature of the design process, Bakhtin's preference for the plural over the singular and for the dialogic over the monologic points toward an open-ended design process of *becoming* that understands users' local situations and conditions, attends to their voices, appreciates their creativity and contributions, respects their subjective experiences, and values their multiple interpretations. This is the essence of a participatory culture, and it is what the CLUE framework strives for in cross-cultural design. Compared to participatory design (Ehn, 1993), which is interested in functional and democratic empowerment of users (see Spinuizzi, 2005) and thus also confines the exploration of user contributions within an organizational context, the CLUE approach seeks to understand user contributions from their cultural contexts and individual experiences and aims to empower users functionally, democratically, emotionally, and spiritually.

This multivoiced, dialogic methodology is the fundamental philosophy behind the CLUE framework, which integrates key concepts explored in Chapter 10—situated action, constructed meaning, a dual mediation process, and affordances—into a coherent framework. Indeed, as the hallmark of genre theory, dialogicality is essential in connecting the mediation of action (see activity theory) and the mediation of meaning (see British cultural studies) if we go back to Chapter 3 to trace the interactions of the three intellectual traditions. With a dialogic emphasis guiding through the whole cross-cultural design process, the CLUE approach argues to foster an ongoing conversation between designers and users and support interactions between technology and users, technology and its surrounding local conditions, and the local and the global, in what McCarthy & Wright (2004) describe as follows: "When we think of design as dialogical, concerned with the ways in which people interacting with technologies consummate themselves in the technologies and the technology in themselves, we point to the openness and unfinalizability of a world that, though already half-designed, is always becoming" (p. 196).

For the rest of the chapter, I discuss the following future directions the cross-cultural design community should take to invoke, initiate, encourage, support, and sustain culturally localized user experiences in the age of participatory culture through a dialogic approach.

- Initiating the dialogue on a cultural circuit
- Expanding the scope of localization
- Meeting local cultural expectations with user localization
- Understanding user experience as cultural consumption

Initiating the Dialogue on a Cultural Circuit

A dialogic approach to cross-cultural design believes that different influences from the milieu of technology, user, and activity interact and mesh in complex ways during technology design and use. These complex interactions do not happen randomly, but occur on a cultural circuit of a globalization age. A cultural circuit comprises five key processes of artifact use: representation, identity, production, consumption, and regulation. These processes *continually* overlap and intertwine with each other. Being a developmental perspective to examine technology use in context, the notion of cultural circuit describes how various contextual and cultural factors act together and interrelate in complex ways from the angle of the signifying practices. In particular, the cultural circuit view of technology use identifies the role of user localization in a design and production cycle.

The complex interactions on a cultural circuit also imply conversations between designers and users. A dialogic cross-cultural design approach considers the design process itself as a dialogue on a cultural circuit. It attends to *glocalization*—the interaction between the local and the global—and regards the efforts of user localization as *local uptakes* (Freadman, 2002) in a global design discourse. A dialogic rhetoric is critical in creating meaningful technology use experience on this circuit. And a mindful design process should encourage conversations between users and designers and initiate a dialogue on a cultural circuit.

Local Uptakes of a Global Design Discourse

So far in this book, much of the discussion has been focused on the interactions between technology and users, and between technology and its surrounding local conditions. The interaction between the local and the global in this globalization age has not been fully explored, yet nobody could overlook the fact that this cultural circuit operates under the forces of globalization. In this section, I argue that efforts of user localization are local uptakes in a global design discourse as they are responding to, taking up, and making use of an original design, in this case, mobile messaging technology.

Text messaging was once marketed and used as a voicemail alert service at its inception—a simple mechanism to inform subscribers that they have a voicemail ready for retrieval (Hill, 2004). Since the first text message sent from the UK in 1992, the mass use of text messaging diffused from Europe to East Asia and North America toward the end of the last century. As presented in the previous chapters, the local uses of mobile text messaging took on different patterns. American participants were interested in sending fun messages to *express* their feelings and share moment-by-moment experiences. Their chats were usually short. A majority of the messages can be regarded as "small talk," in which participants had quick exchanges updating each other about their statuses and other minute life details. Text messaging was reserved for personal and informal use. In contrast, Chinese participants liked to stay in contact with friends via text messaging and sent more messages to *inform*. Long chats exchanged between friends were very common in Chinese message logs, and participants usually had more in-depth conversations over various topics. As a main communication channel for personal life, text messaging was also accepted for use in more formal arenas, such as for sending wedding invitations and holiday greetings, contacting professors or supervisors, and replacing short business email inquiries.

The use difference in the two cultural contexts can be examined by comparing and contrasting local differences in technological, economical, and cultural contexts, which is explicated in Chapter 10, as much of cross-cultural technology use studies would generally do. On the other hand, though an emic (i.e., insider) perspective of and a situated understanding of local use practices are much needed and valuable, we cannot ignore "local-global interplay" (Starke-Meyerring, 2005, p. 483) or fail to realize that "[m]ore is going on locally than just local practice" (Brandt & Clinton, 2002, p. 343).

Local use practices need to be examined in a global context, particularly in this age, when a global telecommunication network links almost everything into a pervasive (and coercive) system. When viewed through the lens of rhetorical genre theory, the local variations of text messaging are not isolated, but form an open, globally networked genre system: Local genres of text messaging share similar technological affordances and some of the same textual features; the technological affordances might evolve at the same time (e.g., the development of multimedia messaging and mobile blogging); local use patterns will influence each other (e.g., the use of text-to-vote has been a common strategy for popular TV programs in countries like the UK, the U.S., and China); and a successful use for a particular task in one locale—the successful response to one situation—is expected to be reproduced in another locale (e.g., American wireless carriers are eager to introduce more business services via text messaging to their customers, like their counterparts in Korea, Japan, and the UK).

As we expect to see "the increasing interdependence and integration of social, cultural, political, and economic processes across local, national, regional, and global levels" (Starke-Meyerring, 2005, p. 470), more local use practices will diffuse through, be copied to, and be imitated by other locales and contexts and take on new generic patterns. Apparently, developing an in-depth understanding of local use practice does not necessarily lead to a full or more complete understanding of that phenomenon. If the text messaging use had been examined in only the Chinese context or only the American context, we would not have been able to notice the dynamic interactions between the local and the global, and we might not have been able to understand why text messaging would be accepted for more formal discourse use in China, instead only taking it as a random and peculiar use phenomenon. Indeed, a technology use practice cannot be just local any more in this age, and every local practice is an *uptake* to the global design discourse as part of globalization.

Having a conceptual implication to cross-cultural technology design, "uptake" refers to a dialogic process of (1) responding to and (2) *taking up* and extending the use of texts/acts/practices responded to. Originating from speech acts theory, it is recast by Freadman (2002) to explore the "bidirectional relation" (i.e., dialogicality) between texts in rhetorical genre theory (p. 40). Though her examples of uptakes are interrelated genres in a genre system, such as a proposal as an uptake to a CFP (call for proposal), she does not rule out the dialogic relation between an instance of a genre and the genre itself. Comparing uptakes to the shots exchanged by tennis players on the tennis court, Freadman (1994) stresses the "enabling and constraining" feature of those shots (i.e., responses) deriving from "the formal-material determinants" (p. 44–45). And an uptake is the outcome of an interaction, which is both constrained and enabled by the utterance to which it responds.

In a technology design and use process, innovative user contributions are shaped in a similar way to an uptake. The value of uptake lies in its nature as a process that "always involves selection and representation that open it up to intention and design" (Kill, 2006, p. 221). Therefore, in the view of Bakhtinian dialogism, uptake is "a negotiation that focuses attention on the translation of intention" (Kill, 2008, p. 68) and "a process of design carried out by a designer in relation to the full complexity of individual intentions and the social purposes that inform them" (p. 73). This characterization precisely describes the virtues of user localization, which helps us to understand that such localization, translation, appropriation, customization, or adaptation from local users are inevitable in this globalization age.

Local uptakes represent the pulling forces that reassert local agency against the pushing force of globalizing trends toward homogeneity and synchronization in a new stage of globalization: glocalization. Glocalization describes the phenomenon that "the globalization of a product or service is more likely to succeed if an attempt at adaptation to the local culture is made" (Paterson, 2006, pp. 80–81). According to Kraidy (2001), the framework of "glocalization" does a better job of exploring contemporary international communication processes between industrialized and developing countries than its two conceptual predecessors: cultural imperialism and globalization. Cultural imperialism, popular between the 1960s and 1980s, is limited with "its assumption of one-way information flow and intentional cultural domination" (p. 39). Globalization, gaining academic ascendency since the 1980s, fails to describe the dialogicality and complexity of contemporary international cultural relations with "its notions of cultural synchronization and world homogenization" (p. 39). Thereby it implies a technology determinist view about development, ignoring local conditions and knowledge (Slack & Wise, 2005). Glocalization, as "a blending of global forces with local elements," recognizes the tension between the global and the local and thus theoretically captures "receding center-periphery international arrangements and emerging decentralized, fragmented, and multifaceted patterns" (Kraidy, 2001, pp. 39–40). However, designers should be aware that this stage of glocalization still functions and is structured under the impact of the postcolonial conditions (Irani, Vertesi, Dourish, Philip, & Grinter, 2010).

The theoretical construct of glocalization helps designers discern the duality issue of technology design, enabling and constraining, on a global level. For example, the well-developed technology infrastructures in industrialized countries might hinder their chances to adopt new technologies as speedily as developing countries do. The world telecommunication report indicates that mobile phone services outnumbered landlines in many developing countries in 2001, while developed countries were working on expanding mobile phone services (Geser, 2005). This phenomenon is called "leapfrogging," which describes how developing countries adopt more advanced technology infrastructure, directly bypassing intermediate technologies. Cell phones have been a major force fueling those documented leapfrogging phenomena (see Donner, 2008), e.g., an ethnographical account of cell phone use by low-income Jamaicans (Horst & Miller, 2006) and a design innovation of using SMS for monitoring drug compliance of the HIV/AIDS patients in remote South African villages (Dray, 2007). Leapfrogging is salient in the case explored in this book—quite a few Chinese participants adopted cell phones directly without ever having a landline phone, and many Chinese participants adopted mobile text messaging before instant messaging.

Localization on a Cultural Circuit

After examining the role user localization plays in a global context, let's trace how user localization functions in a design and production cycle. One question people tend to ask about the phenomenon of text messaging is: Is the mobile text messaging technology well localized or not?

Here we see two contrasting localization phenomena from the developer's site and from the user's site. As discussed in previous chapters, mobile text messaging technology has inherent weaknesses, such as a small display, inconvenient input methods, and a limited message size. When the technology took off, only minimal localization work had been done at the developer's site—primarily the translation of the interface for operational affordances of the technology. Since then, the interface and the functions of the technology have remained almost the same except for the improved inputting methods. The localization work at the developer's site is not exciting. At the user's site, the fieldwork shows that participants worked in various ways to localize the technology successfully into their daily lives: They used mobile text messaging to cope with emotional moments, enhance work and personal life, maintain social contact with old friends, exchange funny jokes, coordinate activities with friends, and so on. Thus, user localization seems to bear fruitful results.

What do the two contrasting localization phenomena suggest for our future cross-cultural design practices? Does this mean that designers might not need to work so hard to address cultural issues in design since interested users will do their homework in their own contexts anyway? This is an unwarranted claim, one that is too optimistic and counts only on user localization for the overall cross-cultural design performance. A cultural circuit view of mobile text messaging (see Figure 11.1) will show us how problematic this conclusion is. On this cultural circuit, five processes—representation, identity, production, consumption, and regulation—link and intertwine with each other. The developer localization occurs during the process of production, designing and initiating the instrumental affordances of mobile text messaging for local users. Then the user localization pervades the processes of consumption,

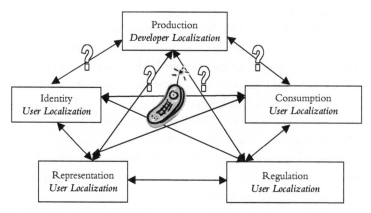

FIGURE 11.1   Localization on a Cultural Circuit (Sun, 2006, p. 475. Used with permission of Taylor & Francis.)

regulation, representation, and identity. Through articulating various cultural factors into the user localization process, users realize the social affordances of the technology through practices. Clearly there is a stronger element of user localization rescuing the weaker developer localization in mobile text messaging, making the circulation of the technology on the circuit possible. However, this might not happen for other technological products. In worse situations, a technological product with poor localization work will not be able to move through this circuit if users refuse to use it or attach social and cultural meanings to it.

The localization success of text messaging technology is an unqualified localization success because it occurs only at the user's site. This technology succeeds despite its inherent use limitations because it offers social affordances that other current technologies are unable to provide. It has its own niche in an ensemble of daily communication technologies available to users: a simple, two-way communication technology with low maintenance that does not have a successor to replace at this moment. With a learning curve not as steep as other more difficult technologies, determined users can get proficient at texting after one or two days of practice. If newer technologies were introduced with similar social affordances as and better instrumental affordances than text messaging, new users would no longer bother to localize text messaging, a technology with such use limitations. The fieldwork already shows this trend: A number of participants reduced the use of text messaging at a later stage due to various reasons: Some American participants thought that text messaging technology was too expensive after their service provider's promotion ended. Several Chinese participants found that other technologies were available to them (for example, email) as the local technology infrastructure improved. Moreover, so many technologies with minimal localization efforts at the developer's site failed on the market, but only mobile text messaging succeeded. The use success of one technology cannot be applied to all technologies.

The circuit view also raises questions for the current developer localization. This view suggests that the mobile messaging technology traverses various processes on the circuit *continually* to accomplish user goals; however, there are problematic links between the production process and the processes of consumption, representation, and identity, which impede a smooth circulation. The links between these processes should be two-way transactions, but the fieldwork seldom found how the production process responded to the use patterns emerging from the processes of consumption, representation, and identity. While it is encouraging to see that, in Lili's case, her phone model ("Dancing Queen") exemplified how a local phone manufacturer responded to the enthusiasm of female users for wireless phones and modified the product to this group of users by adding female-oriented applications, this type of response is still limited in scale. For example, though mobile text messaging technology was used for different communication purposes (fun communication at the American site and relationship communication at the Chinese site), the fieldwork was unable to spot "localized" messaging applications designed to provide instrumental affordances for these different communication functions.

Slowly designers began to notice this trend. For instance, a prototype PDA called "WuKong" developed for Chinese users (Yu & Tng, 2003) rejected the Western conceptual model for applications, documents, and folders, and built on the concept of the *guanxiwang* (i.e., Chinese social network); the Ilkone i800, introduced to the Muslim community in 2004 by a Dubai-based telecommunication company, is equipped with an Arabic-English full text of the Koran and a *kiblah* indicator showing the proper direction to Mecca (Barendregt, 2008). And a few design concepts of localizing text messaging for particular tasks were also advanced in the book *The Inside Text* (Harper, Palen, & Taylor, 2005).

Overall, this circuit view illustrates the importance of a dialogic approach in cross-cultural design: First, a successful cross-cultural design case includes an ongoing interaction between developer's localization and user's localization. These two processes interact with each other in such a way that developer localization provides instrumental affordances for user localization to realize social affordances in use. It also allows the social affordances emerging from the local uses to offer opportunities for developers to design better instrumental affordances and improve localization performance in the next round.

Second, it is possible for a technological product that is poorly localized at the developer's site to still enjoy use success, as long as there is successful user localization that helps close this gap. However, a truly successful localization process will always incorporate a dialogue between developers and users in which developers respond to users' needs in a timely fashion and improve instrumental affordances to support users' activity in context. If this dialogue is problematic or does not exist, any current use success might eventually disappear.

Example: Social Networking Websites as Local Uptakes

The popularity of social networking service (SNS) websites keeps rising globally. The Nielsen Company (2010, 2011) sampled 10 global markets (including the U.S., Australia, Brazil, France, Germany, Italy, Japan, Spain, Switzerland, and the UK) for two years and found "social networks and blogs are the top online destination in each country, accounting for the majority of time spent online and reaching at least 60 percent of active Internet users" (2011, p. 12). The U.S.-based Facebook, which ranked number one among all SNS websites in all those countries, reached only 2% of Japanese users in January 2011. In stark contrast, its reach rate in its home country was 60% at the same time (Tabuchi, 2011). One reason that Japanese users stay away from Facebook is related to a distinctive feature that made this website a huge success in its native culture: using real names and photos for profiles. On the contrary, Japanese users like to keep a high level of anonymity for their profiles—over 75% of Japanese social media users used pseudonyms online around the time of 2009, as supported by the top Japanese SNS website Mixi (Orita & Hada, 2009; Toto, 2008).

Facebook is not the first social networking website that suffers from its insensitivity to local culture. Established in 1999, the most successful SNS website in South Korea, Cyworld, which enjoyed a high penetration rate of 90% of Korean Internet users in their 20s in 2006, had the ambitious plan of trumping MySpace when it entered the American market that year with a $10 million investment (Ali, 2006; Schonfeld, 2006; Tkorea, 2009a). It ended up shutting off its American operation in 2008 and closing the website one year later. However, this three-year record did trump MySpace in one area because MySpace was able to stay in the Korean SNS market for only nine months (Tkorea, 2009b).

Many issues can be blamed for the fall of Cyworld (U.S.), e.g., the poor customer communication they had with their users and the non-connectivity between a user's "friends" on the American Cyworld website and those on the Korean Cyworld (Walton, 2009). When localizing social networking websites, designers need to have a more in-depth understanding of local culture and be prepared to initiate interactions with local users, since social networking websites rely largely on their social affordances to enhance users' social relations within their network. Unfortunately, this might not be obvious for those SNS websites mentioned above. Being extremely successful and popular in their native cultures, they are proud of their unique and winning design features, which they might not realize are closely connected with their localness and come primarily from their designers' intensive local knowledge. For example, a "facebook" is a nickname for a student directory of names, photos, and profiles distributed by American colleges to students, for whom the website was originally designed. While this brand caught American users right away when it was launched, it was hard to translate it into another culture and find a counterpart metaphor,[1] not to mention that the interface features and interaction patterns built on a social networking website are deeply rooted in a local culture. The design of "minihomes," avatars, and virtual currency "acorns" in the Cyworld that has fascinated Korean young people looks childish and cartoon-like to American counterparts, reminding them of the children's websites WebKinz and Club Penguin in North America.

No matter how successful an SNS website is in its local culture, it needs to be conceived and localized as a local uptake when exported to a foreign culture. Designers should seriously consider how to brand the website and how to define its global core, changing their mindset from globalization to glocalization. Simply translating the web interface does not turn a website into a platform for social networking in a foreign context when designers stick to the original social interaction patterns that work for users in the home country, i.e., Korea's social network. The being-localized website should look into rich user activities in the new locale and incorporate the modes of local social interactions as a local uptake.

If the prescribed meaning is not right from the beginning, and designers do not watch or respond to trial users' interactions on the cultural circuit, the social circulation of the technology will not be able to proceed smoothly. At a time when there already existed other SNS websites that better understood local needs—in this case, a rapidly developing Facebook (U.S.) that promoted user localization with its myriad third-party applications—American users did not want to bother to localize a website that did not make sense to them. Therefore, the downfall of the SNS website Cyworld (U.S.) was inevitable.

Expanding the Scope of Localization

The dialogue on the cultural circuit asks the design community to reconsider the localization process in a glocalization age. The localization of technology products and services is both a move from a generic system to local configurations of technology and an active process of "articulation work" in a local context (Hales, 1994). And localization work does not belong only to designers, but also to users. In this "enabling and empowering" system, users work with designers and manufacturers as actors/constructors to co-construct the whole practice.

The scope of localization needs to be expanded to acknowledge and recognize users' contributions. It should go beyond a stage in the software design and engineering cycle (e.g., translation and interface design) to the site of local use and consumption and consider the whole process as a circuit. Below is this expanded vision of the localization process:

> Localization is the adaptation and customization of technological products and services to a locale with a distinctive culture. It includes localization efforts from design through use cyclically, involving developer localization and user localization. The localization process starts at the developer's site, where localization professionals modify a product to make it usable and meaningful to target users based on rich understandings of local use activities in context. It extends to the users' sites, where users develop heterogeneous use strategies from the perceived product affordances and concrete subjective experiences, as well as integrate the product into their everyday lives through use and consumption. These user insights and expertise are channeled into the design process, fueling the next round of localization.

I do not want to suggest that this vision should be interpreted as an official definition of localization, as this is beyond the scope of this book. What I want to maintain with this vision is that localization continues and extends at the user's site, as we see from the case of mobile messaging technology. The use success of mobile text messaging at local sites does not come from the work of localization professionals, but from users' participation and efforts. In this process, users are actively engaged in localization work and integrate the text messaging technology into their lives; they not only make a hard-to-use technology more usable and meaningful for them, but also localize the technology. For example, one American participant localized the text messaging technology into "a handy tool" (participant's description) to maintain daily conversations with her high-school sister back home. Busy with schoolwork, both she and her sister were unable to find a block of time to chat every day, though they cared for each other very much. Then they found text messaging, with which they could send each other quick texts for greetings and sharing right-at-that-moment experiences. Furthermore, design and use are asymmetrical here, and use is actually more important in this process because users' efforts realize localization and propel the process, which is indeed an important link to make a technology "usable and meaningful."

As localization work is expanded to include user localization, the focus of localization work needs to move from localizing for operational affordances to localizing for social affordances. With detailed discussions on instrumental affordances and social affordances in previous chapters, this comparative study illustrates how social affordances arise out of instrumental affordances and how users value social affordances during their use. The translation of menus is an affordance on the operation level, but what users really want and value is an affordance on the activity level. Localization work should address this need. For example, Emma expected to be able to send emotional messages more easily on her phone, and Lili hoped that she would not have to delete words to make the message fit within the size limit most of the time when she texted to her old friends.

This new vision also suggests that localization work be shifted from a single product to the whole system. As the case of mobile messaging technology shows, the localization of this technology is accomplished with the collective efforts of the phone manufacturers, service carriers, and users. In this system, hardware, software, service, and network technology all contribute to the localization work.[2] Clearly it is insufficient to localize only the phone or text messaging application. Usability breakdown will still occur if other components (e.g., network jam or the barrier of sending text messages across the network) fail in this system. During the fieldwork, participants expected to see improvements to the mobile text messaging technology not only in the areas of the messaging application and the handset, but also in the areas of carrier service and network technology. Their feedback suggests that we should think of localization practices as an open activity network—the product quality and usability do not settle only on the artifact but on the whole system. Therefore, an overall cross-cultural design strategy is needed to implement successful localization, deriving from technology vision, design savvy, business acumen, and sensitivity to local cultural, economical, and political conditions. Such a strategic plan will initiate changes, usually affecting many of the structures and processes of an IT company.

Meeting Local Cultural Expectations with User Localization

The expanded vision of localization has its merit in associating localization work with situated use. Localization work does not belong only to the arena of cross-cultural technology design; indeed, all the situated uses are local uses that need "strategies of user localization." Therefore, localization is not only a process in cross-cultural design but a part of the general design cycle as well. In this sense, user localization is a radical view of user-centered design that searches for ways to improve use experience in users' own contexts. It is important in technology design because a technological product would hardly fit into a user's lifestyle without any user initiative.

With the expanded vision of localization, we should start to consider extending the design process to the sites of technology-in-use, where the original and authentic insights of users will be gathered to be incorporated into design, in a cyclical model of the design process instead of the linear model. Individual users are the heroes of this participatory culture. They are not just passive users but active designers who shape, redesign, and localize an available technology to fit into their local contexts. Norman (2004) maintains that designers can make easy-to-use products that fulfill our needs, but they cannot make something to which we would bond. In some sense, who else other than users themselves knows their local culture and contexts better? Users might not be able to articulate those cultural and contextual factors well, but they know what works in their own contexts with their "need expertise" (von Hippel, 2005), and they know how to make use of a technology in their life spheres, if they are able to find the fit. So why not expand the design process to the users' sites and let users participate? Why not let users continue, extend, refine, and stabilize the design—determining the way of using a particular technological artifact?

In previous discussions and research of incorporating users into the design process (e.g., Beyer & Holzblatt, 1998; Hackos & Redish, 1998), researchers and designers examined the contribution of users only during the design phases (from gathering requirements to final testing) and assumed technologies as fixed in the use context once designed and implemented. This is a linear, design-centered model of technology development (Stewart & Williams, 2005), where design and use are separated and staged as different phases. My investigation of user localization in the case of mobile text messaging promotes a cyclical view of technology design, where design and use are linked and combined, and where a user's knowledge, expertise, and contribution are valued and utilized.

Based on this cyclical view of design, I argue that the designers' goal, besides providing functional technological artifacts, is to develop means to initiate practices and fix breakdowns. Generally, designers face two challenges. First, not all design resources are accessible to designers, some of which are "developed in use" (Brown & Duguid, 1996, p. 132). As explored in the previous chapter, much of the meaning about a particular technology is created by users through use. For some technologies, designers would need to wait until after use begins to translate the generated meaning into design resources. The development of social networking websites also demonstrates this. Good responses to emerging user activities, i.e., good translations of user activities into design resources, help to improve and expand a social networking website, while inappropriate ones push users to competitors' websites, as can be seen from the downturns of Friendster and MySpace. Design possibilities and problems also change as technologies and cultures evolve. Second, breakdowns during technology use are inevitable in human–machine communication (Suchman, 1987).

Therefore, one should not expect to create *fully* functional technological artifacts because it is never possible. Instead, what designers should do is the following: First, design with the characteristics of flexibility, adaptability, and tailorability in mind (MacLean, Carter, Lövstrand, & Moran, 1990; Mirel, 2002). For example, when designing technologies for complex tasks, users should be able to "relate actions to conditional factors, to arrange and configure the resources and conditions of work as they see fit, and to plan as they go based on emergent opportunities and constraints" (Mirel, 2002, p. 182). Second, design a technology to be open for interpretation, integration, and change (Höök, 2006; Spinuzzi, 2003; Wright & McCarthy, 2010). An open system "provides a base for workers to build on" and functions as "starter ecology," like an artificial reef "where a genuine ecology can grow" (Spinuzzi, 2003, pp. 204–205).

In fact, designing a flexible technology with an open space to get users involved through use will save manufacturers' money, with which designers might be able to bypass the design paradox: A specific design solution that fits in one local context will be hard to transport to another use context without significant revision, while a general design solution that targets broader markets might need to be customized to work for a particular context. Brown and Duguid (1996) suggest that the future of technology design lies in "not by making more explicit, but by leaving as much as possible implicit, and in the process keeping things simple" (p. 144). Speaking about the case of mobile messaging technology, one explanation states that the success of this technology comes primarily from the simplicity of its design (Jenson, 2005). To put it in another way, though designers and manufacturers continue turning their backs on this technology, its simplicity has still allowed it to survive and sustain over the years by providing an open platform to users who could alter, repurpose, reinvent, and localize the technology.

For cross-cultural technology design, the key here is to include flexibility and openness in the global core from the beginning of the design process. Here, the job of designers is to incorporate better instrumental affordances into a technological artifact to help develop and realize social affordances that resonate with social motives in local contexts, which emerge from the interactions. The core of this vision is founded on a deep understanding of concrete use activities in local contexts while appreciating the cultural and structuring forces behind those activities. It argues that the process of technology design is an open system with built-in design features that could initiate instrumental affordances to invite users to localize the technological artifact and realize its social affordances according to their culture. It is an open space where many possible uses—local uses, actually—have been developed, surrounding the intended use from the beginning.

For new technologies that have not been introduced before, Tuomi (2005) believes that their use depends on a process of social learning, "whereby we have to discover how to use the product to develop new practices" (p. 28), i.e., old social practices are reconfigured into newer ones to accommodate and support this new technology. Because of this, he argues that technology design is "fundamentally a question of designing social relations," which "requires that we define design methodologies where social learning is incorporated" (p. 33). Here the process of social learning is similar to the process of user localization where users are invited to interact, participate, and co-evolve with the design. He found that "socially successful products have historically often resembled oil," which facilitates social relations, and concludes that designers need to consider "the degree of social flexibility that is built into material and functional objects" (p. 36).

In his proposal of democratizing innovation, von Hippel (2005) endorses the "toolkits for user innovation and custom design" that worked for the custom semiconductor industry, with more than $15 billion worth of products in 2003. This approach divides a design project into "solution-information-intensive subtasks" (tasks related to problem solving, which manufacturers tend to know better than users due to their specialties) and "need-information-intensive subtasks" (tasks related to user needs and context-of-use information, which users have more accurate and more detailed knowledge of than manufacturers). He advances that need-intensive subtasks should be "assigned to users along with a kit of tools that enable them to effectively execute the tasks assigned to them" (p. 16). This is evidenced by the booming business of self-assembly furniture and interior design elements nowadays.

I have characterized the approach of user localization as "a rhetoric of locale" where "design and use is naturally associated" in the way that "user localization becomes an inherent consideration from the beginning of design" (Sun, 2009b, p. 259). The dialogical nature of user localization makes it possible to incorporate complex subjectiveness into the objective design process and develop a dynamic and co-constructive relationship between designers and users. The rhetoric of locale suggests ways of linking use back to design and supporting and channeling user contributions in order to make a technology both accessible to culturally diverse users and related to an individual.

To help designers connect use and design on a cultural circuit, I made the following suggestions in an earlier piece (Sun, 2006):

> Designers will not seek to design fully localized interfaces or products (because it is never possible) or regard the product shipment (or developer localization) as the end of design. Instead, they will look for ways of initiating a communication channel and building a support network to enhance user localization and help repair the possible breakdowns in contexts of use. They will also watch the use trends emerging from the user's site and design better instrumental affordances to respond to those trends. (p. 478)

The emergence of participatory culture and the popularity of social media echoed this. Users must be trusted as co-developers, as O'Reilly suggests that "the key to competitive advantage in internet applications is the extent to which users add their own data to that which you provide" (2005). It is important to get users involved "both implicitly and explicitly" to add value to the application with a "perpetual beta" version. This call applies not only to web technologies but also to other technologies. With successes such as the IdeaStorm user community website of Dell and the "My Starbucks Idea" website, these types of "idea partner" programs that turn user's input into actual deliverable are adopted by more companies.

The undertaking of designing for local users has never been so critical. In an emerging digital economy of "the long tail," it is more feasible to design technologies for smaller market niches than in non-digital economies because of the low cost of selling and distributing digital information (Anderson, 2008), but to make this economy work, user localization needs to be the cornerstone.

User localization contributes to the continued successes of mobile text messaging technology in the post period of this cross-cultural study: While the use of text messaging keeps soaring in both countries, it has become a daily communication means among many Chinese people, with a reported penetration rate of 80% in the first quarter of 2009 (Stewart & Quick, 2009). In contrast, the penetration rate was 58% in the U.S. for the same time period (ibid). Text messaging is heavily used by American teenagers and tweens (Entner, 2010; Reardon, 2008b; WTB, 2010) and has metamorphosed into the "twittering" practice of tech-savvy adults (M. Miller, 2007; C. C. Miller, 2009). As we look at the new user localization phenomenon surrounding text messaging at present, we see that the observations made earlier (Sun, 2004, 2006) still apply to these phenomena. For example, in the American context, text messaging is still interpreted and fixated as conversation in both teenagers' and adults' use of mobile messaging technology.

Example: Twitter's Response to User Localization

The success of the Twitter service provides us with a lot of food for thought when it is situated in the developmental trajectories of mobile text messaging technology. Twitter is "a free social networking and micro-blogging service that enables its users to send and read each others' updates, known as *tweets*. Tweets are text-based posts of up to 140 characters" ("Twitter," 2009). Tweets can be sent and received via the Twitter website, text messaging service, and other web applications. Twitter's fast-rising popularity worldwide cannot be separated from the efforts of user localization. The cover story of *Time* announces that Twitter's success comes directly from users' contributions and suggests that these ingenious efforts are the engine of our currently suffering economy since 2008:

> In Twitter's case, the users have been redesigning the tool itself....
> In its short life, Twitter has been a hothouse of end-user innovation:
> the hashtag; searching; its 11,000 third-party applications; all those
> creative new uses of Twitter....All of these adoptions create new
> kinds of value in the wider economy, and none of them actually
> originated at Twitter HQ. (S. Johnson, 2009)

As a key player in social media, Twitter utilizes the power of social media to involve users in the design process. There is a constant dialogue between designers and users behind the success of Twitter: After designers noticed that Twitter users would refer to fellow Twitterers by placing the at sign, @, before their Twitter ID (i.e., @TwitterID), they incorporated it into the design. Later they adopted the users' shorthand "RT" (retweet) and their invention of the hashtag, #. The function of a hashtag, such as #Worldcup 2010, is to group a stream of tweets on the same topic or event for easy search and retrieval. One of the new features added to Twitter is Twitter List, a "groups" feature that allows its users to create streams of the latest tweets from a specific group of users. It was requested by users first and then developed by designers.

Twitter calls this type of design process "an ecosystem of innovation" (Twitter Blog, 2010). In addition to teaming up with users to improve the core of the technology, Twitter also supports third-party applications and collaborates with corporate and individual partners. For example, it buys third-party applications to enhance its service: "Summize" was such a startup company launched by Twitter users, and now it is a part of Twitter that provides a search function for live tweets. The constantly added instrumental affordances bring up more social affordances valuable to users, thus forming a constructive cycle of design process that benefits both designers and users and contributes to the success of the technology itself.

Understanding User Experience as Cultural Consumption

The use success of mobile text messaging attests to the power of consumers. CNN Money claims that "the new culture on the Web is all about consumer creation" (Schonfeld, Malik, & Copeland, 2006). In this participatory culture, when social software and participatory technologies are reshaping our lives with a huge amount of user-generated content, the lens of cultural consumption can help the cross-cultural design community to design for better local user experience: Cultural consumption contributes to the active meaning-making process in technology use, as explored in the previous chapter.

One thing that tends to be forgotten by the design community is that a usable technology does not equal a meaningful technology for local users. And when users cannot relate to a technology, they will not use it. To make a usable technology relate to individual users with diverse cultural backgrounds, designers need to help users to *consummate* their experiences into culturally localized user experiences. The "genius loci" coming out of user localization certainly consummates user experience. Through creative cultural consumption activities, active users-as-designers develop their use-design expertise, and they bring this developed expertise to the next technology for user localization.

I discussed how cultural consumption functions as production and as identity formation during the meaning-construction process in the last chapter. Based on that, I would further discuss that cultural consumption also performs as communication, linking it to the dialogic methodology. It is not just a material activity, but a symbolic activity (Bourdieu, 1984). Consumption involves multiple communications on different levels. First, a consumer communicates with the artifact being used. Like reading a text, using technology involves the same communication process, in which meanings are prescribed and encoded in its design and are transcribed, decoded, and deciphered in its use—a process that has been called consumption, appropriation, transcription, or localization. In this process, new meanings will be added and old meanings may be altered, as discussed in Chapter 10. A technology most likely will be read/used in different ways than what it was originally designed for. For instance, who still remembers that the initial purpose of the telephone was for the transmission and reception of religious services, concerts, and sporting events? The second level of communication occurs between consumers. First, a purchased artifact is a way of expressing oneself in one's own cultural habitus (ibid). Second, cultural consumption acts as a "ritual activity" in which people consume in order to communicate with "fellow consumers, of a universe of values" (Douglas & Isherwood, 1996, as cited in Storey, 1999, p. 44). The popularity of user forums surrounding various technological products attests to this. The third level is between production and consumption, or between design and use, as is discussed in the previous sections.

Next I discuss how the view of cultural consumption as production, as identity construction, and as communication will open up new avenues for technology design and provide space to leverage user agency, identity, and expertise in technological systems.

The notion of cultural consumption has its merit in showing us how meaning is constructed, interpreted, and appropriated dynamically during technology use on a cultural circuit. Contesting the biases about a passive consumer image, it theoretically sketches the value of consumption and technology use in the process of making culture. Storey (1999) explains his particular use of cultural consumption in this way: He is not referring to "the consumption of culture" as most people do, but to "make the point that cultural consumption produces culture" (p. xxi). Following his line of logic, I would like to argue that the notion of cultural consumption will help designers and researchers see that those active and creative consumer activities are making part of the culture. "Culture is, therefore, neither the products produced by the culture industries, nor simply their appropriation by consumers; it is always the result of an active combination of the two" (p. xxii). Here consumption is "the continual struggle to appropriate goods and services made in alienating circumstances and transform them into inalienable culture" (D. Miller, 1987, as cited in Storey, 1999, p. 162), and it is "a means for creating authentic culture" (D. Miller, 1997, p. 19), which is exactly the user localization process of turning a technology into a meaningful part of life. Coming from the field of design history, Julier (2008) observes that the consumption lens has greatly contributed to the development of design culture. He suggests that designers should take "the polysemic nature of consuming—that it can mean several things at various levels" and filter, interpret, and recycle it into "an endless circuit" of design and consumption (p. 73).

Regarding user localization as cultural consumption links a material use experience to a subjective and symbolic one by including self, identity, personality, and lifestyle into a design process. It shows the necessity and ways of designing for multiple interpretations of a technology through a culture-making process from "being" to "becoming." For example, in this culture-making process, how could we design a technology to support its use as production, as identity construction, and as communication for creative cultural consumers/experts? What could we do to facilitate and respond to users' production work at their sites? What social affordances could we aim for as far as identity, agency, and expertise are concerned? What communication mechanism and supportive network could be built in this participation age?

Example: Selling and Shopping as Cultural Consumption

Taobao.com, a Chinese C2C (consumer-to-consumer) giant with online shopping and auction services, was regarded as one of eBay's local competitors in China when launched in 2003. Taobao means "searching for treasures" in Chinese. Three years later, it found the treasure and won with a C2C Chinese market share of more than 80%, which made eBay quit the China market. As of October 2011, it was ranked as the third most visited website in China and the 16th globally, higher than eBay.com, according to Alexa.com.

There are many factors contributing to the sweeping success of Taobao in this fierce competition—for example, the "Glocal Advantages" Taobao has over eBay (Ou & Davison, 2009). As an indigenous e-commerce website, Taobao understands Chinese consumers' concerns about e-commerce and the high risk of Internet fraud. In particular, it designed interface features to help build "swift trust" between buyers and sellers with an embedded instant messaging application, WangWang, which supports texting, voice chat, video chat, and file transfer. There is an icon next to a product's listing picture to show whether the seller is online; if the seller is online, the buyer can use WangWang to communicate with the seller right away. Chinese users reported that this system is more trustworthy than the seller rating system that is commonly seen in other e-commerce websites. At the same time, this social affordance is beneficial in forming relationships between two parties. Smart shoppers even negotiate product prices or shipping fees via this communication channel, just like people do face to face at a flea market.

More significant differences between eBay and Taobao are the cultural consumption practices surrounding online shopping and auction Taobao has designed and nurtured in recent years. While eBay (China) is just a place for doing business or shopping to Chinese users, Taobao provides a world of *Jianghu*, a peculiar culture based on the popular Chinese *Wuxia* (martial artists) novels and movies. *Jianghu*, which can be translated literally as "rivers and lakes," refers to a fictional universe, world, and milieu where the adventurers, rebels, wanderers, unemployed laborers, gangsters, and outcasts of society gather. In that world, everyone has a dream of becoming a hero in the end, even the most powerful one who governs the world of *Jianghu*, with superb martial arts skills honed from years of earnest practice and undertaking demanding trials, all the while earning love. A famous representation of this culture can be seen in Ang Lee's movie *Crouching Tiger, Hidden Dragon*. Built on the social affordances resonating with local culture, Taobao's *Jianghu* matches the imagination of many ordinary Chinese people who dream of quickly becoming rich through adventure and luck at this time of the market economy.

With its free-of-charge business model, Taobao has enticed millions of new users to open online shops and thus developed the largest online C2C community in China, which recursively shaped the design of the website. For example, Taobao's embedded SNS platform combines shopping and social networking with fun games. Users are encouraged to seek hidden treasures such as gadgets for photo albums and a voting feature, useful for product promotion, and join the product-related gangster communities to expand the business.

A comparison of Taobao's homepage, which is updated annually, shows how Taobao identifies itself with the local culture in an interesting way. The homepage of 2003 imitates the designs of many American successful e-business websites: a simple and easy-to-use interface with a modular layout. In contrast, the homepage of 2011 would overwhelm most Western users with its huge listing of product categories occupying one fourth of the four-screen-long home page—the opposite of minimalist design. Indeed, it looks more like an online portal than an e-commerce website with links to news, entertainment, leisure, online communities, and blogs, scattered with flashy product ads. To be honest, it is not very user friendly for Chinese beginner users either.

However, this might be what a *Jianghu*, full of turbulence and strife, looks like. This open market attracts many frequent users, both shoppers and sellers, who come to the website for doing business, fulfilling shopping goals, searching for deals, making friends, having fun, and seeking treasures. It is an e-commerce *Jianghu* where business and game are subtly blended, and where a dream of rising to be a powerful millionaire hero can come true.

Coda: Thinking Globally, Designing Locally

It has never been more important to design for local users in this age of participatory culture, when social software and interactive web technologies are reshaping our lives with an ever-growing amount of user-generated content, connections, and relationships. For researchers, practitioners, educators, and students in fields such as human–computer interaction, professional and technical communication, computer-supported collaborative work, information design, and information studies, and for those who want to gain an understanding of and develop expertise in designing for culturally diverse users, I hope the CLUE approach discussed in this book will meet your needs and spark your design ideas.

Yet this book is not only about cross-cultural technology design, but about culture and design in general (i.e., culturally sensitive design) as well. The design issues I examined in this book also occur in general technology design and in other design areas, such as information design and communication design. The conversation I want to start with this book is to develop an integrated, balanced perspective in order to better design a mindful, ethical, and responsible relationship between us and our surrounding nature, which consists mostly of mediated technologies nowadays.

Obviously, the heading of this section comes from the famous slogan of the 20th-century environmental movement, "Think globally, act locally." This influential, iconic statement was first used by Rene Dubos at the United Nations Conference on the Human Environment in 1972 ("Think,"1994). It states that responsible actions to solve global environmental problems should start from the local community with a full consideration of the ecological, economic, and cultural differences in local contexts. Adapting this to cross-cultural technology design, "think globally, design locally" advocates a design philosophy that promotes that, to successfully create a technology across cultures, an ethical and responsible design should start from a full understanding of the local context where the technology will be used. While this problem-solving heuristic suggests that global problems should be approached and solved from the local—as most of this book does in arguing for the importance of the local, showcasing the value of local efforts, and advancing suggestions of designing for the local—we should not forget to *think globally* as the premise. Every local becomes the local due to the existence of the global. In the end of this book, I will discuss how to integrate the local and the global in cross-cultural design, which is more than the interplay between the global and the local as discussed in an earlier section. The principle of "think globally, design locally" should be regarded as the guiding philosophy of design in an age of *glocalization*. Particularly when designing for the developing world, the design community will find it instructive to better balance the issues such as power, value, and equality in addressing the design reality of "postcolonial computing" (Irani et al., 2010).

My take on "think globally" stands on the double meaning of the word *global*. First, it means worldwide, international, and cross-cultural, as in the instances of a global village, global politics, and globalization. Second, it suggests an overall, holistic, and constituting perspective. So the phrase "thinking globally" leads to a holistic cross-cultural design philosophy that stresses integration in the design process: integrating the global and the local, integrating action and meaning, integrating situatedness and constructiveness, integrating implementation and interpretation, integrating instrumental affordance and social affordance, integrating design and use, and integrating production and consumption, to name a few. Philosophically, it implies integrating human beings and their mediated and non-mediated environments. Only with the guiding philosophy of integration in mind can we "design locally"—designers would begin the design process from the local (including both the user's local and designer's local), listening to local folks, becoming embedded in the local culture, making well-informed design decisions locally, etc.

This philosophy of integration is an essential feature of the CLUE framework, as shown from five of the seven CLUE principles, highlighting this integration from different angles:

- Local culture constitutes the dynamic nexus of contextual interactions and manifests numerous articulations of practices and meanings.
- User experience is both situated activity and constructed meaning.
- Technology use is a dual mediation process, including tool-mediated production and sign-mediated communication.
- Structured affordance comes from dialogic interactions between operational, instrumental, and social affordances.
- Design is both problem solving and engaged conversation.

As I have stated throughout this book, the goal of the CLUE framework is to advocate a design philosophy that integrates action and meaning in technology design in order to make a technology usable and meaningful to culturally diverse users. However, integration will not happen automatically. To achieve the unity between "thinking globally" and "designing locally," a dialogic approach to integration is critical. The integration emphasis is tightly related to the dialogic methodology that underlines the CLUE framework, and all the integration occurs through this dialogic methodology. The four implications presented in this chapter, based on the collective case study and the CLUE model, aim to chart new paths of starting this dialogic journey to integration; at the same time, more innovative routes are called for in order to invoke, initiate, support, nurture, and sustain the multivoiced dialogue. Generally, a dialogic methodology leads to an integrated approach to cross-cultural technology design, which attempts to achieve the unity of the subject and the surrounding contexts, the unity of human beings and their created technologies, with a deep appreciation of the "enabling and constraining" nature of technology.

Then we come to the hefty topic of the relationship of technology and human beings, which seems to be unavoidable in the conclusion of a book about a cross-cultural design approach that aims for integration. Clearly, the integrated design approach—the CLUE framework I advocate and outline in this book—is inspired by great musings about technology of this age in the Western world, which overshadows my earlier discussion. It also comes from my own cultural background, the traditional Chinese philosophical principle of *"Tian ren he yi"* ("the unity of Heaven and human") that is promoted by Chinese traditional philosophical schools, which is a perspective of intersubjectivity for the synergy and the harmony of the human being and the world. While tracing the influences of different schools of thought to contemporary technology design deserves more than one book from a big group of diverse authors, my purpose for indicating these influences, even briefly at the end, is to show the "enabling and constraining" characteristic of the CLUE methodology itself, echoing the thesis of this section.

There is another reason that dialogism is emphasized in the end of the book: because the design model itself and its broader implications for future research and practice should also be evaluated first in terms of local appropriateness or, more accurately, should expect a dialogue or an interaction between the local and the global. Design philosophies and principles are cultural artifacts themselves that carry invisible local values from where they originated. For example, it is no accident that participatory design was advanced and accepted in Scandinavian culture, a culture with a lower power distance index than many other countries and where low-level workers are treated in a more egalitarian way by the upper management. Naturally, such a design philosophy will not be easily introduced to cultures that have a higher power distance index. As a result, participatory design is treated as a design technique rather than a design philosophy in the U.S. (Spinuzzi, 2005; Svanæs, 2000).

In this age of glocalization, cross-cultural design expertise is required not just for those researchers and practitioners who engage in cross-cultural design and communication projects on a daily basis, but is also needed by every researcher, practitioner, or communicator who is conscious of their living existence in this contemporary global society and who seeks to have meaningful and engaging conversations with his or her culturally diverse users. While I am unable to cover everything about cross-cultural technology design in this book, such as the influences of the political, economic, and infrastructural conditions, what I hope to achieve is to start a "situated" conversation about usable and meaningful technology design at a time when diverse, multivoiced thoughts are valued and articulated into plural, mindful cross-cultural design methodologies for analysis and design to accomplish the unity and harmony of the global and the local.

Now it is your turn...

Notes

1. For example, the Chinese translation for Facebook in mass media is "Lian Pu" ("mask"). In online street language, Facebook is jokingly referred to as "must-die" by some Chinese SNS users, based on the Chinese translation of its pronunciation. It does partially tell the truth: If Facebook fails to consider local cultural expectations, then it will die in a foreign context.
2. In this case, the Chinese site did a better localization job of text messaging considering its service design.

Appendix A

Mobile Messaging User Survey

Background

1. Age
2. Gender
3. Occupation
4. Educational background
5. Who are the other people in your house?
6. How would you describe your daily schedule?
7. Which of the following best describes your usual place of work? (Circle one)
   a. Home
   b. Location away from home
   c. Mix of home and location away from home
   d. On the road
   e. Not working

Phone Info

8. What is your phone model?
9. How much money did you pay for your current phone?

10. Please choose the functions your cell phone has (circle all those apply):
    a. Text messaging
    b. Web browsing
    c. Downloadable games
    d. Downloadable ringtones
    e. Color
    f. Camera
    g. MP3
    h. Other _____
11. When did you start to use your first cell phone (month, year)?
12. When did you start to use mobile messaging for the first time (month, year)?
13. What's your wireless service plan (plan name, services, and cost)?
14. How much money do you spend on your cell phone monthly?
15. How much money do you spend on text messaging monthly?

SMS Use

16. How did you learn to use text messaging? Please circle one number to best describe your situation (*on a scale from 1 to 5 representing five categories: strongly agree, agree, not sure, disagree, and strongly disagree*).
    a. Figured it out by myself with trial and error
    b. Watched people to see how they did it
    c. Consulted manuals or tutorials
    d. Asked friends to show me
    e. Other methods such as _____
17. How much time (in term of minutes, hours, or days) did it take you to learn how to text message?
18. What text inputting method do you use? Please circle one number for each method to show how frequently you use it (*on a scale from 1 to 10 representing five categories: always, usually, sometimes, seldom, and never*).
    a. Multi-tap
    b. T9 (predictive typing)
    c. Other _____

19. How do you send text messages to other people? Please circle one number to best describe your situation (*on a scale from 1 to 10 representing five categories: always, usually, sometimes, seldom, and never*).
    a. By phone
    b. By email
    c. Via websites
20. What kinds of mobile messaging services do you use? Please circle one number to best describe your situation (*on a scale from 1 to 10 representing five categories: always, usually, sometimes, seldom, and never*).
    a. One-way text messaging
    b. Two-way text messaging
    c. Multimedia (or picture) messaging
    d. Chat room
    e. IM services on mobile phones (e.g., AIM, MSN messenger)
21. For what purpose do you usually communicate via mobile messaging? Please circle one number to best describe your situation (*on a scale from 1 to 5 representing five categories: strongly agree, agree, not sure, disagree, and strongly disagree*).
    a. To arrange or adjust appointments
    b. To have fun conversations with friends
    c. To stay in contact with friends or loved ones at every moment
    d. To send a stealth message from a place where I can't talk
    e. To connect with people without disturbing them
    f. To kill time
    g. To avoid lengthy phone conversations
    h. To save phone cost
    i. To email people when computers are not accessible
    j. To get or exchange information instantly
    k. To show people I'm cool
    l. Other _____
22. Do you subscribe to text alert services (e.g., weather forecasts, breaking news, etc.)? If yes, what kinds of alerts do you subscribe to?

Use of Other ITs

23. What communication tools do you use generally? Please circle one number for each tool to show how frequently you use it (*on a scale from 1 to 10 representing five categories: always, usually, sometimes, seldom, and never*).
    a. Emails
    b. Letters
    c. Faxes
    d. IM (instant messaging)
    e. Landline phones
    f. Wireless phones
    g. Mobile messaging
    h. Other _____

24. How would rate your knowledge of these technologies below? Please circle one number to best describe your situation (*on a scale from 1 to 5 representing three categories: beginner user, intermediate user, and expert user*).
    a. Computer
    b. Instant messaging
    c. Email application
    d. Mobile text messaging

25. Do you have a landline phone in the place where you live?
    a. Yes
    b. No

Appendix B

Workbook of "Experiences with Mobile Messaging"

Sample questions are provided below to show the design of the diary workbook.

Where I go and stay

1. Inside the circles, name the places where you stay a lot at work (e.g., offices, labs, and classrooms), at home (e.g., living rooms, bedrooms), at play (e.g., theaters, bars), and on the go (e.g., cars, streets). You don't have to fill in all the circles.
2. Around the circles, write down words that describe what you do most in those places (e.g., create documents, watch movies).

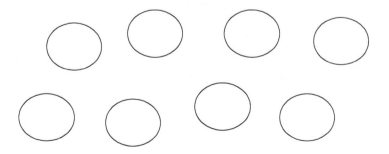

3. In a circle for a specific place, mark "M" if you've used mobile phones and mark "T" if you've used mobile text messaging.
4. Rank all of these places in order from where you stay the most to where you stay the least.

Where I use mobile messaging

On this page you will create a diagram of how you use your mobile text messaging in your daily life.

1. Select *three places that you use mobile messaging most often* and write down the names of those places inside the three circles.
   These three places can be *similar* to those on the previous two pages *or different* from them.
2. List people (e.g., family, friends, and/or coworkers) with whom you spend time in those places in and around the circles:
   a. Draw *triangles* to represent people.
   b. Write down who the person is next to or inside the triangle.
   c. Draw *arrows* between "Me" and the triangles.

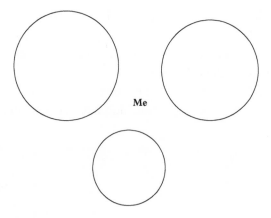

Text message log form

Day 1

Shorthand: **R**—Message Received, **SP**—Message Sent By Phone, **SE**—Message Sent By Email, **SW**—Message Sent Via Websites

Today's date: _____

Q*: Would you still send the same message with other communication tools if you didn't have a mobile messaging service available?

#	Time	Type				From / To Whom	Reply to Message #	Message Content	Place	Situation	Q*	
		R	SP	SE	SW						Y	N
3	7:00 a	x				Jane	2	City kitty	driving	She went to NYC		x
1												
2												

How I feel about mobile messaging

Please complete the following sentences:

I use mobile messaging instead of calling people directly when...

I use mobile messaging instead of emailing people when...

I use mobile messaging instead of IMing (instant messaging) people when...

I use mobile messaging because...

Mobile messaging is *a) important, b) ok, c) not important* (please circle one) to me because...

Appendix C

Coding Scheme: Mobile Text Messaging Use in Context

Below is a brief description of the coding scheme.

Dimension 1: Rhetorical Purposes of Mobile Text Messaging

Text messages are coded into the following categories:

- Informing: Any message or reply that is sent to inform about something going on and to share information in which one or both of the parties might be interested
- Co-experiencing: Any message or reply that is sent to share the current status or experience with the other party
- Instructing: Any message or reply where the recipient is asked to help or propose something in order to accomplish a task
- Coordinating: Any message or reply that is sent to coordinate tasks, events, and schedules
- Expressing: Any message or reply that is used to express feelings or views
- Switching: Any message or reply that suggests having a follow-up phone or text conversation shortly

- Other: Any message or reply that does not fit one of the above categories

Dimension 2: Life Spheres of Mobile Text Messaging

Text messages are coded into the follow categories:

- Work: Any message or reply that is about the life sphere of work related to the sender or the recipient
- School: Any message or reply that is about the life sphere of the school or the educational institution related to the sender or the recipient
- Family: Any message or reply that is about the life sphere of the family related to the sender or the recipient
- Personal leisure other than with family: Any message or reply that is about the life sphere of personal leisure other than with family related to the sender or the recipient
- Other: Any message or reply that doesn't fit into any other categories or is a system message from phone carriers or advertisers

References

3GAmericas. (2004). *Short Messaging Services (SMS) for Success.* Retrieved May 20, 2004, from http://www.3gamericas.org/English/Services/sms_for_success.cfm

Adler, P. S., & Winograd, T. A. (Eds.). (1992). *Usability: Turning technologies into tools.* New York: Oxford University Press.

Albrechtsen, H., Andersen, H. H. K., Bødker, S., & Pejtersen, A. M. (2001). *Affordances in activity theory and cognitive systems engineering.* Roskilde: Riso National Laboratory.

Ali, R. (2006, July 28). *Cyworld's U.S. Launch; $10 Million Investment.* Retrieved July 8, 2010, from http://paidcontent.org/article/cyworlds-us-launch-10-million-investment/

Andersen, J. (2008). The concept of genre in information studies. *Annual Review of Information Science and Technology, 42,* 339–367.

Anderson, C. (2008). *The long tail: Why the future of business is selling less of more.* New York: Hyperion.

Aykin, N. (Ed.). (2004). *Usability and internationalization of information technology.* Mahwah, NJ: Lawrence Erlbaum Associates.

Aykin, N., & Milewski, A. (2004). Practical issues and guidelines for international information display. In N. Aykin (Ed.), *Usability and internationalization of information technology* (pp. 21–50). Mahwah, NJ: Lawrence Erlbaum Associates.

Aykin, N., Chavan, A. L., Dray, S. M., & Prabhu, G. (2007). Panel discussion: Global innovative design for social change. In *HCI International 2007 Proceedings,* (Vol. 10, pp. 3–9). Berlin: Springer.

Badre, A. (2002). *Shaping web usability: Interaction design in context*. Indianapolis, IN: Pearson Education.

Baerentsen, K., & Trettvik, J. (2002). An activity theory approach to affordance. In O. W. Bertelsen, S. Bodker, & K. Kuuti (Eds.), *Proceedings of the Second Nordic Conference on Human-Computer Interaction* (pp. 51–60). New York: ACM Press.

Bakhtin, M., M. (1981). *The dialogic imagination: Four essays*. Austin: University of Texas Press.

Bakhtin, M., M. (1986). *Speech genres and other late essays*. Austin: University of Texas Press.

Bannon, L. J., & Bødker, S. (1991). *Beyond the interface: Encountering artifacts in use*. Retrieved June 15, 2004, from http://www.ul.ie/~idc/library/papersreports/LiamBannon/13/LBsb9.html

Barber, W., & Badre, A. (1998). Culturability: The merging of culture and usability. In *Proceedings of the Fourth Conference on Human Factors and the Web*. Basking Ridge, NJ. Retrieved April 5, 2000, from http://zing.ncsl.nist.gov/hfweb/att4/proceedings/barber/

Bardzell, J., & Bardzell, S. (2008). Interaction criticism: A proposal and framework for a new discipline of HCI. In *Extended Abstracts of Conference on Human Factors in Computing Systems (CHI 2008)* (pp. 2463–2472). New York: ACM Press.

Barendregt, B. (2008). Sex, cannibals, and the language of cool: Indonesian tales of the phone and modernity. *The Information Society, 24*, 160–170.

Baron, N. S. (2008). *Always on: Language in an online and mobile world*. New York: Oxford University Press.

Barton, D., & Hamilton, M. (1998). *Local literacies: Reading and writing in one community*. New York: Routledge.

Batteau, A. W. (2010). *Technology and culture*. Long Grove, IL: Waveland.

Baumgartner, V. J. (2003). *A practical set of cultural dimensions for global user-interface analysis and design*. Unpublished graduate thesis, University of Vienna, Vienna, Austria.

Bazerman, C. (1998). The production of technology and the production of human meaning. *Journal of Business and Technical Communication, 12*(3), 381–387.

Bazerman, C. (1999). *The language of Edison's light*. Cambridge, MA: MIT Press.

Bazerman, C. (2000). Letters and the social grounding of differentiated genres. In D. Barton & N. Hall (Eds.), *Letter writing as a social practice* (pp. 15–29). Philadelphia: John Benjamins.

Beaton, J., & Kumar, R. (2010). Indian cultural effects on user research methodologies. In *Extended Abstracts of Conference on Human Factors in Computing Systems (CHI 2010)* (pp. 4267–4272). Atlanta, GA: ACM.

Bell, G. (2005). The age of the thumb: A cultural reading of mobile technologies from Asia. In P. Glotz, S. Bertschi, & C. Locke (Eds.), *Thumb culture: The meaning of mobile phones for society* (pp. 67–88). Bielefeld: transcript Verlag.

Beyer, H., & Holtzblatt, K. (1998). *Contextual design: Defining customer-centered systems*. San Francisco: Morgan Kaufman.

Blom, J., Chipchase, J., & Lehikoinen, J. (2005, July). Contextual and cultural challenges for user mobility research. *Communications of the ACM, 48,* 37–41.

Blythe, M. A., Overbeeke, K., Monk, A. F., & Wright, P. C. (Eds.). (2004). *Funology: From usability to enjoyment.* Dordrecht, The Netherlands: Kluwer.

Bourges-Waldegg, P., & Scrivener, S. (1998). Meaning, the central issue in cross-cultural HCI design. *Interacting with Computers, 9*(3), 287–309.

Bødker, S., & Andersen, P. B. (2005). Complex mediation. *Human–Computer Interaction, 20*(4), 353–402.

Bradner, E. (2001). *Social factors in the design and use of computer-mediated communication technology.* Unpublished doctoral dissertation, University of California, Irvine.

Brandt, D., & Clinton, K. (2002). Limits of the local: Expanding perspectives on literacy as a social practice. *Journal of Literacy Research, 34*(3), 337–356.

Broadbent, S., & Bauwens, V. (2008). Understanding convergence. *Interactions, 15*(1), 23–27.

Brown, J. S., & Duguid, P. (1994). Borderline issues: Social and material aspects of design. *Human-Computer Interaction. Special Issue on Context in Design, 9*(1), 4–36.

Brown, J. S., & Duguid, P. (1996). Keeping it simple. In T. Winograd (Ed.), *Bringing design to software* (pp. 129–150). New York: Addison Wesley.

Campbell, H. (2008). 'What hath God wrought?' Considering how religious communities culture (or kosher) the cell phone. In G. Goggin (Ed.), *Mobile phone cultures* (pp. 53–65). Abingdon, Oxon: Routledge.

Carroll, J., Howard, S., Vetere, F., Peck, J., & Murphy, J. (2002). Just what do the youth of today want? Technology appropriation by young people. In *Proceedings of the 35th Hawaii International Conference on System Sciences* (pp. 1777–1785). Hawaii: IEEE.

Chen, K.-H. (1995). Cultural studies and the politics of internationalization: An interview with Stuart Hall by Kuan-Hsing Chen. In S. Hall, D. Morley, & K.-H. Chen (Eds.), *Stuart Hall: Critical dialogues in cultural studies* (pp. 392–408). New York: Routledge.

Chochinov, A. (2007). *1000 words: A manifesto for sustainability in design.* Retrieved May 20, 2010, from http://www.core77.com/reactor/04.07_chochinov.asp

Chochinov, A. (2009). A good long tradition. In E. Pilloton (Ed.), *Design revolution: 100 products that empower people* (pp. 6–9). New York: Metropolis.

Choi, B., Lee, I., Kim, J., & Jeon, Y. (2005). A qualitative cross-national study of cultural influences on mobile data service design. In *Proceedings of Conference on Human Factors in Computing Systems (CHI 2005)* (pp. 661–670). New York: ACM Press.

Choi, B., Lee, I., & Kim, J. (2006). Culturability in mobile data services: A qualitative study of the relationship between cultural characteristics and user-experience attributes. *International Journal of Human-Computer Interaction, 20*(3), 171–206.

Churchill, E. F., & Wakeford, N. (2001). Framing mobile collaborations and mobile technologies. In B. Brown, N. Green, & R. Harper (Eds.), *Wireless world: Social and interactional aspects of wireless technology* (pp. 154–179). London: Springer-Verlag.

Clark, B., Drugan, J., Hartley, T., & Wu, D. (2003). *Training for localization (Replies to a questionnaire).* Retrieved December 28, 2003, from http://www.ice.urv. es/trans/future/localization2/leeds.html

Clement, A. (1994). Computing at work: Empowering action by "low-level users." *Communications of the ACM, 37*(1), 52–63.

Clemmensen, T., & Plocher, T. (2007). The Cultural Usability (CULTUSAB) Project: Studies of cultural models in psychological usability evaluation methods. In *HCI International 2007 Proceedings* (Vol. 10, pp. 274–280). Berlin: Springer.

Comaroff, J., & Comaroff, J. (1992). *Ethnography and the historical imagination.* Boulder, Colorado: Westview Press.

Costall, A. (1995). Socializing affordances. *Theory & Psychology, 5*(4), 467–481.

Covey, N. (2008, November). *Flying fingers.* Retrieved June 30, 2010, from http:// en-us.nielsen.com/content/nielsen/en_us/insights/consumer_insight/ issue_12/flying_fingers.html

Cox, A. L., Cairns, P. A., Walton, A., & Lee, S. (2008). Tlk or txt? Using voice input for SMS composition. *Personal and Ubiquitous Computing, 12*, 567–588.

Coyne, R. (1995). *Designing information technology in the postmodern age: From method to metaphor.* Cambridge, MA: MIT Press.

Crumlish, C., & Malone, E. (2009). *Designing social interfaces.* Sebastopol, CA: O'Reilly Media.

CTIA. (2010). *Wireless quick facts: Year-end figures.* Retrieved June 30, 2010, from http://www.ctia.org/advocacy/research/index.cfm/AID/10323

Cutting, J. (2002). *Pragmatics and discourse: A resource book for students.* Florence, KY: Routledge.

Davis, F. D. (1989). Perceived usefulness, perceived, ease of use, and user acceptance of information technology. *MIS Quarterly, 13*(3), 319–340.

de Certeau, M. (1984). *The practice of everyday life.* Berkeley, CA: University of California Press.

Deleuze, G., & Guattari, F. (1987). *A thousand plateaus: Capitalism and schizophrenia* (B. Massumi, Trans.). Minneapolis: University of Minnesota Press.

DeSanctis, G., & Poole, M. S. (1994). Capturing the complexity in advanced technology use: Adaptive structuration theory. *Organization Science, 5*(2), 121–147.

DeVoss, D., Jasken, J., & Hayden, D. (2002). Teaching intracultural and intercultural communication: A critique and suggested method. *Journal of Business and Technical Communication, 16*(1), 69–94.

Dias, P., Freedman, A., Medway, P., & Pare, A. (1999). *Worlds apart: Acting and writing in academic and workplace contexts.* Mahwah, NJ: Lawrence Erlbaum Associates.

Donner, J. (2008). Research approaches to mobile use in the developing world: A review of the literature. *The Information Society, 24,* 140–159.

Dourish, P. (2001). *Where the action is.* Cambridge, MA: MIT Press.

Dourish, P. (2003). The appropriation of interactive technologies: Some lessons from placeless documents. *Computer-Supported Cooperative Work: Special Issue on Evolving Use of Groupware, 12,* 465–490.

Dray, S. M., & Mrazek, D. (1996). A day in the life of a family: An international ethnographic study. In D. Wixon & J. Ramey (Eds.), *Field methods casebook for software design* (pp. 145–157). New York: John Wiley & Sons.

Dray, S. (2007). *Global innovative design for social change: Susan Dray's Statement.* Paper presented at the 12th Human-Computer Interaction International, Beijing.

Dray, S., & Siegel, D. (2007). Understanding users in context: An in-depth introduction to fieldwork for user centered design. In *Proceedings of the 11th IFIP TC 13 International Conference on Human-Computer Interaction* (Vol. Part II, pp. 712–713). Berlin: Springer-Verlag.

Drouin, P. (2003). *Training for localization (Replies to a questionnaire).* Retrieved December 28, 2003, from http://www.ice.urv.es/trans/future/localization2/drouin.html

du Gay, P., Hall, S., Janes, L., Mackay, H., & Negus, K. (1997). *Doing cultural studies: The Story of the Sony Walkman.* London: Sage.

Dumas, J. S., & Redish, J. (1993). *A practical guide to usability testing.* NJ: Ablex Publishing Corp.

Duncker, E. (2002). Cross-cultural usability of the library metaphor. In *Proceedings of Joint Conferences on Digital Libraries 2002* (pp. 223–230). New York: ACM Press.

Edwards, E. C., & Kasik, D. J. (1974). User experience with the CYBER graphics terminal. In *Proceedings of VIM-21* (pp. 284–286). New York: ACM Press.

Eglash, R., Bennett, A., O'Donnell, C., Jennings, S., & Clintorino, M. (2006). Culturally situated design tools: Ethnocomputing from field site to classroom. *American Anthropologist, 108*(2), 347–362.

Ehn, P. (1993). Scandinavian design: On participation and skill. In D. Schuler & N. Aki (Eds.), *Participatory design: Principles and practices* (pp. 41–77). Hillsdale, NJ: Erlbaum.

Eldridge, M., & Grinter, R. E. (2001, April). *Studying text messaging in teenagers.* Paper presented at the CHI 2001 Workshop: Mobile Communications: Understanding Users, Adoption & Design, Seattle, WA.

Elwood-Clayton, B. (2005). Desire and loathing in the cyber Philippines. In R. Harper, L. A. Palen & A. S. Taylor (Eds.), *The inside text: Social, cultural and design perspectives on SMS* (pp. 195–219). Dordrecht: Springer.

Engeström, Y. (1999). Activity theory and individual and social transformation. In Y. Engeström, R. Miettinen, & R.-L. Punamäki (Eds.), *Perspectives on activity theory* (pp. 19–38). Cambridge: Cambridge University Press.

Entner, R. (2010, January 27). *Under-aged texting: Usage and actual cost.* Retrieved June 30, 2010, from http://blog.nielsen.com/nielsenwire/online_mobile/under-aged-texting-usage-and-actual-cost/

Erickson, T. (1999). Rhyme and punishment: The creation and enforcement of conventions in an on-line participatory limerick genre. In *Proceedings of the 32nd Hawaii International Conference on System Sciences* (pp. 1–10). Hawaii: IEEE.

Eriksén, S. (2002). Localizing self on the Internet: Designing for "genius loci" in a global context. In Y. Dittrich, C. Floyd, & R. Klischewski (Eds.), *Social thinking-software practice* (pp. 425–450). Cambridge, MA: MIT Press.

Ess, C., & Sudweeks, F. (Eds.). (2005). Special theme: Culture and computer-mediated communication. In *Journal of Computer-Mediated Communication* 11(1). Retrieved August 5, 2008, from http://jcmc.indiana.edu/vol11/issue1/

Esselink, B. (2000). *A Practical guide to localization.* Philadelphia: John Benjamins.

European Telecommunications Standards Institute (ETSI). (2010). *Cellular history.* Retrieved June 16, 2010, from http://www.etsi.org/website/technologies/Cellularhistory.aspx

Faiola, A. (2002). A visualization pilot study for hypermedia: Developing cross-cultural user profiles for new media interfaces. *The Journal of Educational Multimedia and Hypermedia, 11*(3), 51–70.

Feenberg, A. (1999). *Questioning technology.* New York: Routledge.

Feenberg, A. (2002). *Transforming technology: A critical theory revisited.* New York: Oxford University Press.

Feenberg, A. (2004). *Critical theory of technology.* Retrieved September 12, 2009, from http://www.sfu.ca/~andrewf/ctt.htm

Figliola, P. M. (2008). *Text and multimedia messaging: Emerging issues for Congress* (No. RL34632): GalleryWatch.com.

Fiske, J. (1987). British cultural studies and television. In R. Allen (Ed.), *Channels of discourse, reassembled: Television and contemporary criticism* (2nd ed., pp. 284–326). Chapel Hill, NC: University of North Carolina Press.

Flanagan, M., Howe, D. C., & Nissenbaum, H. (2008). Embodying values in technology: Theory and practice. In J. v. d. Hoven & J. Weckert (Eds.), *Information technology and moral philosophy* (pp. 322–353). Cambridge: Cambridge UP.

Fogg, B. J. (2003). *Persuasive technology: Using computers to change what we think and do.* San Francisco: Morgan Kaufmann.

Ford, D. P., Connelly, C. E., & Meister, D. B. (2003). Information systems research and Hofstede's culture's consequences: An uneasy and incomplete partnership. *IEEE Transactions on Engineering Management, 50*(1), 8–25.

Frantz, W. (2003, June 8). *SendNote.* Retrieved July 10, 2003, from http://www.apgap.com/sendnote.php

Freadman, A. (1994). Anyone for tennis? In A. Freedman & P. Medway (Eds.), *Genre and the new rhetoric* (pp. 43–66). London: Taylor and Francis.

Freadman, A. (2002). Uptake. In R. Coe, L. Lingard, & T. Teslenko (Eds.), *The rhetoric and ideology of genre: Strategies for stability and change* (pp. 39–53). Cresskill, NJ: Hampton Press.

Friedman, B. (1996). Value-sensitive design. *Interactions, 3*(6), 17–23.

Friedman, B. (Ed.). (1997). *Human values and the design of computer technology.* New York: Cambridge UP.

Garrett, J. J. (2003). *The elements of user experience: User-centered design for the Web.* Indianapolis, IN: New Riders.

Gaver, W. (1991). Technology affordances. In *Proceedings of Conference on Human Factors in Computing Systems (CHI'91)* (pp. 79–84). New York, NY: ACM Press.

Geertz, C. J. (1973). *The interpretation of cultures.* New York: Basic Books.

Geisler, C. (2004). *Analyzing streams of language: Twelve steps to the systematic coding of text, talk and other verbal data.* NY: Pearson/Longman.

Geser, H. (2005). Towards a sociological theory of the mobile phone. In A. Zerdick, A. Picot, K. Schrape, J.-C. Burgelmann, R. Siverstone, V. Feldmann, C. Wernick, & C. Wolff (Eds.), *E-merging media: Communication and the media economy of the future* (pp. 235–260). Berlin: Springer.

Gibson, J. J. (1979). *The ecological approach to visual perception.* Boston: Houghton Mifflin.

Giddens, A. (1984). *The constitution of society.* Berkeley, CA: University of California Press.

Gillan, D. J., & Bias, R. G. (2001). Usability science I: Foundations. *International Journal of Human-Computer Interaction, 13*(4), 351–372.

Glotz, P., Bertschi, S., & Locke, C. (Eds.). (2005). *Thumb culture: The meaning of mobile phones for society.* Bielefeld: transcript Verlag.

Goggin, G. (2006). *Cell phone culture: Mobile technology in everyday life.* London: Routledge.

Gould, E. W. (2004). Synthesizing the literature on cultural values. In N. Aykin (Ed.), *Usability and internationalization of information technology* (pp. 66–102). Mahwah, NJ: Lawrence Erlbaum Associates.

Gray, W. D., & Salzman, M. C. (1998). Damaged merchandise? A review of experiments that compare usability evaluation methods. *Human-Computer Interaction. Special Issue on Context in Design, 13,* 203–261.

Green, W. S., & Jordan, P. W. (Eds.). (2002). *Pleasure with products: Beyond usability.* New York: Taylor & Francis.

Grossberg, L. (1992). *We gotta get out of this place: Popular conservatism and postmodern culture.* New York: Routledge.

Hackos, J. T., & Redish, J. C. (1998). *User and task analysis for interface design.* New York: John Wiley & Sons.

Haddon, L. (2003). Domestication and mobile telephony. In J. E. Katz (Ed.), *Machines that become us: The social context of personal communication technology* (pp. 43–56). New Brunswick, NJ: Transaction Publisher.

Hales, M. (1994). Where are designers? Styles of design practices, objects of design and views of users in CSCW. In D. Rosenberg & C. Hutchison (Eds.), *Design issues in CSCW* (pp. 151–177). London: Springer Verlag.

Hall, E. (1983). *The dance of life.* New York: Anchor Books.

Hall, S. (Ed.). (1997). *Representation: Cultural representations and signifying practices.* London: Sage.

Harper, R., Palen, L. A., & Taylor, A. S. (Eds.). (2005). *The inside text: Social, cultural and design perspectives on SMS.* Dordrecht: Springer.

Hart-Davidson, W., Cushman, E., Grabill, J., DeVoss, D., & Porter, J. (2005). Why teach digital writing? *Kairos, 10*(1). Retrieved June 10, 2009, from http://kairos.technorhetoric.net/10.1/binder2.html?coverweb/wide/index.html

Harvey, F. (1997). National cultural differences in theory and practice: Evaluating Hofstede's national cultural framework. *Information Technology & People, 10*(2), 132–146.

Hassenzahl, M. (2008). Aesthetics in interactive products: Correlates and consequences of beauty. In H. N. J. Schifferstein & P. Hekkert (Eds.), *Product experience* (pp. 287–302). San Diego, CA: Elsevier.

Hassenzahl, M. (2010). *Experience design: Technology for all the right reasons.* San Rafael, CA: Morgan & Claypool.

Heskett, J. (2005). *Design: A very short introduction.* New York: Oxford University Press.

Hill, T. (2004). New revenue alert from SMS. *Telecommunications International, 38*(2), 43–44.

Hillebrand, F. (2010). Global market development. In F. Hillebrand (Ed.), *Short Message Service (SMS): The creation of personal global text messaging* (pp. 125–130). Chichester, West Sussex: John Wiley and Sons.

Hjorth, L. (2009). *Mobile media in the Asia Pacific: Gender and the art of being mobile.* New York: Routledge.

Hofstede, G. (2001). *Culture's consequences: Comparing values, behaviors, institutions, and organizations across nations* (2nd ed.). Thousand Oaks, CA: Sage.

Hofstede, G., & Hofstede, G. J. (2005). *Culture and organizations: Software of the mind.* New York: McGraw-Hill.

Hoft, N. L. (1995). *International technical communication: How to export information about high technology.* New York: John Wiley & Sons.

Holtzblatt, K., Wendell, J. B., & Wood, S. (2005). *Rapid contextual design: A how-to guide to key techniques for user-centered design.* San Francisco: Morgan Kaufman.

Horst, H., & Miller, D. (2006). *The cell phone: An anthropology of communication.* Oxford: Berg.

Horton, W. (2004). Graphics: The not quite universal language. In N. Aykin (Ed.), *Usability and internationalization of information technology* (pp. 157–188). Mahwah, NJ: Lawrence Erlbaum Associates.

House, R. J., Hanges, P. J., Javidan, M., Dorfman, P. W., & Gupta, V. (Eds.). (2004). *Culture, leadership, and organizations: The GLOBE study of 62 societies.* Thousand Oaks, CA: Sage.

Höök, K. (2006). Designing familiar open surfaces. In *Proceedings of the 4th Nordic Conference on Human-Computer Interaction* (pp. 242–251). New York: ACM Press.

Hsieh, A., Hausman, T., Titus, N., & Miller, J. (2008). "If you build it, they will come... if they can": Pitfalls of releasing the same product globally. In *Extended Abstracts of Conference on Human Factors in Computing Systems (CHI 2008)* (pp. 2591–2596). New York: ACM.

Hughes, T. P. (1999). Edison and electric light. In D. MacKenzie & J. Wajcman (Eds.), *The social shaping of technology* (2nd ed., pp. 50–63). Buckingham: Open UP.

Hutchby, I. (2001). *Conversation and technology: From the telephone to the Internet.* Cambridge, UK: Polity Press.

Hutchins, E. (1995). *Cognition in the wild.* Cambridge, MA: MIT Press.

IDEO. (2008). *Design for social impact: How-to guide.* Retrieved April 5, 2010, from http://www.ideo.com/images/uploads/news/pdfs/IDEO_RF_Guide.pdf

Igarashi, T., Takai, J., & Yoshida, T. (2005). Gender differences in social network development via mobile phone text messages: A longitudinal study. *Journal of Social & Personal Relationships, 22*(5), 691–713.

Iivari, N. (2006). 'Representing the User' in software development—a cultural analysis of usability work in the product development context. *Interacting with Computers, 18*(4), 635–664.

Impiö, J. (2010). Give man a fish and you'll feed him for a day, teach him how to fish and he will overfish. *Interactions, 17*(3), 22–25.

Informa Telecoms & Media. (2011, January 26). *Global SMS traffic to reach 8.7 trillion in 2015.* Retrieved March 9, 2011, from http://www.informatm.com/itmgcontent/icoms/whats-new/20017843617.html

Inglehart, R. (1997). *Modernization and postmodernization: cultural, economic, and political change in 43 societies.* Princeton, NJ: Princeton UP.

Irani, L., Vertesi, J., Dourish, P., Philip, K., & Grinter, R. E. (2010). Postcolonial computing: A lens on design and development. In *Proceedings of Conference on Human Factors in Computing Systems (CHI 2010)* (pp. 1311–1320). New York: ACM.

ISO 9241. (1998). Ergonomic requirements for office work with visual display terminals: Part 11: Guidance on usability.

Issacs, E., Walendowski, A., Whittaker, S., Schiano, D., & Kamm, C. (2002). The character, functions, and styles of instant messaging in the workplace. In *Proceedings of the 2002 Conference on Computer Supported Cooperative Work* (pp. 11–20). New Orleans, Louisiana.

Ito, M. (2006). Introduction: Personal, portable, pedestrian. In M. Ito, D. Okabe, & M. Matsuda (Eds.), *Personal, portable, pedestrian mobile phones in Japanese life* (pp. 1–16). Cambridge, MA: MIT Press.

Ito, M., Okabe, D., & Matsuda, M. (Eds.). (2006). *Personal, portable, pedestrian mobile phones in Japanese life*. Cambridge, MA: MIT Press.

Jenson, S. (2005). Default thinking: Why consumer products fail. In R. Harper, L. A. Palen, & A. S. Taylor (Eds.), *The inside text: Social, cultural and design perspectives on SMS* (pp. 305–325). Dordrecht: Springer.

Jiang, H. (2007). Shou ji duan xin/cai xin [mobile messaging/multimedia messaging]. In C. Gong (Ed.), *Xin mei ti gai lun [Intro to New Media]* (pp. 248–258). China Radio & Television Publishing House.

Johnson, R. R. (1998). *User-centered technology: A rhetorical theory for computers and other mundane artifacts*. Albany, NY: SUNY Press.

Johnson, R. R., Salvo, M., & Zoetewey, M. (2007). User-centered technology in participatory culture: Two decades "Beyond a narrow conception of usability testing." *IEEE Transactions on Professional Communication, 50*(4), 320–332.

Johnson, S. (2009, June 5). *How Twitter will change the way we live*. Retrieved June 13, 2009, from http://www.time.com/time/printout/0,8816,1902604,00.html

Johnson-Eilola, J. (1996). Relocating the value of work: Technical communication in a post-industrial age. *Technical Communication Quarterly, 5*(3), 245–270.

Jokinen, P., Karimäki, K., & Kangas, A.-M. (2003). Demanding needs for mobile phones: A qualitative user study on the young urban lower middle class in China. In V. Evers, K. Rose, P. Honold, J. Coronado, & D. L. Day (Eds.), *Designing for global markets 5—IWIPS 2003—Fifth International Workshop on Internationalisation of Products and Systems* (pp. 105–114). Berlin: IWIPS.

Jordan, P. W. (2000). *Designing pleasurable products: An introduction to the new human factors*. London: Taylor & Francis.

Julier, G. (2008). *The culture of design* (2nd ed.). London: Sage.

Kano, N. (1995). *Developing international software for Windows 95 and Windows NT: A handbook for international software design*. Redmond, WA: Microsoft Press.

Kaptelinin, V. (1996). Computer-mediated activity: Functional organs in social and developmental contexts. In B. Nardi (Ed.), *Context and consciousness: Activity theory and human-computer interaction* (pp. 45–68). Cambridge, MA: MIT Press.

Kaptelinin, V., & Nardi, B. (2006). *Acting with technology: Activity theory and interaction design*. Cambridge, MA: MIT Press.

Keeker, K. (1997). *Improving web-site usability and appeal: Guidelines compiled by msn usability research*. Retrieved March 20, 2010, from http://msdn.microsoft.com/en-us/library/cc889361(office.11).aspx

Kill, M. (2006). Acknowledging the rough edges of resistance: Negotiation of identities for first year composition. *College Composition and Communication, 58*(2), 213–235.

Kill, M. K. (2008). *Challenging communication: A genre theory of innovative uptake*. Unpublished doctoral dissertation, University of Washington, Seattle, WA.

Klass, G. M. (2008). *Just plain data analysis: Finding, presenting, and interpreting social science data*. Lanham, MD: Rowman & Littlefield.

Knies, R. (2009, March 5). *boyd: Taking the Pulse of Social Networks*. Retrieved April 10, 2009, from http://research.microsoft.com/en-us/news/features/boyd-032009.aspx

Kraidy, M. M. (2001). From imperialism to glocalization: A theoretical framework for the Information Age. In B. L. Ebo (Ed.), *Cyberimperialism? Global relations in the new electronic frontier* (pp. 27–42). Westport, CT: Greenwood Publishing.

Krippendorff, K. (2006). *The semantic turn: A new foundation for design*. Boca Raton, FL: CRC Press.

Kuniavsky, M. (2003). *Observing the user experience: A practitioner's guide to user research*. San Francisco: Morgan Kaufmann.

Kuutti, K. (2001). *Hunting for the lost user: From sources of errors to active actors-and beyond*. Paper presented at the Cultural Usability Seminar, University of Art and Design, Helsinki.

Latour, B. (2005). *Reassembling the social: An introduction to actor-network-theory*. New York: Oxford University Press.

Lee, C. (2003). Towards a framework for culturally responsive design in multimedia computer environments: Cultural modeling as a case. *Mind, Culture, and Activity, 10*(1), 42–61.

Lenhart, A., Rainie, L., & Lewis, O. (2001, June). *Teenage life online: The rise of the instant-message generation and the Internet's impact on friendships and family relationships*. Retrieved February 10, 2003, from http://www.pewinternet.org

Lenhart, A., Ling, R., Campbell, S., & Purcell, K. (2010, April 20). *Teens and mobile phones*. Retrieved June 30, 2010, from http://pewinternet.org/Reports/2010/Teens-and-Mobile-Phones.aspx

Leont'ev, A. N. (1978). *Activity. Consciousness. Personality*. Upper Saddle River, NJ: Prentice-Hall.

Lin, A. (2005). Gendered, bilingual communication practices: Mobile text-messaging among Hong Kong college students. *Fibreculture Journal* (6). Retrieved from http://six.fibreculturejournal.org/fcj-031-gendered-bilingual-communication-practices-mobile-text-messaging-among-hong-kong-college-students/

Lin, A. M. Y., & Tong, A. H. M. (2008). Text-messaging cultures of college girls in Hong Kong: SMS as resources for achieving intimacy and gift-exchange with multiple functions. In G. Goggin (Ed.), *Mobile phone cultures* (pp. 158–170). Abingdon, Oxon: Routledge.

Ling, R. S. (2004). *The mobile connection: The cell phone's impact on society*. San Francisco: Morgan Kaufmann.

Ling, R. (2008). Mobile communication and teen emancipation. In G. Goggin & L. Hjorth (Eds.), *Mobile technologies: From telecommunications to media* (pp. 50–61). New York: Routledge.

Ling, R. (2008). *New tech, new ties: How mobile communication is reshaping social cohesion*. Cambridge, MA: MIT Press.

Ling, R. (2010). Texting as a life phase medium. *Journal of Computer-Mediated Communication, 15*, 277–292.

Lingo Systems. (2000). *The guide to translation and localization: Preparing products for the global marketplace.* Portland, OR: Lingo Systems.

Lingo Systems. (2009). *The guide to translation and localization: Communicating with the global marketplace* (7th ed.). Portland, OR: Lingo Systems.

LISA. (2007). *The globalization industry primer.* Switzerland: The Localization Industry Standards Association.

Liu, Y., & Räihä, K. J. (2010). Predicting Chinese text entry speeds on mobile phones. In *Proceedings of Conference on Human Factors in Computing Systems (CHI 2010)* (pp. 2183–2192). New York: ACM.

Livingstone, S. (2003). On the challenges of cross-national comparative media research. *European Journal of Communication, 18*(4), 477–500.

Lowe, S. (2003, March 3). Upwardly mobile girls stay in close touch with technology. *Sydney Morning Herald.* Retrieved May 1, 2003, from http://www.smh.com.au/articles/2003/03/14/1047583701261.html

Mackay, H. (Ed.). (1997). *Consumption and everyday life.* London: Sage.

MacKenzie, D., & Wajcman, J. (Eds.). (1999). *The social shaping of technology* (2nd ed.). Buckingham: Open UP.

MacLean, A., Carter, K., Lövstrand, L., & Moran, T. (1990). User-tailorable systems: Pressing the issues with buttons. In *Proceedings of the SIGCHI Conference of Human Factors in Computing Systems (CHI 1990)* (pp. 175–182). New York: ACM Press.

Mallick, M. (2003). *Mobile and wireless design essentials.* New York: John Wiley & Sons.

Mante, E., & Heres, J. (2003). Face and place: The mobile phone and Internet in the Netherlands. In J. E. Katz (Ed.), *Machines that become us: The social context of personal communication technology* (pp. 127–146). New Brunswick, NJ: Transaction Publisher.

Marcus, G. E. (1995). Ethnography in/of the world system: The emergence of multi-sited ethnography. *Annual Review Anthropology, 24,* 95–117.

Marcus, A. (1996). Icon and symbol design issues for graphical user interfaces. In E. M. D. Galdo & J. Nielsen (Eds.), *International user interfaces* (pp. 257–270). New York: John Wiley and Sons.

Marcus, A., & Gould, E. W. (2000, June 19). *Cultural dimensions and global web user-interface design: What? So what? Now what?* Paper presented at the 6th Conference on Human Factors and the Web, Austin, Texas.

Marcus, A., & Krishnamurthi, N. (2009). Cross-cultural analysis of social network services in Japan, Korea, and the USA. In N. Aykin (Ed.), *HCI International 2009 Proceedings (Internationalization, Design, LNCS 5623)* (pp. 59–68). Berlin: Springer-Verlag.

Marková, I. (2003). Dialogicality in the Prague School of Linguistics: A theoretical retrospect. In I. E. Josephs (Ed.), *Dialogicality in development* (pp. 3–34). Westport, CT: Greenwood.

Maxwell, J. A. (1996). *Qualitative research design: An interactive approach*. Thousand Oaks, CA: Sage.

McCarthy, J., & Wright, P. (2004). *Technology as experience*. Cambridge, MA: MIT Press.

McCool, M. (2006). Information architecture: Intercultural human factors. *Technical Communication, 53*(2), 167–183.

McCoy, S., Galletta, D. F., & King, W. R. (2007). Applying TAM across cultures: The need for caution. *European Journal of Information Systems, 16*, 81–90.

McLaughlin, M. L. (1984). *Conversation: How talk is organized*. Beverly Hills, CA: Sage.

Merholz, P., Wilkens, T., Schauer, B., & Verba, D. (2008). *Subject to change: Creating great products & services for an uncertain world*. Sebastopol, CA: O'Reilly Media.

Meso, P., Musa, P., & Mbarika, V. (2005). Towards a model of consumer use of mobile information and communication technology in LDCs: The case of sub-Saharan Africa. *Information Systems Journal, 15*, 119–146.

MIIT. (2008). *Monthly statistical report on the telecommunications industry of December 2007*. Retrieved August 18, 2009, from http://www.miit.gov.cn/n11293472/ n11293832/n11294132/n11302706/11766761.html

MIIT. (2009). *Report of major benchmarks accomplished by the telecommunications industry in December 2008*. Retrieved August 18, 2009, from http://www.miit.gov. cn/n11293472/n11295057/n11298508/11912660.html

MIIT. (2010). *2009 Annual statistical report of the telecommunications industry*. Retrieved June 29, 2010, from http://www.miit.gov.cn/n11293472/n11293832 /n11294132/n12858447/13011909.html

Miller, C. R. (1984). Genre as Social Action. *Quarterly Journal of Speech, 70*(2), 151–167.

Miller, C. R. (1994). Rhetorical community: The cultural basis of genre. In A. Freedman & P. Medway (Eds.), *Genre and the new rhetoric* (pp. 67–78). London: Taylor & Francis.

Miller, C. R., & Shepherd, D. (2009). Questions for genre theory from the blogsphere. In J. Giltrow & D. Stein (Eds.), *Genres in the Internet: Issues in the theory of genre* (pp. 263–290). Amsterdam: John Benjamins.

Miller, D. (1997). Consumption and its consequences. In H. Mackay (Ed.), *Consumption and everyday life* (pp. 13–50). London: Sage.

Miller, M. (2007, March 15). *Is Twitter popular because no one has "real" friends who text message?* Retrieved June 15, 2008, from http://www.zdnet.com/blog/ mobile-gadgeteer/is-twitter-popular-because-no-one-has-real-friends-who-text-message/316

Miller, C. C. (2009, August 26). *Who's driving Twitter's popularity? Not teens*. Retrieved July 7, 2010, from http://www.nytimes.com/2009/08/26 /technology/internet/26twitter.html

Mirel, B. (2002). Advancing a vision of usability. In B. Mirel & R. Spilka (Eds.), *Reshaping technical communication* (pp. 165–188). Mahwah, NJ: Lawrence Earlbaum Associates.

Mirel, B. (2004). *Interaction design for complex problem solving: Developing useful and usable software.* San Francisco: Morgan Kaufmann.

MobileSMS. (2004). *SMS History Zone.* Retrieved May 5, 2004, from http://www.mobilesms.com/history.asp

Morgan Stanley. (2004, April 14). *Chinese Internet report.* Retrieved June 3, 2004, from http://www.morganstanley.com/institutional/techresearch/pdfs/China_Internet_Report0404.pdf

Morville, P. (2004). *User experience design.* Retrieved July 20, 2007, from http://semanticstudios.com/publications/semantics/000029.php

MultiLingual. (2010). *Guide archives.* Retrieved June 12, 2010, from http://www.multilingual.com/guides.php

Murphie, A., & Potts, J. (2003). *Culture and technology.* New York: Palgrave Macmillan.

Musale, S. (2001). *Localizing for mobile devices: A primer.* Féchy: LISA.

Myers, M. D., & Tan, F. B. (2002). Beyond models of national culture in information systems research. *Journal of Global Information Management, 10*(1), 24–32.

Nardi, B. (1996a). Studying context: A comparison of activity theory, situated action models, and distributed cognition. In B. Nardi (Ed.), *Context and consciousness: Activity theory and human-computer interaction* (pp. 69–102). Cambridge, MA: MIT Press.

Nardi, B. (1996b). Activity theory and human-computer interaction. In B. Nardi (Ed.), *Context and consciousness: Activity theory and human-computer interaction* (pp. 7–16). Cambridge, MA: MIT Press.

Nielsen, J. (1993). *Usability engineering.* London: AP Professional.

Nielsen, J. (1994). Heuristic evaluation. In J. Nielsen & R. L. Mack (Eds.), *Usability inspection methods* (pp. 25–64). New York: John Wiley & Sons.

Nielsen Norman Group. (2008). *User experience—our definition.* Retrieved June 20, 2008, from http://www.nngroup.com/about/userexperience.html

Nieminen-Sundell, R., & Vaananen-Vainio-Mattila, K. (2003). Usability meets sociology for richer consumer studies. In C. Lindholm, T. Keinonen, & H. Kiljander (Eds.), *Mobile usability: How Nokia changed the face of the mobile phone* (pp. 113–130). New York, NY: McGraw-Hill.

Nissenbaum, H. (2005). Values in technical design. In *Encyclopedia of science, technology and ethics* (pp. ixvi–ixx). New York: Macmillan.

Norman, D. A. (1988). *The design of everyday things.* New York: Basic Books.

Norman, D. A. (1999, May/June). Affordance, conventions and design. *Interactions,6*(3), 38–42.

Norman, D. A. (2004). *Emotional design: Why we love (or hate) everyday things.* New York: Basic Books.

O'Reilly, T. (2005, September 30). *What is Web 2.0.* Retrieved July 10, 2006, from http://oreilly.com/pub/a/web2/archive/what-is-web-20.html

Ong, W. (1982). *Orality and literacy*. New York: New Accents.

Orita, A., & Hada, H. (2009). Is that really you? An approach to assure identity without revealing real-name online. In *Proceedings of the 5th ACM Workshop on Digital Identity Management* (pp. 17–20). New York: ACM.

Orlikowski, W. J. (1992). The duality of technology: Rethinking the concept of technology in organizations. *Organization Science, 3*(3), 398–427.

Orlikowski, W. J. (2000). Using technology and constituting structures: A practice lens for studying technology in organizations. *Organization Science, 11*(4), 404–428.

Ou, C. X., & Davison, R. M. (2009). Why eBay lost to Taobao in China: The Glocal advantage. *Communications of the ACM, 52*(1), 145–148.

Page, C. (2005). Mobile research strategies for a global market. *Communications of the ACM, 48*(7), 42–48.

Palen, L., & Salzman, M. (2002a). Beyond the handset: Designing for wireless communications usability. *ACM Transactions on Computer-Human Interaction, 9*(2), 125–151.

Palen, L., & Salzman, M. (2002b). Voice-mail diary studies for naturalistic data capture under mobile conditions. In *Proceedings of the 2002 Conference on Computer Supported Cooperative Work*. New Orleans, Louisiana.

Paterson, M. (2006). *Consumption and everyday life*. London: Routledge.

Pertierra, R. (2005). Mobile phones, identity and discursive intimacy. *Human Technology, 1*(1), 23–44.

Peters, O., Almekinders, J., van Buren, R., Snippers, R., & Wessels, J. (2003). *Motives for SMS use*. Paper presented at the 2003 International Communication Association Annual Convention, San Diego CA.

Petroski, H. (1989). *The pencil: A history of design and circumstances*. New York: Knopf.

Pilloton, E. (2009). *Design revolution: 100 products that empower people*. New York: Metropolis.

Pinch, T. J., & Bijker, W. E. (1987). The social construction of facts and artifacts. In W. E. Bijker, T. P. Hughes, & T. J. Pinch (Eds.), *The social construction of technological systems* (pp. 17–50). Cambridge, MA: MIT Press.

Pine, B. J., & Gilmore, J. H. (1999). *The experience economy: Work is theater & every business a stage*. Cambridge, MA: Harvard Business School Press.

Porter, J. (2008). *Designing for the social web*. Berkeley, CA: New Riders.

Prabhu, G. (2007). *Global innovative design for social change: Girish Prabhu's Statement*. Paper presented at the 12th Human-Computer Interaction International, Beijing.

Prahalad, C. K. (2006). *The fortune at the bottom of the pyramid: Eradicating poverty through profits*. Upper Saddle River, NJ: Wharton School Publishing.

Rakow, L. F. (1992). *Gender on the line: Women, the telephone, & community life*. Urbana, IL: University of Illinois Press.

Rakow, L. F., & Navarro, V. (1993). Remote mothering and the parallel shift: Women meet the cellular phone. *Critical Studies in Mass Communication, 10*(2), 144–157.

Randall, D., Harper, R., & Rouncefield, M. (2007). *Fieldwork for design: Theory and practice*. London: Springer-Verlag.

Reardon, M. (2008a, September 10). *U.S. text usage hits record despite price increases*. Retrieved June 7, 2009, from http://news.cnet.com/8301-1035_3-10038634-94.html

Reardon, M. (2008b, September 23). *Text messaging explodes in America*. Retrieved June 7, 2009, from http://www.cbsnews.com/stories/2008/09/23/tech/cnettechnews/main4471183.shtml

Rheingold, H. (2002). *Smart mobs: The next social revolution*. Cambridge, MA: Perseus.

Richtel, M. (2004, June 26). For liars and loafers, cellphones offer an alibi. *New York Times*. Retrieved June 27, 2004, from http://www.nytimes.com/2004/06/26/business/for-liars-and-loafers-cellphones-offer-an-alibi.html

Rogers, E. M. (1995). *Diffusion of innovations* (5th ed.). New York: Free Press.

Rubin, H., & Rubin, I. (1995). *Qualitative interviewing: The art of hearing data*. San Diego: Sage.

Saffer, D. (2007). *Designing for interaction: Creating smart applications and clever devices*. Berkeley, CA: New Riders.

Salvador, T., Bell, G., & Anderson, K. (1999). Design ethnography. *Design Management Journal, 10*(4), 35–41.

Salvo, M. (2001). Ethics of engagement: User-centered design and rhetorical methodology. *Technical Communication Quarterly, 10*(3), 273–290.

Sassen, S. (1998). *Globalization and its discontents*. New York: New Press.

Satchell, C. (2008). Cultural theory and real world design—Dystopian and utopian outcomes. In *Proceedings of Conference on Human Factors in Computing Systems (CHI 2008)* (pp. 1593–1602). New York: ACM Press.

Schiano, D., Chen, C., Ginsberg, J., Gretarsdottir, U., Huddleston, M., & Issacs, E. (2002). *Teen use of messaging media*. Paper presented at the CHI 2002 Short Talk, Minneapolis, MN.

Schmitt, B. (2003). *Customer experience management*. New York: The Free Press.

Schneider-Hufschmidt, M. (2005). Usability issues of sending text messages. In R. Harper, L. A. Palen, & A. S. Taylor (Eds.), *The inside text: Social, cultural and design perspectives on SMS* (pp. 223–236). Dordrecht: Springer.

Schonfeld, E., Malik, O., & Copeland, M. V. (2006, March 1). *The Next Net 25: Social media*. Retrieved March 15, 2006, from http://money.cnn.com/2006/02/24/smbusiness/business2_nextnet_social/index.htm

Schonfeld, E. (2006, July 27). *Cyworld ready to attack MySpace*. Retrieved July 8, 2010, from http://money.cnn.com/2006/07/27/technology/cyworld0727.biz2/index.htm

Schryer, C. F. (1994). The lab versus the clinic. In A. Freedman & P. Medway (Eds.), *Genre and the new rhetoric* (pp. 105–124). London: Taylor & Francis.

Schumacher, R. M. (Ed.). (2010). *Handbook of global user research*. Burlington, MA: Morgan Kaufmann.

Selfe, C. L., & Richard J. Selfe, J. (1994). The politics of the interface: Power and its exercise in electronic contact zones. *College Composition and Communication, 45*(4), 480–504.

Sengers, P., Kaye, J. J., Boehner, K., Fairbank, J., Gay, G., Medynskiy, Y., et al. (2004). Culturally embedded computing. *Pervasive Computing, 3*(1), 14–21.

Sengers, P., & Gaver, W. (2005). Designing for interpretation. In *Proceedings of the 11th International Conference on Human-Computer Interaction.* Mahwah, NJ: Lawrence Erlbaum Associates. Retrieved from http://cemcom.infosci. cornell.edu/mainsite/uploads/pubs/DesigningForInterpretation.pdf

Sengers, P., & Gaver, W. (2006). Staying open to interpretation: Engaging multiple meanings in design and evaluation. In *Proceedings of the 6th conference on designing interactive systems* (pp. 99–108). New York: ACM Press.

Shade, L. R. (2008). Feminizing the mobile: Gender scripting of mobiles in North America. In G. Goggin (Ed.), *Mobile phone cultures* (pp. 42–52). Abingdon, Oxon: Routledge.

Sheppard, C., & Scholtz, J. (1999). The effects of cultural markers on web site use. In *Proceedings of the Fifth Conference on Human Factors and the Web.* Gaithersburg, MD. Retrieved April 5, 2000, from http://zing.ncsl.nist.gov/ hfweb/proceedings/sheppard/index.html

Shneiderman, B. (1998). *Designing the user interface: Strategies for effective human-computer interaction.* Reading, MA: Addison-Wesley.

Silfverberg, M., MacKenzie, I. S., & Korhonen, P. (2000). Predicting text entry speed on mobile phones. In *Proceedings of Conference on Human Factors in Computing Systems (CHI 2000)* (pp. 9–16). New York: ACM.

Silverstone, R., & Haddon, L. (1996). Design and the domestication of information and communication technologies: Technical change and everyday life. In R. Mansell & R. Silverstone (Eds.), *Communication by design: The politics of information and communication technologies* (pp. 44–74). Oxford: Oxford University Press.

SINA. (2006, January 28). *Beijing shiwei shizhengfu tongguo duanxin xiang shimin bainian* [Beijing city government sent text message greetings to citizens]. Retrieved April 15, 2006, from http://news.sina.com.cn/c/2006-01-28/ 02088098887s.shtml

Singh, N., & Pereira, A. (2005). *The culturally customized web site: Customizing web sites for the global marketplace.* Burlington, MA: Elsevier (Butterworth-Heinemann).

SJInfo. (2003). *An overview of Chinese input on cell phones.* Retrieved June 20, 2004, from http://www.sjinfo.net/syzn/59.html

Slack, J. D. (1989). Contextualizing technology. In B. Dervin, L. Grossberg, B. J. O'Keefe, & E. Wartella (Eds.), *Rethinking communication: Volume 2: Paradigm exemplars* (pp. 329–345). Newbury Park, CA: Sage.

Slack, J., Miller, D., & Doak, J. (1993). The technical communicator as author: Meaning, power, authority. *Journal of Business and Technical Communication, 7*(1), 12–36.

Slack, J. (1996). The theory and method of articulation in cultural studies. In D. Morley & K.-H. Chen (Eds.), *Stuart Hall: Critical dialogues in cultural studies* (pp. 112–127). New York: Routledge.

Slack, J. D., & Wise, J. M. (2005). *Culture + Technology: A primer.* New York: Peter Lang.

Smith, C. E. (Ed.). (2007). *Design for the other 90%.* New York: Smithsonian Organization & Cooper-Hewitt, National Design Museum.

Spinuzzi, C. (1999a). *Designing for lifeworlds: Genre and activity in information systems design and evaluation.* Unpublished PhD dissertation, Iowa State University, Ames, IA.

Spinuzzi, C. (1999b). Grappling with distributed usability: A cultural-historical examination of documentation genres over four decades. In *ACM SIGDOC Conference Proceedings* (pp. 16–21). New York, NY: ACM Press.

Spinuzzi, C. (2002). Toward integrating our research scope: A sociocultural field methodology. *Journal of Business and Technical Communication, 16*(1), 3–32.

Spinuzzi, C. (2003). *Tracing genres through organizations: A sociocultural approach to information design.* Cambridge, MA: MIT Press.

Spinuzzi, C. (2005). Lost in the translation: Shifting claims in the migration of a research technique. *Technical Communication Quarterly, 14*(4), 411–446.

Spinuzzi, C. (2008). *Network: Theorizing knowledge work in telecommunications.* New York: Cambridge UP.

Stake, R. E. (1995). *The art of case study research.* Thousand Oaks, CA: Sage Publications.

Starke-Meyerring, D. (2005). Meeting the challenges of globalization: A framework for cultural literacies in professional communication programs. *Journal of Business and Technical Communication, 19*(4), 468–499.

Stewart, J., & Williams, R. (2005). The wrong trousers? Beyond the design fallacy: Social learning and the user. In D. Howcroft & E. M. Trauth (Eds.), *Handbook of critical information systems research: Theory and application* (pp. 195–221). Cheltenham, Glos: Edward Elgar Publishing.

Stewart, J., & Quick, C. (2009, October 6). *Global mobile—Strategies for growth.* Retrieved June 30, 2010, from http://blog.nielsen.com/nielsenwire/online_mobile/global-mobile-strategies-for-growth/

Storey, J. (1999). *Cultural consumption and everyday life.* London: Arnold.

Straub, D. W. (1994). The effect of culture on IT diffusion: E-mail and FAX in Japan and the U.S. *Information Systems Research, 5*(1), 23–47.

Straub, D., Keil, M., & Brenner, W. (1997). Testing the technology acceptance model across cultures: A three country study. *Information and Management, 33*(1), 1–11.

Suchman, L. (1987). *Plans and situated actions: The problem of human-computer communication.* New York: Cambridge University Press.

Suchman, L., Blomberg, J., Orr, J. E., & Trigg, R. (1999). Reconstructing technologies as social practice. *American Behavioral Scientist, 43*(3), 392–408.

Suchman, L. (2002). *Located accountabilities in technology production.* Retrieved October 10, 2004, from http://www.lancs.ac.uk/fass/sociology/papers/suchman-located-accountabilities.pdf

Sullivan, P. (1989). Beyond a narrow conception of usability testing. *IEEE Transactions on Professional Communication, 32*(4), 256–264.

Sullivan, P., & Porter, J. E. (1997). *Opening spaces: Writing technologies and critical research practices.* Greenwich, CT: Ablex.

Sun, H. (2001). Building a culturally-competent corporate Web site: An exploratory study of cultural markers in multilingual Web design. In *Proceedings of ACM Special Interest Group for Design of Communications (SIGDOC) 2001* (pp. 95–102). New York: ACM.

Sun, H. (2002a). Exploring cultural usability. In *Proceedings of 2002 IEEE International Professional Communication Conference* (pp. 319–330). Portland, OR: IEEE. Copyright 2002 IEEE.

Sun, H. (2002b). Why cultural contexts are missing: A rhetorical critique of localization practices. In *Proceedings of STC 49th Annual Conference.* Arlington, VA: STC Publications.

Sun, H. (2004). *Expanding the scope of localization: A cultural usability perspective on mobile text messaging use in American and Chinese contexts.* Doctoral dissertation, Rensselaer Polytechnic Institute, Troy, NY. Available from Proquest Digital Dissertations database (AAT 3140970).

Sun, H. (2006). The triumph of users: Achieving cultural usability goals with user localization. *Technical Communication Quarterly, 15*(4), 457–481.

Sun, H. (2009a). Designing for a dialogic view of interpretation in cross-cultural IT design. In *HCI International 2009 Proceedings (Internationalization, Design and Global Development, LNCS 5623)* (Vol. 4, pp. 108–116). Berlin: Springer-Verlag.

Sun, H. (2009b). Towards a rhetoric of locale: Localizing mobile messaging technology into everyday life. *Journal of Technical Writing and Communication, 39*(3), 245–261. ©2009, Baywood Publishing Co., Inc.

Sutcliffe, A. (2010). *Designing for user engagement: Aesthetic and attractive user interfaces.* San Rafael, CA: Morgan & Claypool.

Svanaes, D. (2000). *Understanding interactivity: Steps to a phenomenology of human-computer interaction.* Unpublished PhD dissertation, Norwegian University of Science and Technology, Trondheim.

Tabuchi, H. (2011, January 9). Facebook Wins Relatively Few Friends in Japan. Retrieved October 17, 2011, from http://www.nytimes.com/2011/01/10/technology/10facebook.html

Tannen, D. (1990). *You just don't understand: Women and men in conversation.* New York: Bellantine Books.

Tarkka, M., & Tikka, H. (2001). *Cultural usability: Towards a design sensibility.* Retrieved October 10, 2001, from http://mlab.uiah.fi/culturalusability/introduction.html

Taylor, D. (1992). *Global software: Developing applications for the international market.* New York: Springer-Verlag.

Taylor, A. S., & Harper, R. (2001). *Talking 'activity': Young people and mobile phones.* Paper presented at the CHI 2001 Workshop: Mobile Communications: Understanding Users, Adoption & Design, Seattle, WA.

Texting: The (near) silent revolution. (2004). Retrieved June 10, 2004, from http://www.science.ie/scopetv/content/content.asp?section_id=665#links

Thackara, J. (2005). *In the bubble: Designing for a complex world.* Cambridge: MIT Press.

The Nielsen Company. (2010, March 19). *Global audience spends two hours more a month on social networks than last year.* Retrieved June 23, 2010, from http://blog.nielsen.com/nielsenwire/global/global-audience-spends-two-hours-more-a-month-on-social-networks-than-last-year/

The Nielsen Company. (2011, September). *The Social Media Report: Q3 2011.* Retrieved October 17, 2011, from http://cn.nielsen.com/documents/Nielsen-Social-Media-Report_FINAL_090911.pdf

Think globally, act locally. (1994). Retrieved March 30, 2006, from http://capita.wustl.edu/ME567_Informatics/concepts/global.html

Thomas, P., & Macredie, R. (2002). Introduction to the new usability. *ACM Transactions on Computer-Human Interaction, 9*(2), 69–73.

Thomas, F., Haddon, L., Gilligan, R., Heinzmann, P., & de Gournay, C. (2005). Cultural factors shaping the experience of ICTs: An exploratory review. In L. Haddon (Ed.), *International collaborative research: Cross-cultural differences and cultures of research* (pp. 15–30). Brussels: COST.

TKorea. (2009a, February 5). *Myspace pulls out of Korea.* Retrieved July 8, 2010, from http://www.telecomskorea.com/business-3797.html

TKorea. (2009b, November 9). *Korean SNS Cyworld to withdraw from U.S. and Taiwan.* Retrieved July 8, 2010, from http://www.telecomskorea.com/business-8268.html

Toffler, A. (1980). *The third wave.* London: Collins.

Toto, S. (2008, August 3). *Taking social networks abroad—Why MySpace and Facebook are failing in Japan.* Retrieved July 8, 2010, from http://techcrunch.com/2008/08/03/taking-social-networks-abroad-why-myspace-and-facebook-are-failing-in-japan/

Trompernaars, F. (1993). *Riding the waves of culture: Understanding cultural diversity in business.* London: Nicole Brealey.

Tuomi, I. (2002). *Networks of innovation: Change and meaning in the age of the Internet.* New York: Oxford University Press.

Tuomi, I. (2005). Beyond user-centric models of product creation. In L. Haddon, E. Mante, B. Sapio, K.-H. Kommonen, L. Fortunati, & A. Kant (Eds.), *Everyday innovators: Researching the role of users in shaping ICT's* (pp. 21–38). Dordrecht: Springer.

Twitter. (2009). In *Wikipedia*. Retrieved June 10, 2009, from http://en.wikipedia. org/wiki/Twitter

Twitter Blog. (2010, March 1). *Enabling a rush of innovation*. Retrieved July 10, 2010, from http://blog.twitter.com/2010/03/enabling-rush-of-innovation.html

User Experience Network. (2008). *UXnet: The User Experience Network*. Retrieved June 20, 2008, from http://www.uxnet.org/

Uy-Tioco, C. (2008). Overseas Filipino workers and text messaging: Reinventing transnational mothering. In G. Goggin (Ed.), *Mobile phone cultures* (pp. 111–123). Abingdon, Oxon: Routledge.

Vaananen-Vainio-Mattila, K., & Ruuska, S. (2000). Designing mobile phones and communicators for consumers' needs at Nokia. In E. Bergman (Ed.), *Information appliances and beyond: Interaction design for consumer products* (pp. 169–204). San Francisco: Morgan Kaufmann.

Verbeek, P.-P. (2005). *What things do—Philosophical reflections on technology, agency, and design* (R. P. Crease, Trans.). University Park, PA: Penn State UP.

Victor, D. A. (1992). *International business communication*. New York: Harper Collins.

Virkkunen, J., & Engeström, Y. (2001). *Usability and the changing producer-user relationship*. Retrieved October 8, 2003, from http://mlab.uiah.fi/culturalusability/ papers/Virkkunen_Engestrom.pdf

von Hippel, E. (2005). *Democratizing innovation*. Cambridge, MA: MIT Press.

Vredenburg, K. (2002). Designing the total user experience at IBM: An examination of case studies, research findings, and advanced methods. *International Journal of Human-Computer Interaction, 14*(3/4), 275–278.

Vyas, D., Chisalita, C., & van de Veer, G. (2006). Affordance in interaction. In *Proceedings of the 13th European Conference on Cognitive Ergonomics* (pp. 92–99). New York: ACM Press.

Vyas, D., & van de Veer, G. (2006). Experience as meaning: Some underlying concepts and implications for design. In *Proceedings of the 13th European Conference on Cognitive Ergonomics* (pp. 81–91). New York: ACM Press.

Walton, R. (2009, November 7). *Give me two minutes to tell you why Cyworld US failed*. Retrieved July 8, 2010, from http://thenextweb.com/asia/2009/11/07/ give-minutes-cyworld-failed/

Water hyacinth. (2010). In *Wikipedia*. Retrieved June 15, 2010, from http:// en.wikipedia.org/wiki/Water_hyacinth

Watson, S. (2008). The business of customer experience: Lessons learned at Wells Fargo. *Interactions, 15*(1), 38–43.

Wei, R. (2006). Lifestyles and new media: Adoption and use of wireless communication technologies in China. *New Media & Society, 8*(6), 991–1008.

Weilenmann, A. (2010). Learning to text: An interaction analytic study of how seniors learn to enter text on mobile phones. In *Proceedings of Conference on Human Factors in Computing Systems (CHI 2010)* (pp. 1135–1144). New York: ACM.

Weisinger, J. Y., & Salipante, P. F. (2000). Cultural knowing as practicing: Extending our conceptions of culture. *Journal of Management Inquiry, 9*(4), 376–390.

Weisinger, J. Y., & Trauth, E. M. (2002). Situating culture in the global information sector. *Information Technology & People, 15*(4), 306–320.

Wertsch, J. V. (1991). *Voices of the mind: A sociocultural approach to mediated action.* Cambridge, MA: Harvard University Press.

Wheeler, J. V. (1999). *The impact of social environments on self-directed change and learning.* Unpublished doctoral dissertation, Case Western Reserve University, Cleveland, OH.

Winner, L. (1980). Do artifacts have politics? *Daedalus, 109*(1), 121–136.

Winograd, T., & Flores, F. (1986). *Understanding computers and cognition: A new foundation for design.* Norwood, NJ: Ablex.

Woods, J. (2004). Managing multicultural content in the global enterprise. In N. Aykin (Ed.), *Usability and internationalization of information technology* (pp. 123–155). Mahwah, NJ: Lawrence Erlbaum Associates.

World Salaries. (2008). *China average salaries & expenditures.* Retrieved July 10, 2010, from http://www.worldsalaries.org/china.shtml

Wright, P., McCarthy, J., & Meekison, L. (2003). Making sense of experience. In M. Blythe, A. Monk, K. Overbeeke, & P. Wright (Eds.), *Funology: From usability to user enjoyment* (pp. 43–53). Dordrecht: Kluwer.

Wright, P., & McCarthy, J. (2010). *Experience-centered design: Designers, users, and communities in dialogue.* San Rafael, CA: Morgan & Claypool.

WTB. (2002, 2003, 2004, 2005, 2006, 2008, 2009, 2010). *Annual Commercial Mobile Radio Services (CMRS) competition reports.* Retrieved June 1, 2010, from http://wireless.fcc.gov/index.htm?job=cmrs_reports

Xinhua Net. (2006, March 20). *Yin Mingshan duanxin qing shengli* [Yin Mingshan celebrates victory with text messaging]. Retrieved April 15, 2006, from http://www.xinhuanet.com/chinanews/2006-03/20/content_6511670.htm

Xinhua News. (2002). *55 million users have been using SMS.* Retrieved March 20, 2003, from http://it.sohu.com/03/10/article203961003.shtml

Yan, X. (2003). Mobile data communications in China. *Communications of the ACM, 46*(12), 80–85.

Yang, K. S. (1986). Chinese personality and its change. In M. H. Bond (Ed.), *The psychology of the Chinese people* (pp. 106–170). New York: Oxford University Press.

Yates, J., & Orlikowski, W. J. (1992). Genres of organizational communication: A structurational approach to studying communication and media. *The Academy of Management Review, 17*(2), 299–326.

Yesky. (2003, June 17, 2003). *Text entry for SMS, which way is better?* Retrieved June 20, 2004, from http://www.yesky.com/Fashion/73753040967958528/200306 17/1708453.shtml

Yi, J. C. (2010). User-research-driven mobile user interface innovation: A success story from Seoul. *Interactions, 17*(1), 48–51.

Yli-Jokipii, H. (2001). The local and the global: An exploration into the Finnish and English websites of a Finnish company. *IEEE Transactions on Professional Communication, 44*(2), 104–113.

Yu, L., & Tng, T. H. (2003). Culture and design for mobile phones for China. In J. E. Katz (Ed.), *Machines that become us: The social context of personal communication technology* (pp. 187–198). New Brunswick, NJ: Transaction Publisher.

Yu, H. (2004). The power of thumbs: The politics of SMS in urban China. *Graduate Journal of Asia-Pacific Studies, 2*(2), 30–43.

Zahedi, M., Pelt, W. V., & Song, J. (2001). A conceptual framework for international Web design. *IEEE Transactions on Professional Communication, 44*(2), 83–103.

Zappen, J. P. (2004). *The rebirth of dialogue: Bakhtin, Socrates, and the rhetorical tradition.* Albany, NY: SUNY Press.

Index

NOTE: In this index "text messaging" and "texting" are used interchangeably. Page numbers followed by *f* refer to figures; page numbers followed by *t* refer to tables; page numbers followed by "n" refer to notes.